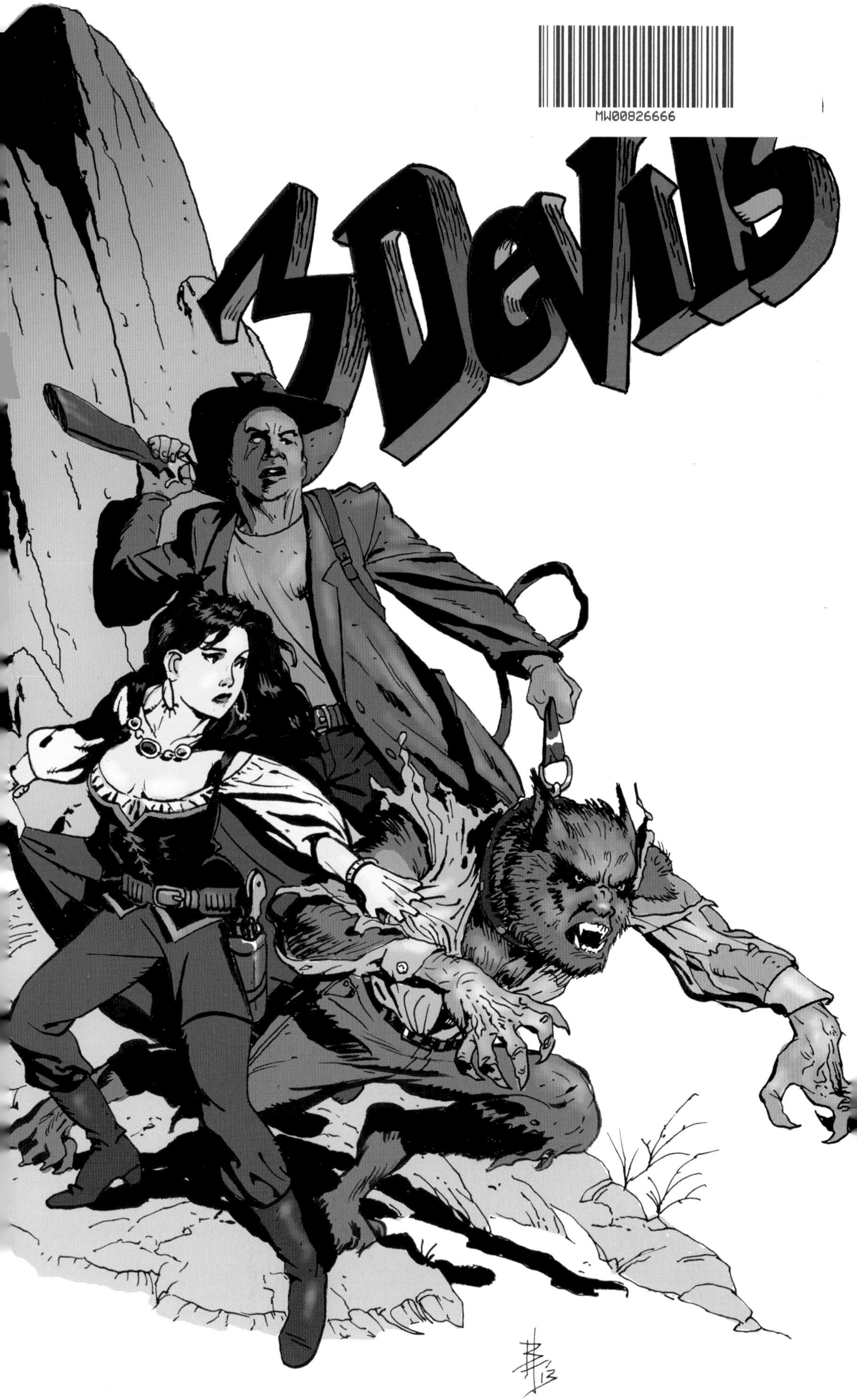
3 Devils

3 Devils

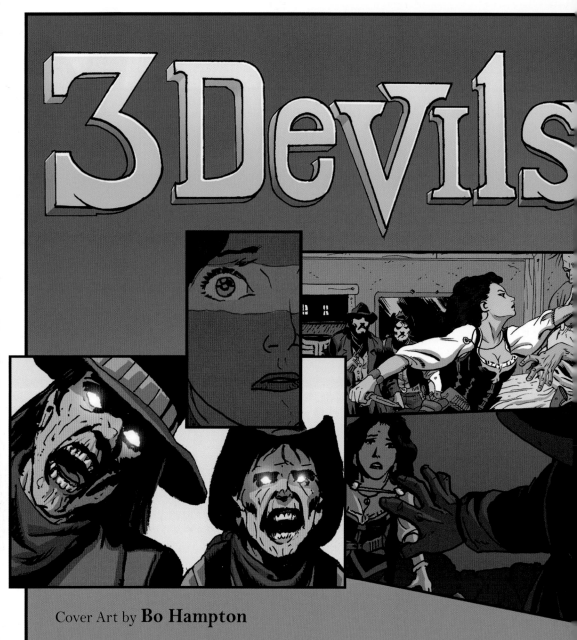

Cover Art by **Bo Hampton**

Collection Edits by **Justin Eisinger** and **Alonzo Simon**

Collection Design by **Ron Estevez**

Publisher: **Ted Adams**

ISBN: 978-1-63140-698-0

19 18 17 16   1 2 3 4

IDW®
www.IDWPUBLISHING.com

Ted Adams, CEO & Publisher
Greg Goldstein, President & COO
Robbie Robbins, EVP/Sr. Graphic Artist
Chris Ryall, Chief Creative Officer/Editor-in-Chief
Matthew Ruzicka, CPA, Chief Financial Officer
Dirk Wood, VP of Marketing
Lorelei Bunjes, VP of Digital Services
Jeff Webber, VP of Licensing, Digital and Subsidiary Rights
Jerry Bennington, VP of New Product Development

Facebook: **facebook.com/idwpublishing**
Twitter: **@idwpublishing**
YouTube: **youtube.com/idwpublishing**
Tumblr: **tumblr.idwpublishing.com**
Instagram: **instagram.com/idwpublishing**

Originally published as 3 DEVILS issues #1–4.

Story and Art by **Bo Hampton**

Colors by **Jeremy Mohler**

Letters by **Bo Hampton**

Series Edits by **Tom Waltz**

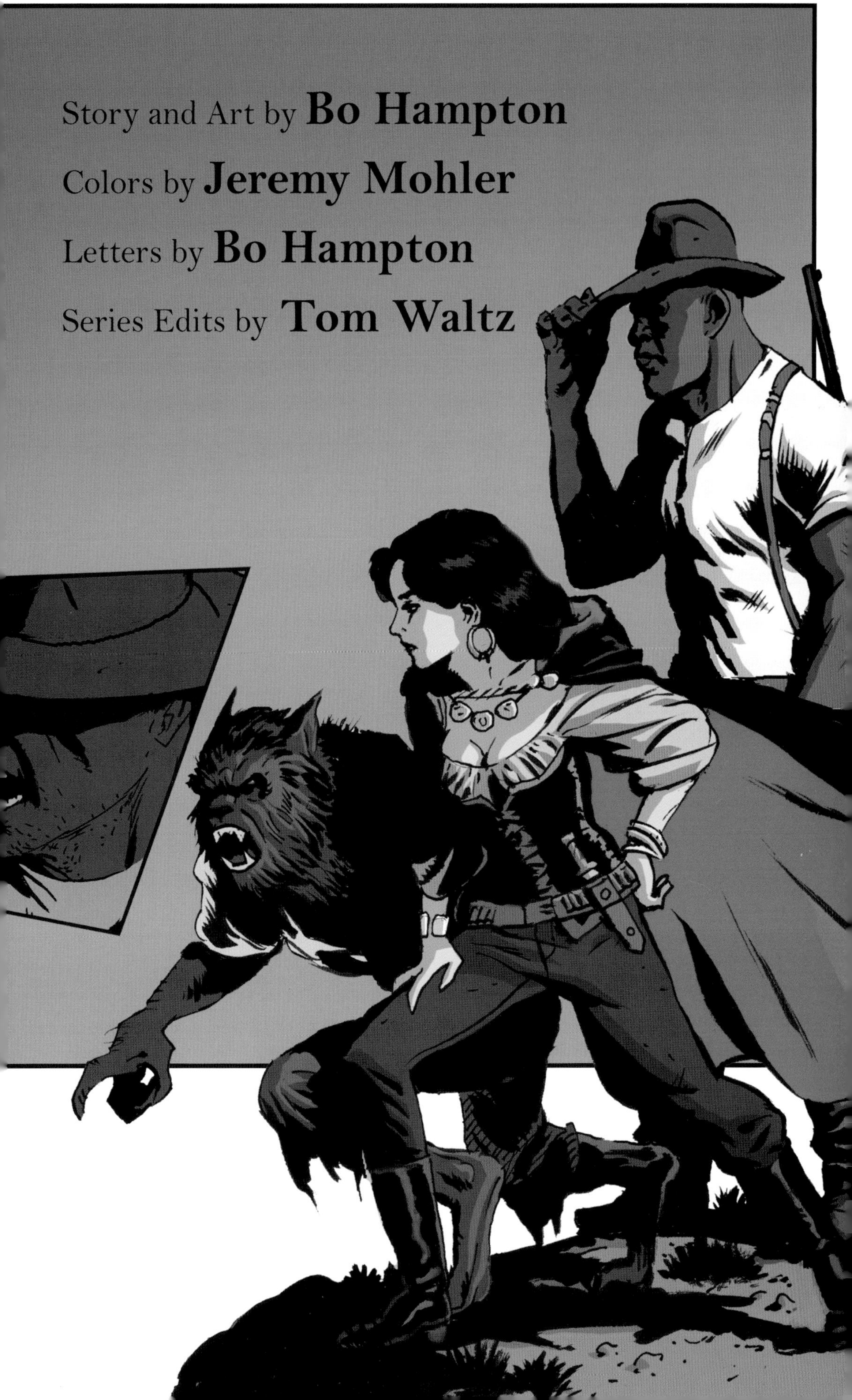

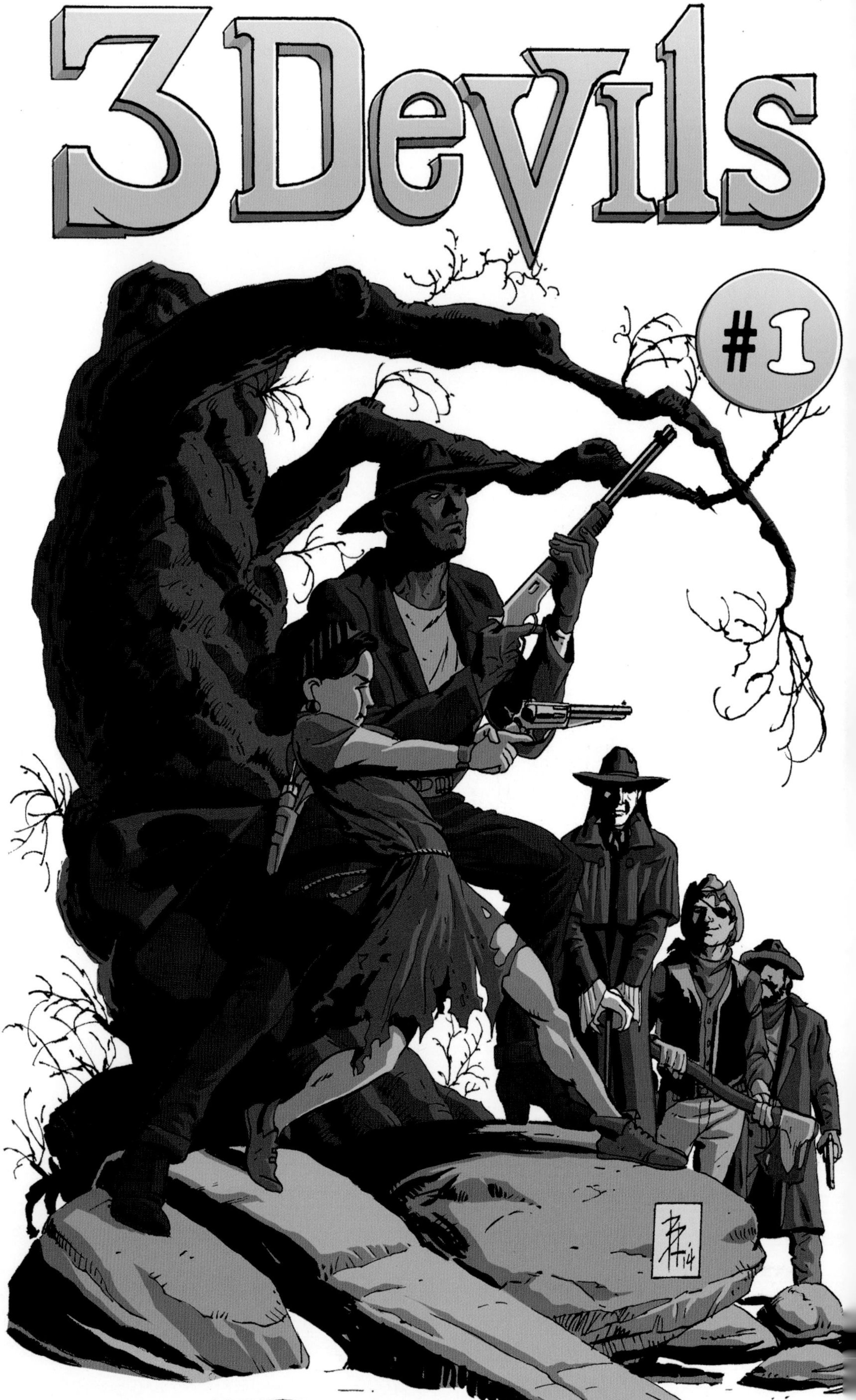
3Devils
#1

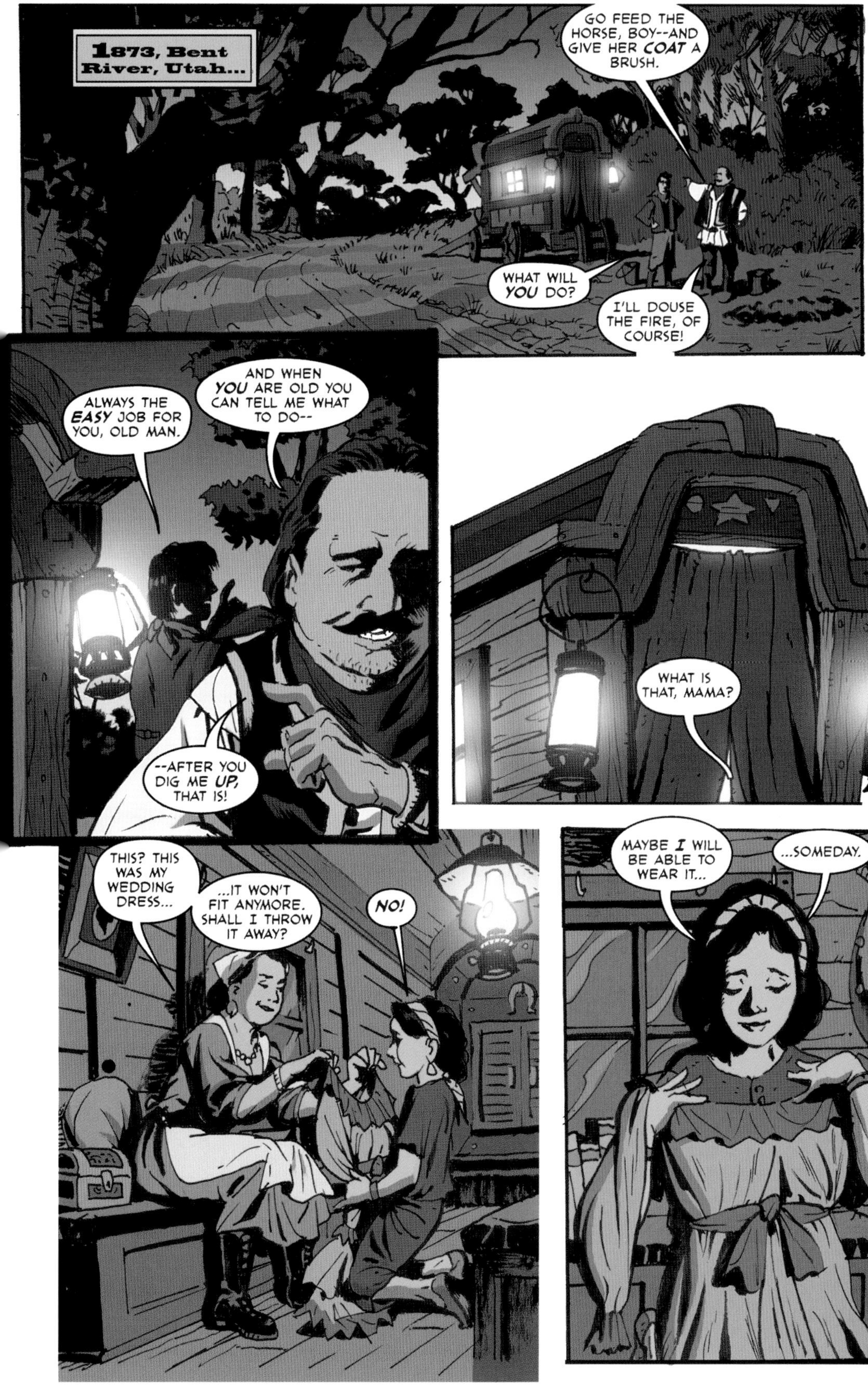
1873, Bent River, Utah...
GO FEED THE HORSE, BOY--AND GIVE HER COAT A BRUSH.
WHAT WILL YOU DO?
I'LL DOUSE THE FIRE, OF COURSE!
ALWAYS THE EASY JOB FOR YOU, OLD MAN.
AND WHEN YOU ARE OLD YOU CAN TELL ME WHAT TO DO--
--AFTER YOU DIG ME UP, THAT IS!
WHAT IS THAT, MAMA?
THIS? THIS WAS MY WEDDING DRESS...
...IT WON'T FIT ANYMORE. SHALL I THROW IT AWAY?
NO!
MAYBE I WILL BE ABLE TO WEAR IT...
...SOMEDAY.

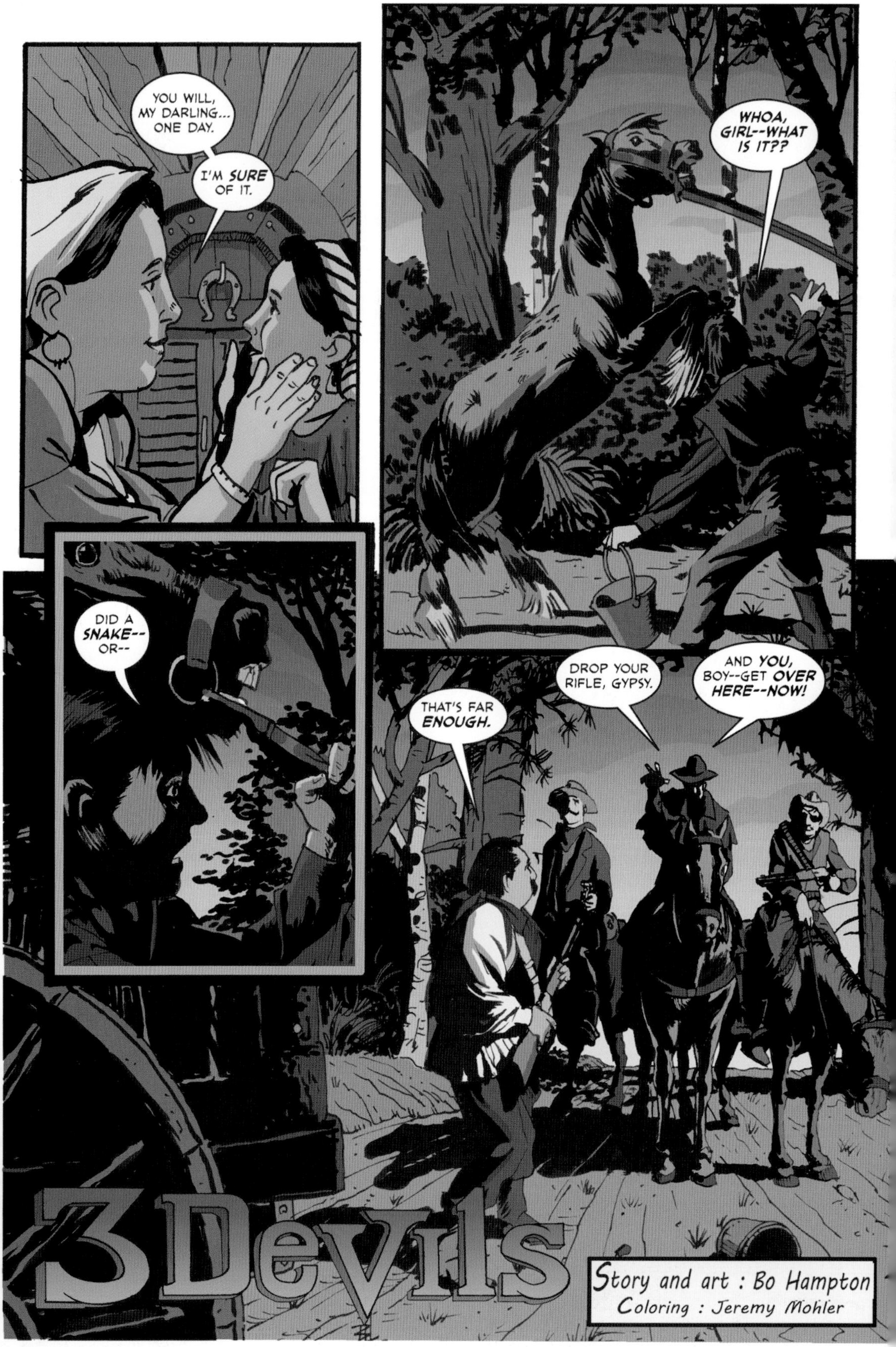
YOU WILL, MY DARLING... ONE DAY.
I'M SURE OF IT.
WHOA, GIRL--WHAT IS IT??
DID A SNAKE--OR--
THAT'S FAR ENOUGH.
DROP YOUR RIFLE, GYPSY.
AND YOU, BOY--GET OVER HERE--NOW!
3 Devils
Story and art : Bo Hampton
Coloring : Jeremy Mohler

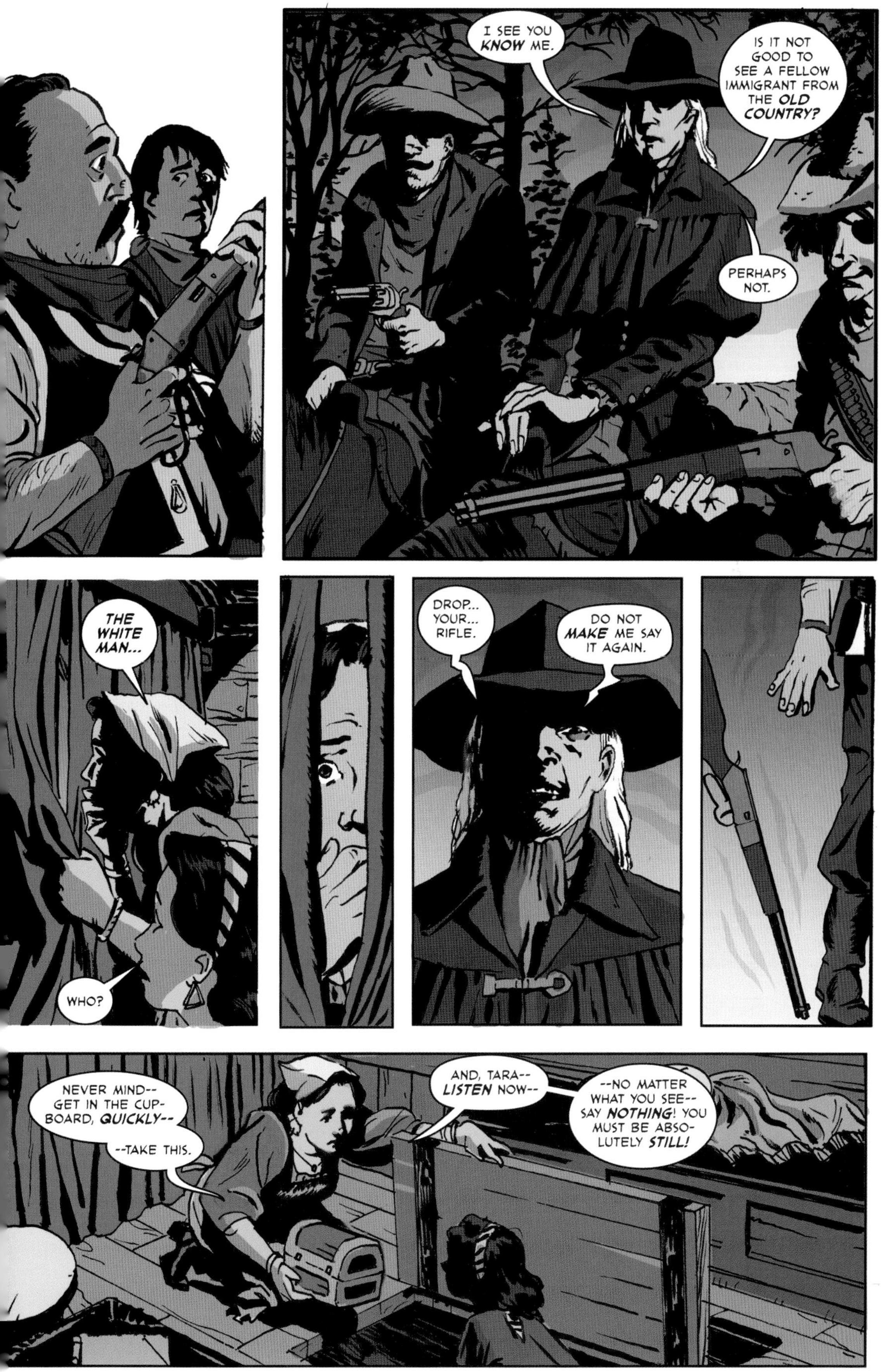
I SEE YOU KNOW ME.
IS IT NOT GOOD TO SEE A FELLOW IMMIGRANT FROM THE OLD COUNTRY?
PERHAPS NOT.
THE WHITE MAN...
WHO?
DROP... YOUR... RIFLE.
DO NOT MAKE ME SAY IT AGAIN.
NEVER MIND-- GET IN THE CUP-BOARD, QUICKLY--
--TAKE THIS.
AND, TARA-- LISTEN NOW--
--NO MATTER WHAT YOU SEE-- SAY NOTHING! YOU MUST BE ABSO-LUTELY STILL!

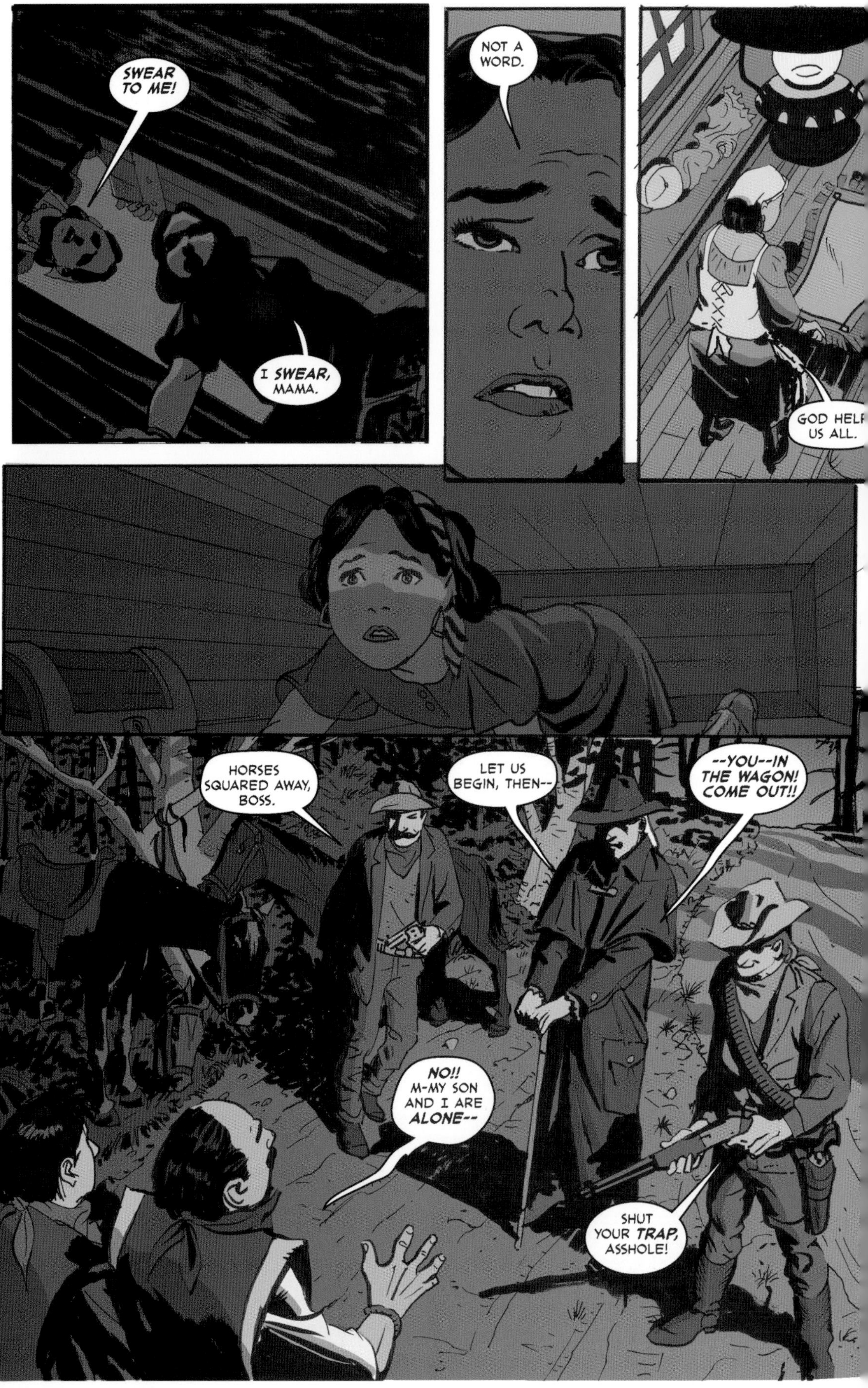
SWEAR TO ME!
I SWEAR, MAMA.
NOT A WORD.
GOD HELP US ALL.
HORSES SQUARED AWAY, BOSS.
LET US BEGIN, THEN--
--YOU--IN THE WAGON! COME OUT!!
NO!! M-MY SON AND I ARE ALONE--
SHUT YOUR TRAP, ASSHOLE!

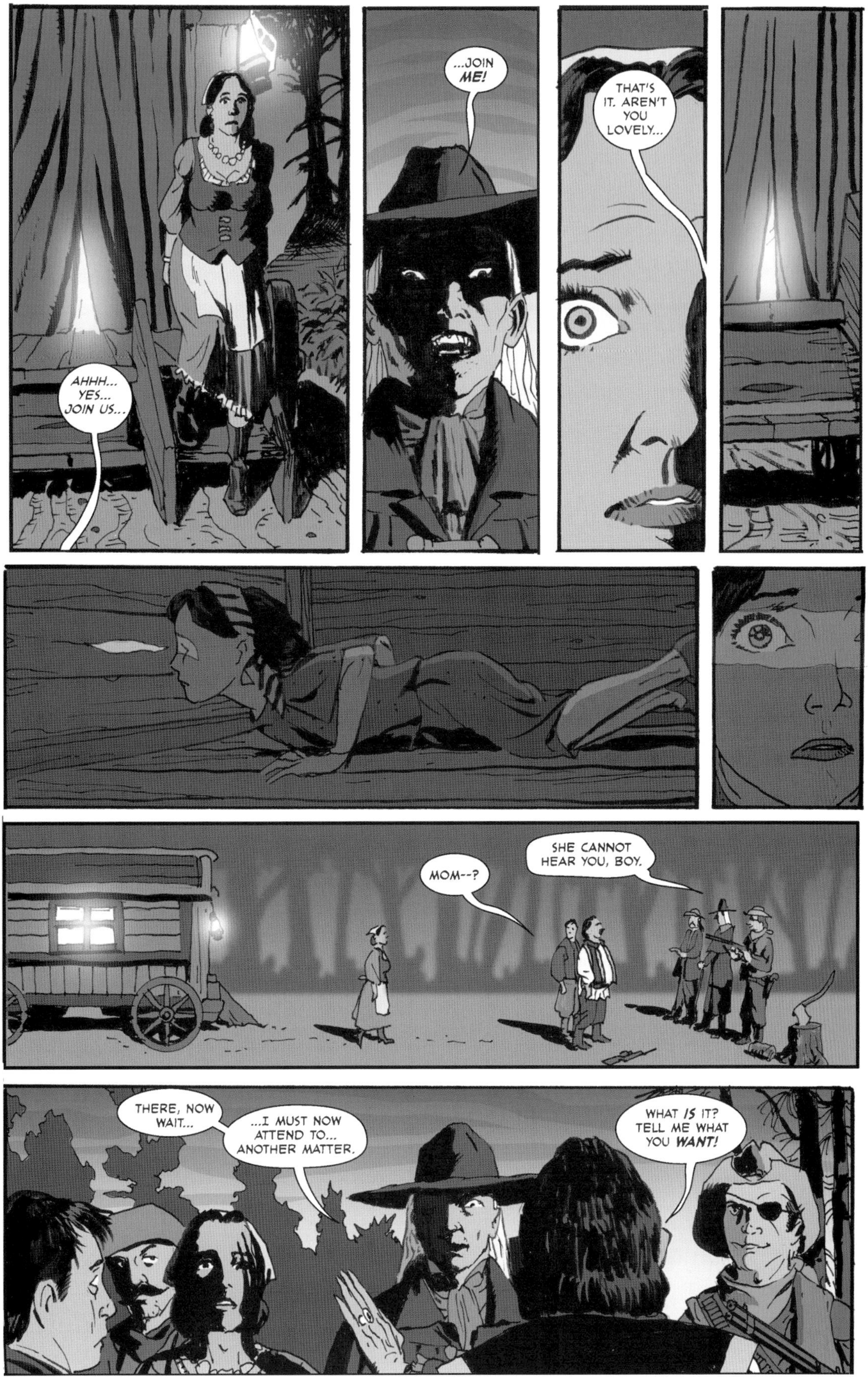
AHHH... YES... JOIN US...
...JOIN ME!
THAT'S IT. AREN'T YOU LOVELY...
MOM--?
SHE CANNOT HEAR YOU, BOY.
THERE, NOW WAIT...
...I MUST NOW ATTEND TO... ANOTHER MATTER.
WHAT IS IT? TELL ME WHAT YOU WANT!

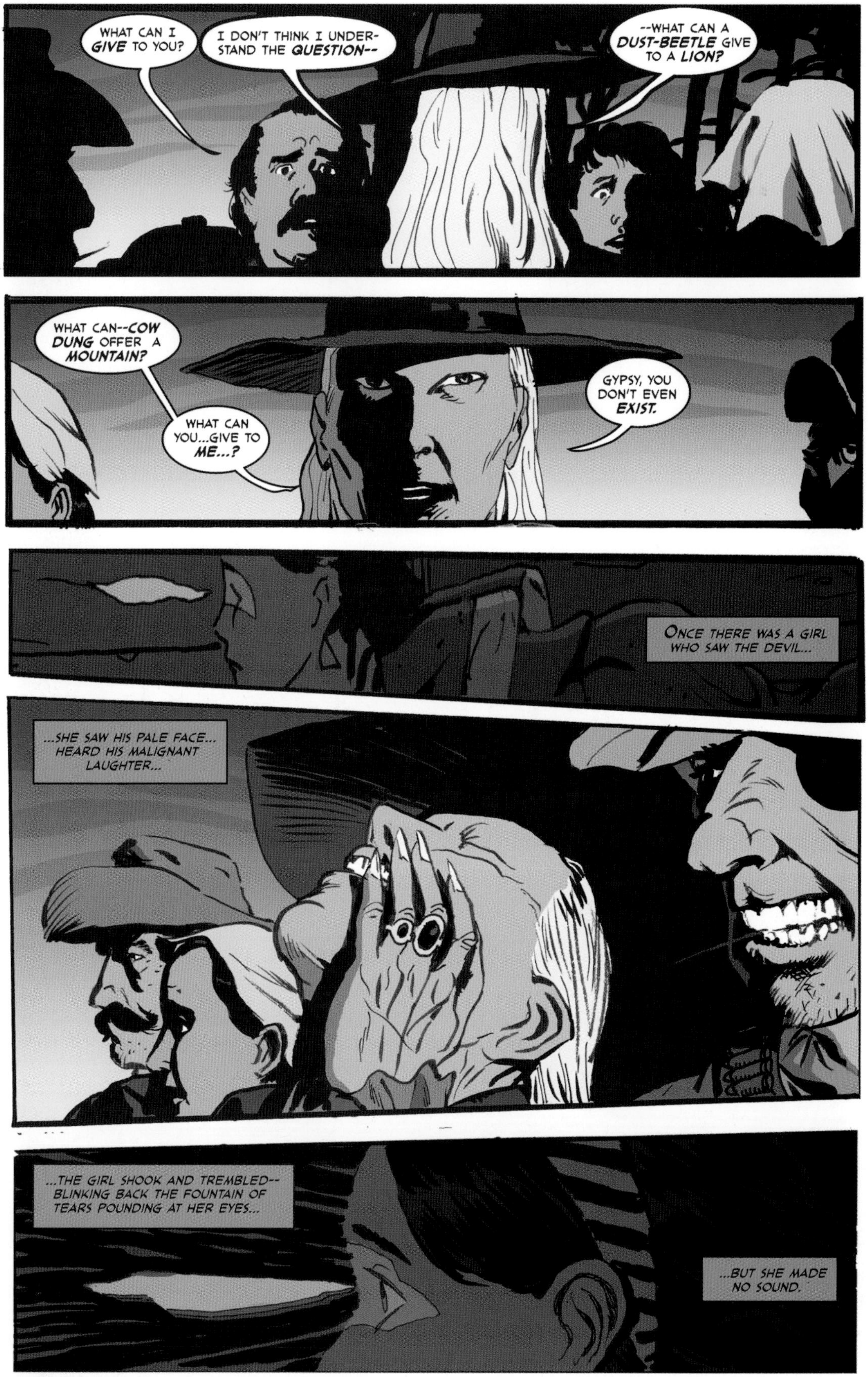

WHAT CAN I GIVE TO YOU?
I DON'T THINK I UNDERSTAND THE QUESTION--
--WHAT CAN A DUST-BEETLE GIVE TO A LION?
WHAT CAN--COW DUNG OFFER A MOUNTAIN?
WHAT CAN YOU...GIVE TO ME...?
GYPSY, YOU DON'T EVEN EXIST.
ONCE THERE WAS A GIRL WHO SAW THE DEVIL...
...SHE SAW HIS PALE FACE... HEARD HIS MALIGNANT LAUGHTER...
...THE GIRL SHOOK AND TREMBLED--BLINKING BACK THE FOUNTAIN OF TEARS POUNDING AT HER EYES...
...BUT SHE MADE NO SOUND.

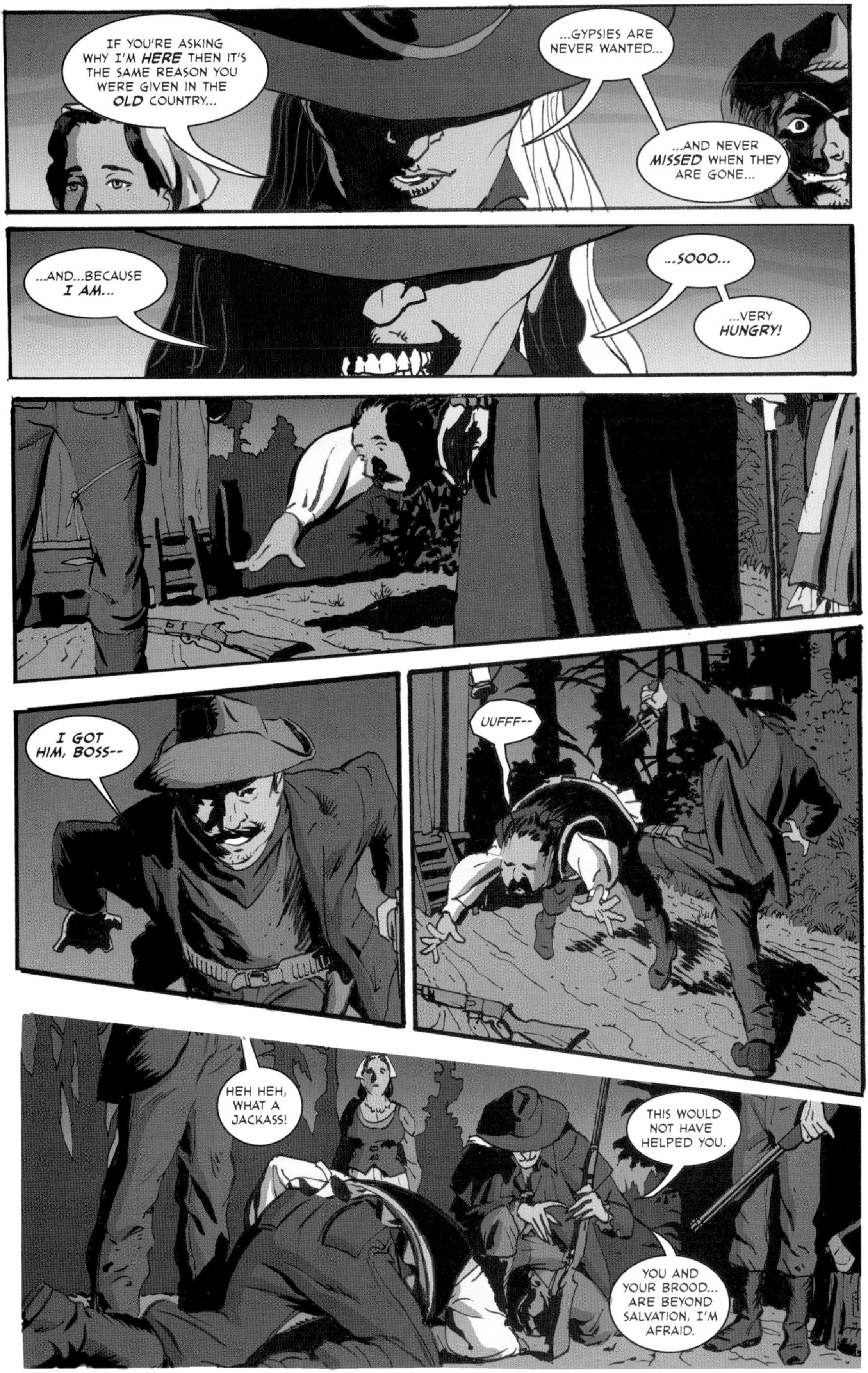
IF YOU'RE ASKING WHY I'M HERE THEN IT'S THE SAME REASON YOU WERE GIVEN IN THE OLD COUNTRY...
...GYPSIES ARE NEVER WANTED...
...AND NEVER MISSED WHEN THEY ARE GONE...
...AND...BECAUSE I AM...
...SOOO...
...VERY HUNGRY!
I GOT HIM, BOSS--
UUFFF--
HEH HEH, WHAT A JACKASS!
THIS WOULD NOT HAVE HELPED YOU.
YOU AND YOUR BROOD... ARE BEYOND SALVATION, I'M AFRAID.

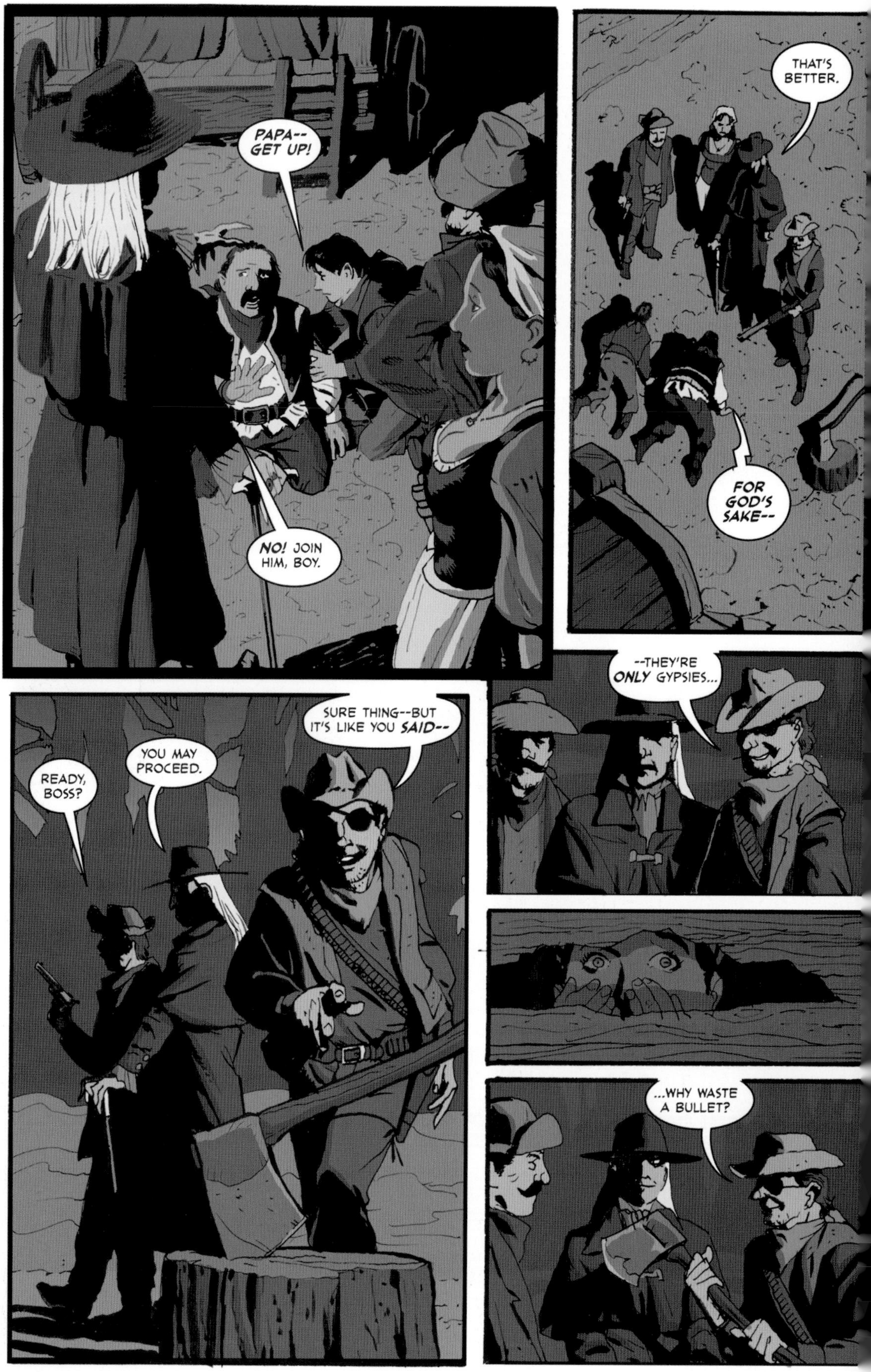
PAPA--
GET UP!
NO! JOIN HIM, BOY.
THAT'S BETTER.
FOR GOD'S SAKE--
READY, BOSS?
YOU MAY PROCEED.
SURE THING--BUT IT'S LIKE YOU SAID--
--THEY'RE ONLY GYPSIES...
...WHY WASTE A BULLET?

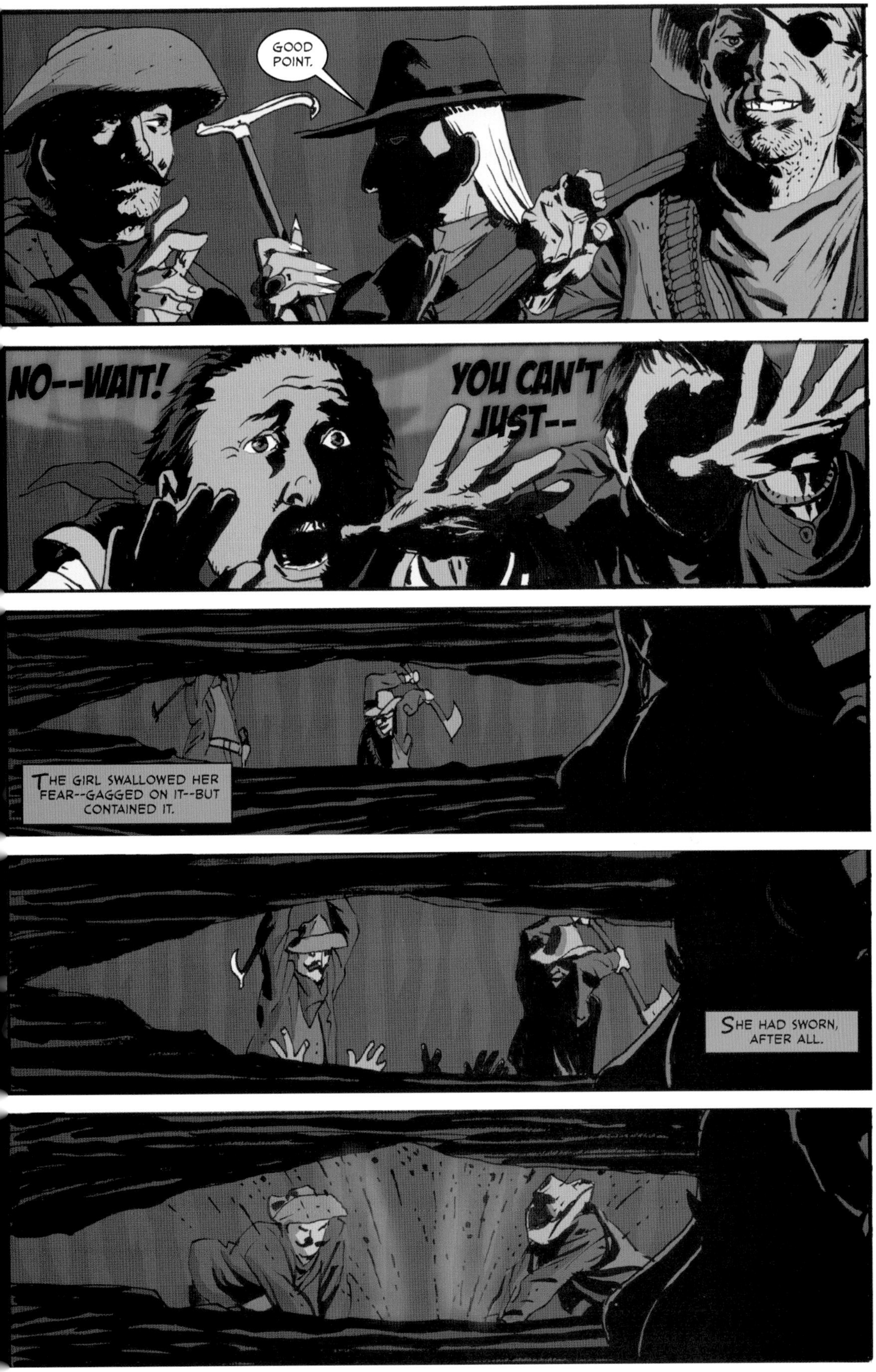
GOOD POINT.
NO--WAIT!
YOU CAN'T JUST--
THE GIRL SWALLOWED HER FEAR--GAGGED ON IT--BUT CONTAINED IT.
SHE HAD SWORN, AFTER ALL.

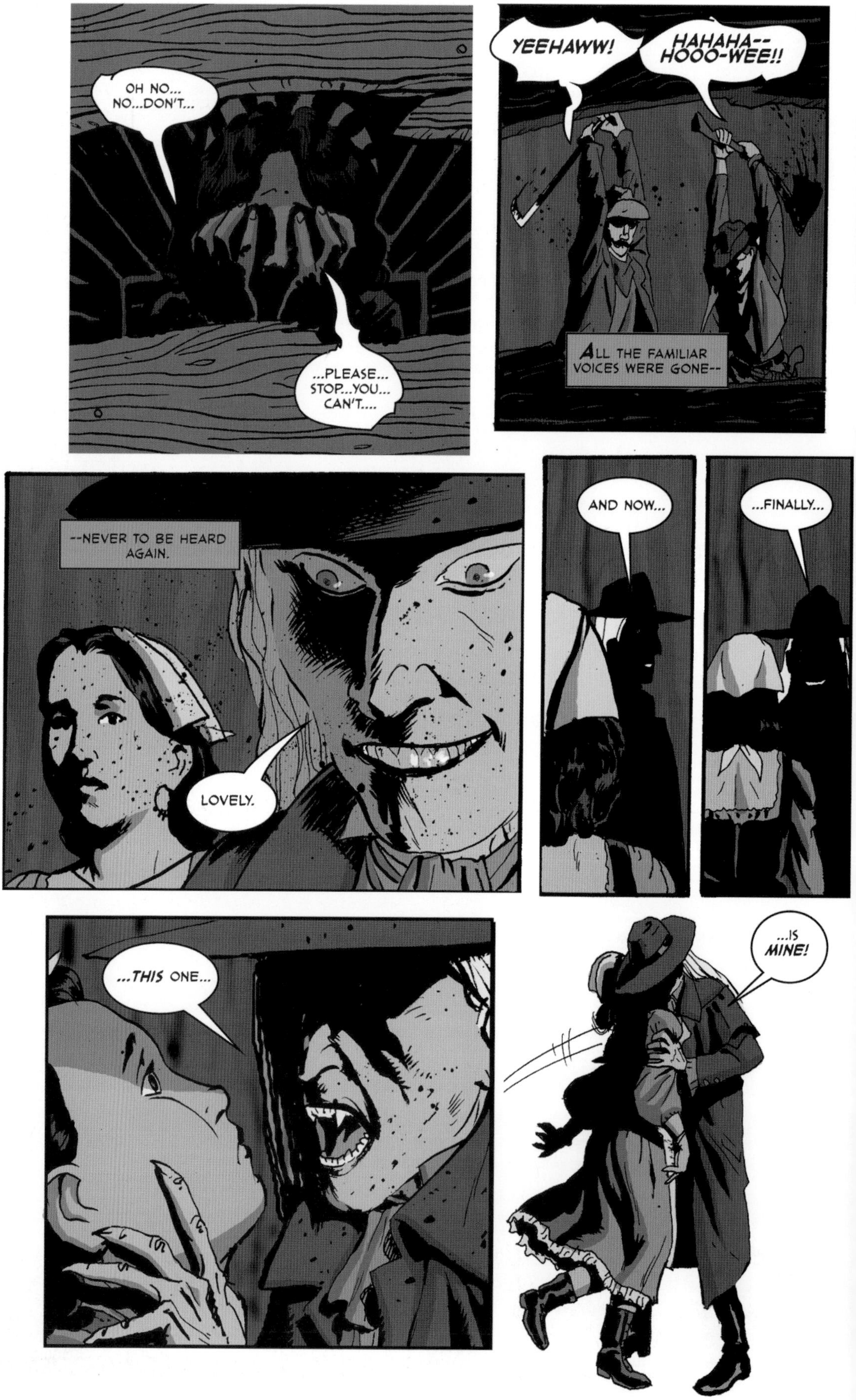
OH NO... NO...DON'T...
...PLEASE... STOP...YOU... CAN'T....
YEEHAWW!
HAHAHA-- HOOO-WEE!!
ALL THE FAMILIAR VOICES WERE GONE--
--NEVER TO BE HEARD AGAIN.
LOVELY.
AND NOW...
...FINALLY...
...THIS ONE...
...IS MINE!

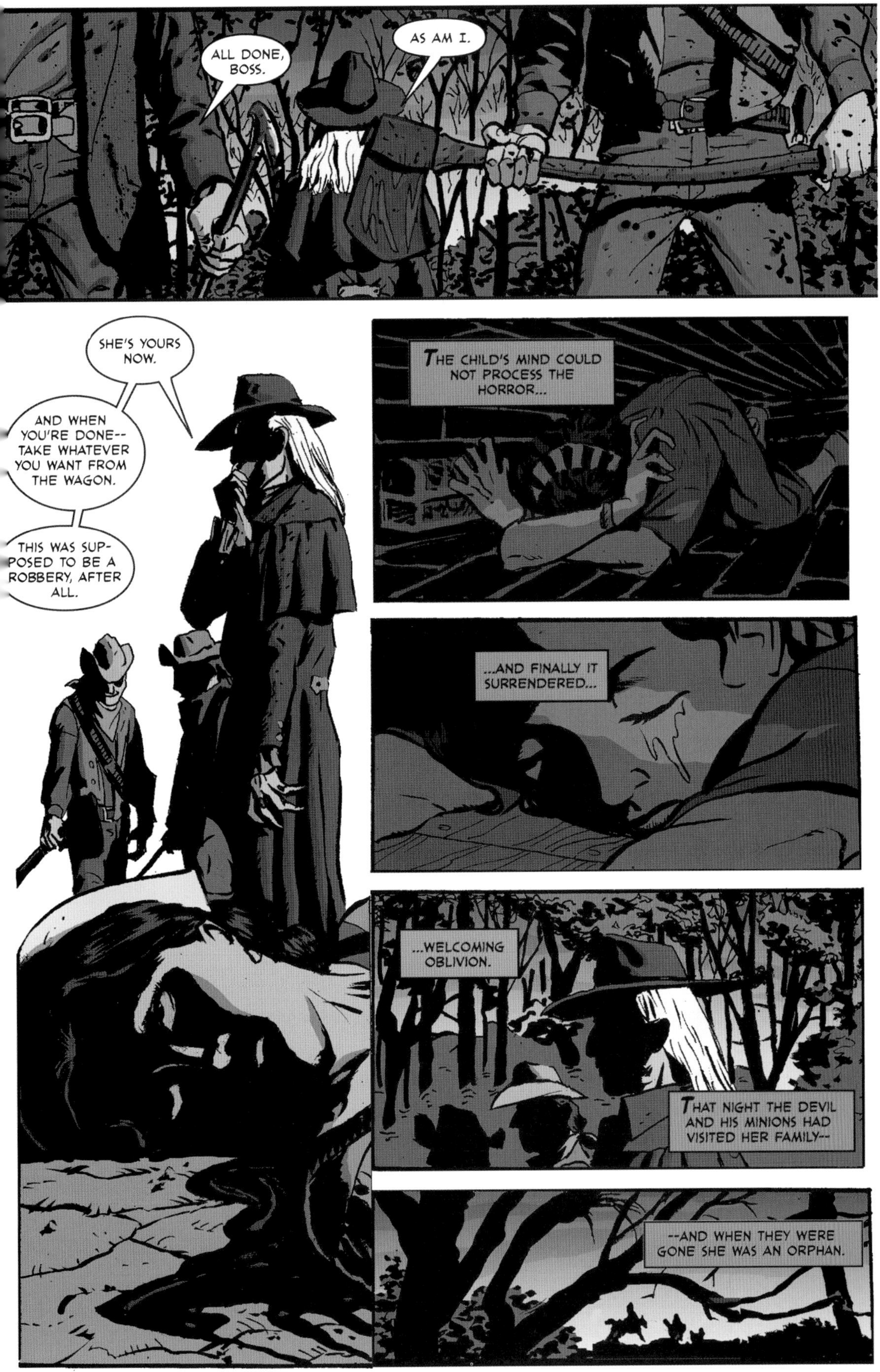
ALL DONE, BOSS.
AS AM I.
SHE'S YOURS NOW.
AND WHEN YOU'RE DONE-- TAKE WHATEVER YOU WANT FROM THE WAGON.
THIS WAS SUPPOSED TO BE A ROBBERY, AFTER ALL.
THE CHILD'S MIND COULD NOT PROCESS THE HORROR...
...AND FINALLY IT SURRENDERED...
...WELCOMING OBLIVION.
THAT NIGHT THE DEVIL AND HIS MINIONS HAD VISITED HER FAMILY--
--AND WHEN THEY WERE GONE SHE WAS AN ORPHAN.

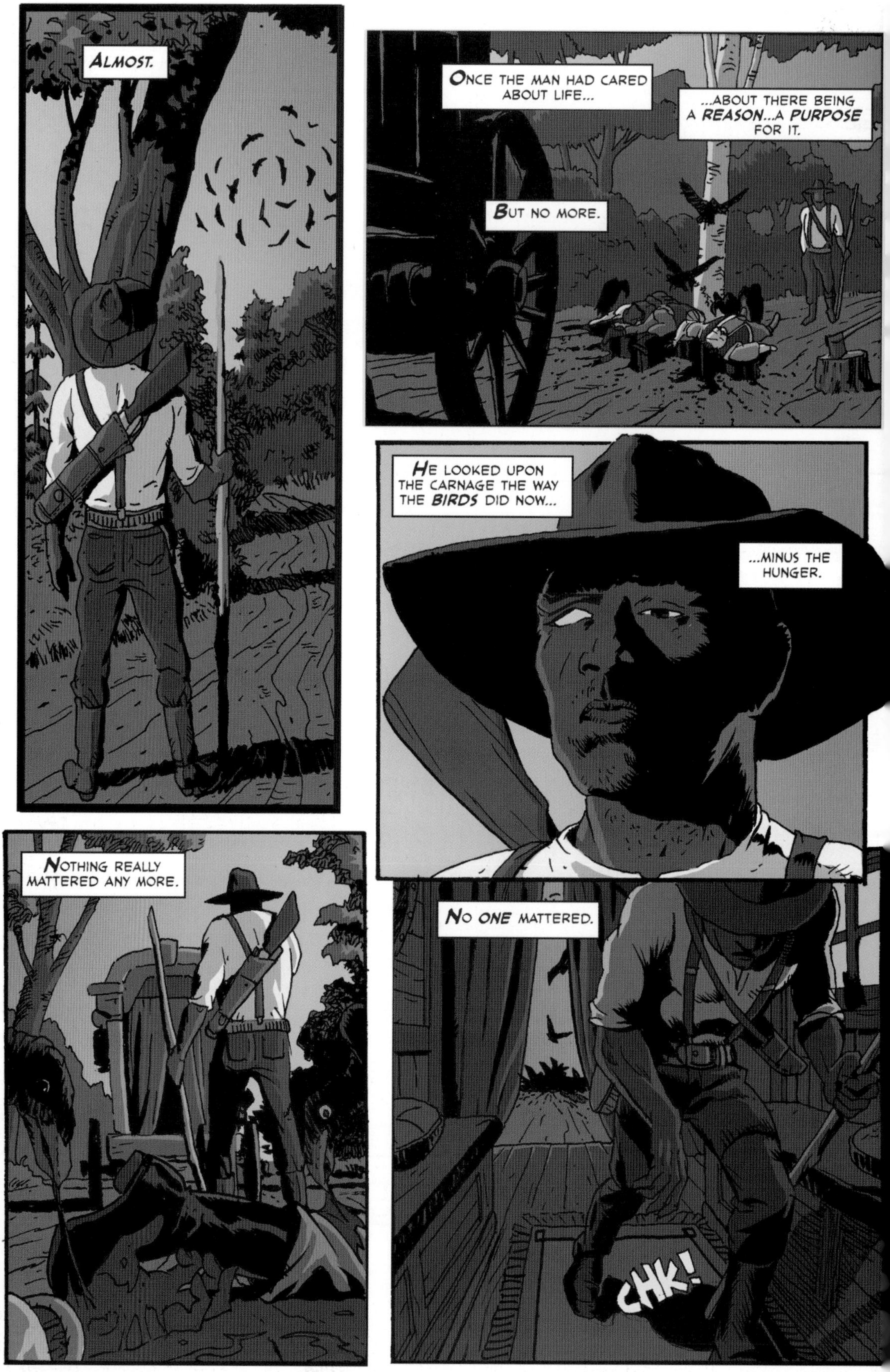
ALMOST.
ONCE THE MAN HAD CARED ABOUT LIFE...
...ABOUT THERE BEING A REASON...A PURPOSE FOR IT.
BUT NO MORE.
HE LOOKED UPON THE CARNAGE THE WAY THE BIRDS DID NOW...
...MINUS THE HUNGER.
NOTHING REALLY MATTERED ANY MORE.
NO ONE MATTERED.
CHK!

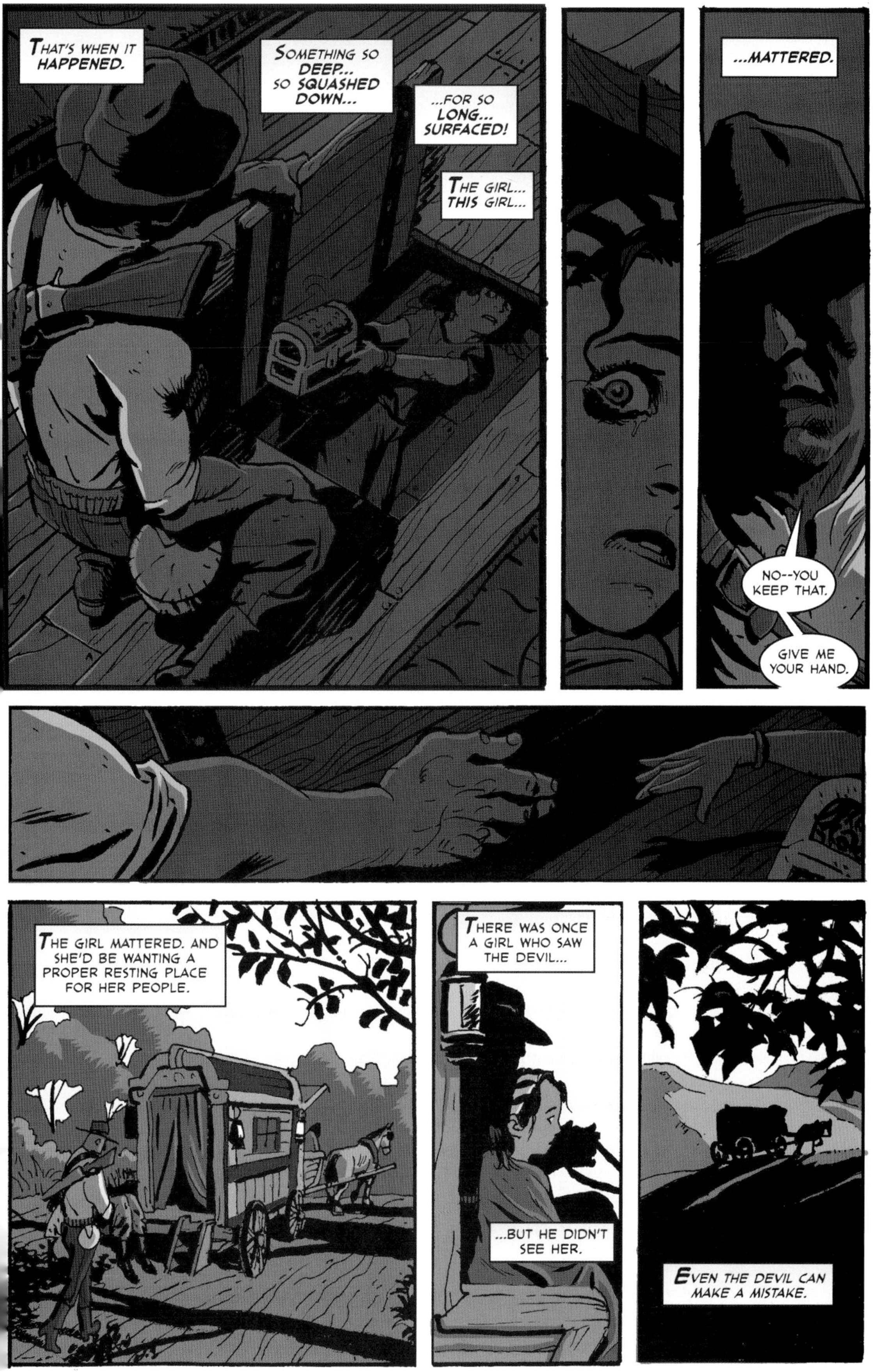
THAT'S WHEN IT HAPPENED.
SOMETHING SO DEEP... SO SQUASHED DOWN...
...FOR SO LONG... SURFACED!
THE GIRL... THIS GIRL...
...MATTERED.
NO--YOU KEEP THAT.
GIVE ME YOUR HAND.
THE GIRL MATTERED. AND SHE'D BE WANTING A PROPER RESTING PLACE FOR HER PEOPLE.
THERE WAS ONCE A GIRL WHO SAW THE DEVIL...
...BUT HE DIDN'T SEE HER.
EVEN THE DEVIL CAN MAKE A MISTAKE.

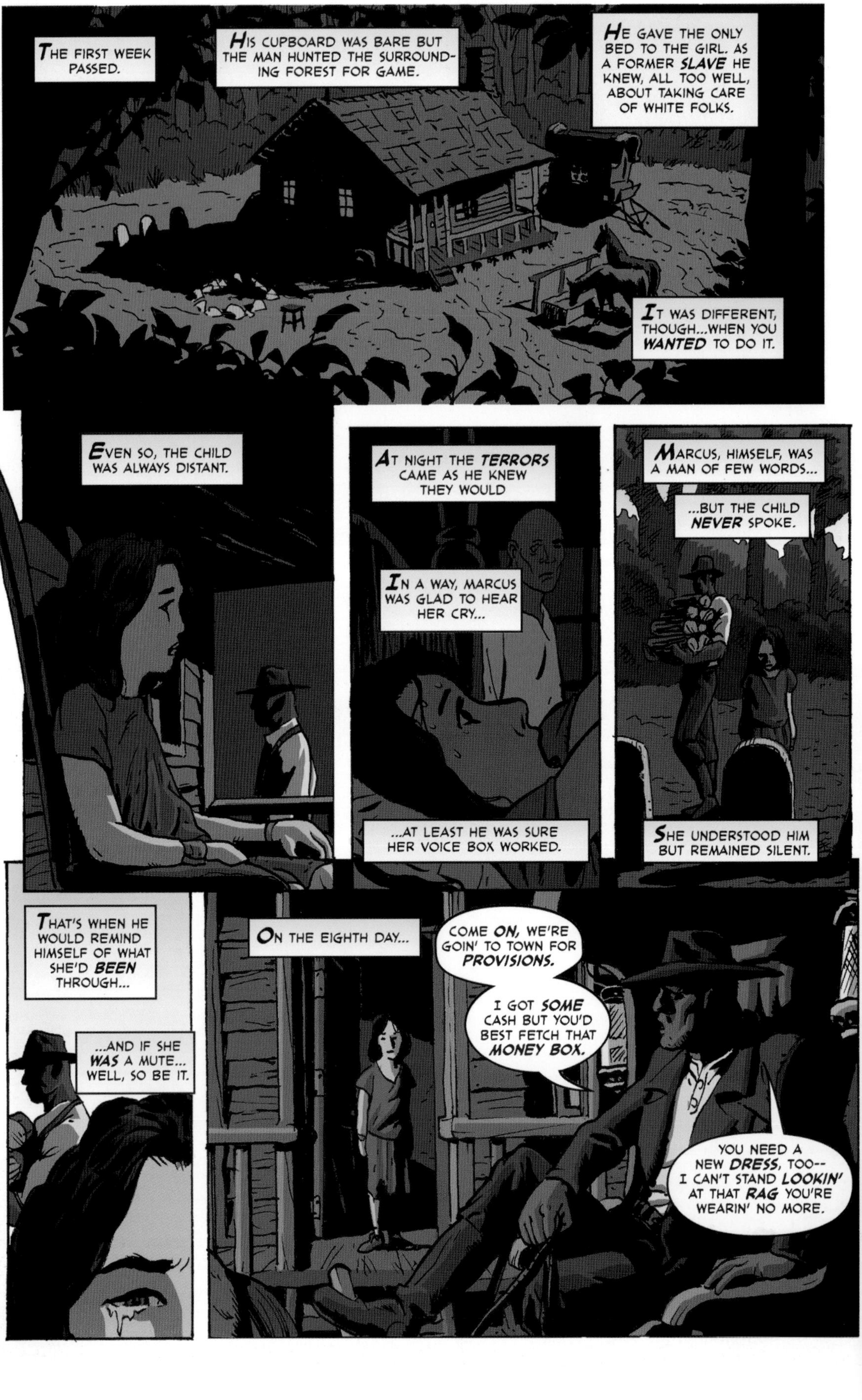
THE FIRST WEEK PASSED.
HIS CUPBOARD WAS BARE BUT THE MAN HUNTED THE SURROUNDING FOREST FOR GAME.
HE GAVE THE ONLY BED TO THE GIRL. AS A FORMER SLAVE HE KNEW, ALL TOO WELL, ABOUT TAKING CARE OF WHITE FOLKS.
IT WAS DIFFERENT, THOUGH...WHEN YOU WANTED TO DO IT.
EVEN SO, THE CHILD WAS ALWAYS DISTANT.
AT NIGHT THE TERRORS CAME AS HE KNEW THEY WOULD
IN A WAY, MARCUS WAS GLAD TO HEAR HER CRY...
...AT LEAST HE WAS SURE HER VOICE BOX WORKED.
MARCUS, HIMSELF, WAS A MAN OF FEW WORDS...
...BUT THE CHILD NEVER SPOKE.
SHE UNDERSTOOD HIM BUT REMAINED SILENT.
THAT'S WHEN HE WOULD REMIND HIMSELF OF WHAT SHE'D BEEN THROUGH...
...AND IF SHE WAS A MUTE... WELL, SO BE IT.
ON THE EIGHTH DAY...
COME ON, WE'RE GOIN' TO TOWN FOR PROVISIONS.
I GOT SOME CASH BUT YOU'D BEST FETCH THAT MONEY BOX.
YOU NEED A NEW DRESS, TOO-- I CAN'T STAND LOOKIN' AT THAT RAG YOU'RE WEARIN' NO MORE.

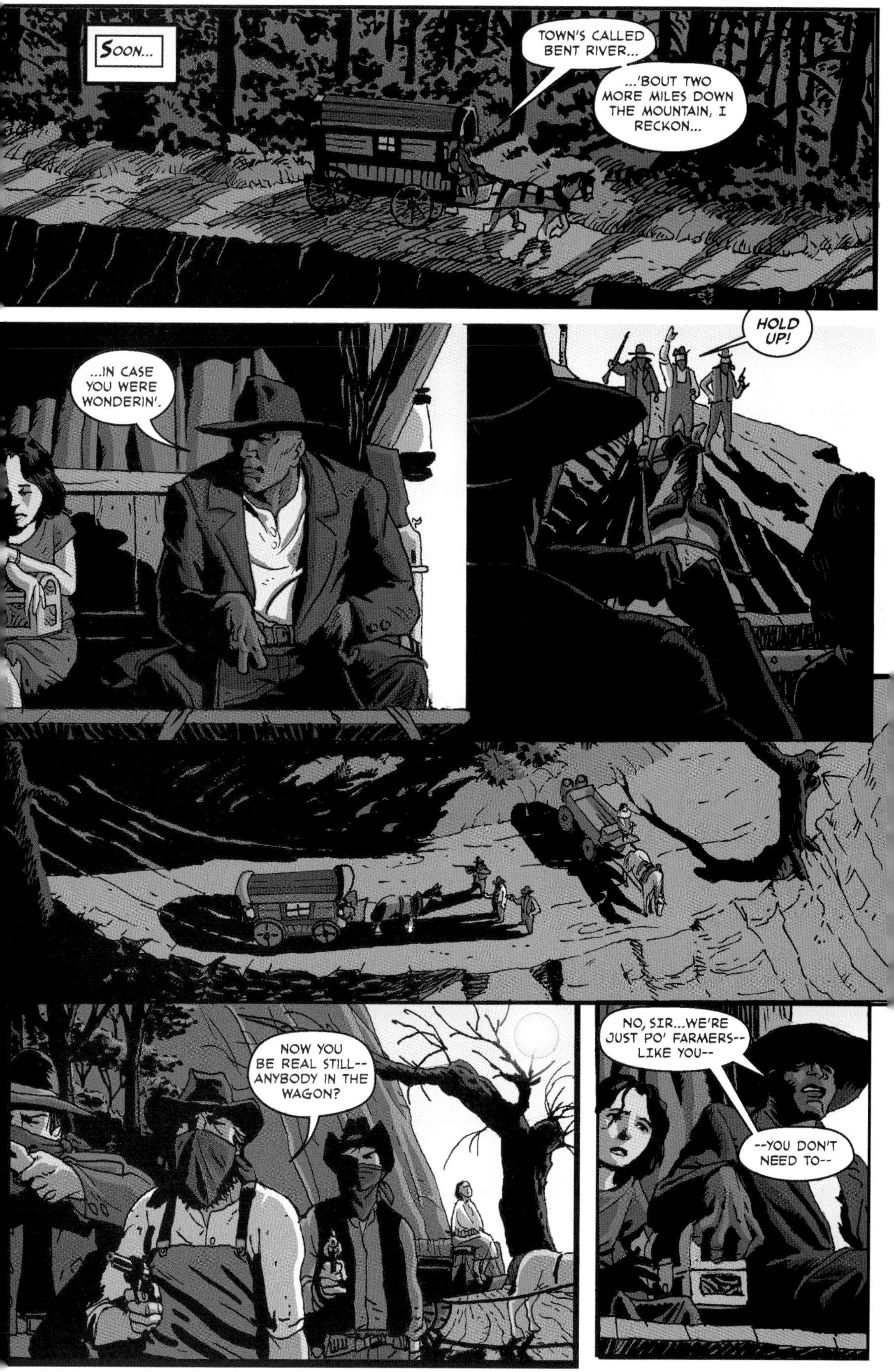
SOON...
TOWN'S CALLED BENT RIVER...
...'BOUT TWO MORE MILES DOWN THE MOUNTAIN, I RECKON...
...IN CASE YOU WERE WONDERIN'.
HOLD UP!
NOW YOU BE REAL STILL-- ANYBODY IN THE WAGON?
NO, SIR...WE'RE JUST PO' FARMERS-- LIKE YOU--
--YOU DON'T NEED TO--

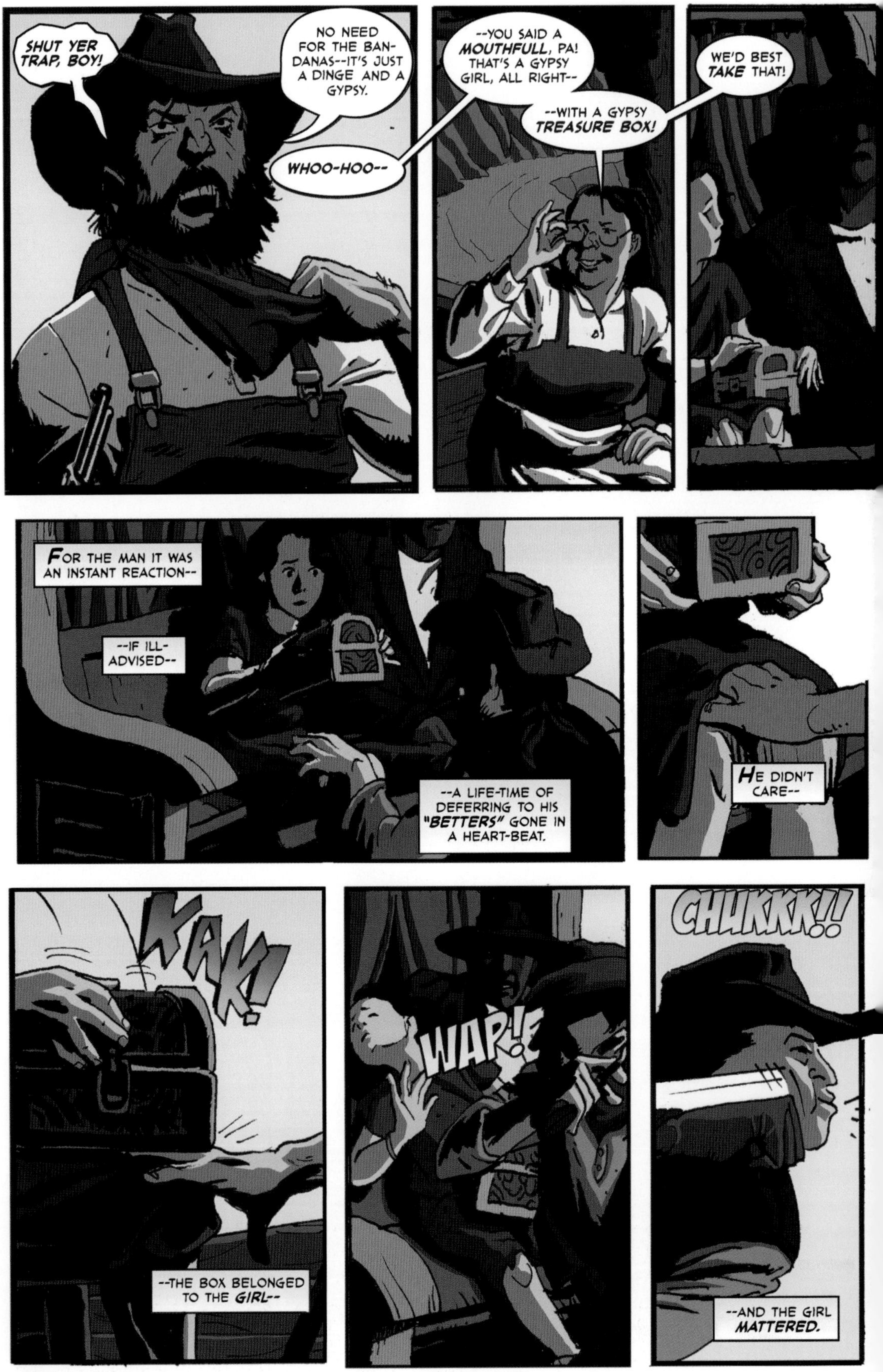
SHUT YER TRAP, BOY!
NO NEED FOR THE BAN-DANAS--IT'S JUST A DINGE AND A GYPSY.
WHOO-HOO--
--YOU SAID A MOUTHFULL, PA! THAT'S A GYPSY GIRL, ALL RIGHT--
--WITH A GYPSY TREASURE BOX!
WE'D BEST TAKE THAT!
FOR THE MAN IT WAS AN INSTANT REACTION--
--IF ILL-ADVISED--
--A LIFE-TIME OF DEFERRING TO HIS "BETTERS" GONE IN A HEART-BEAT.
HE DIDN'T CARE--
KAK!
--THE BOX BELONGED TO THE GIRL--
WAP!E
CHUKKK!!
--AND THE GIRL MATTERED.

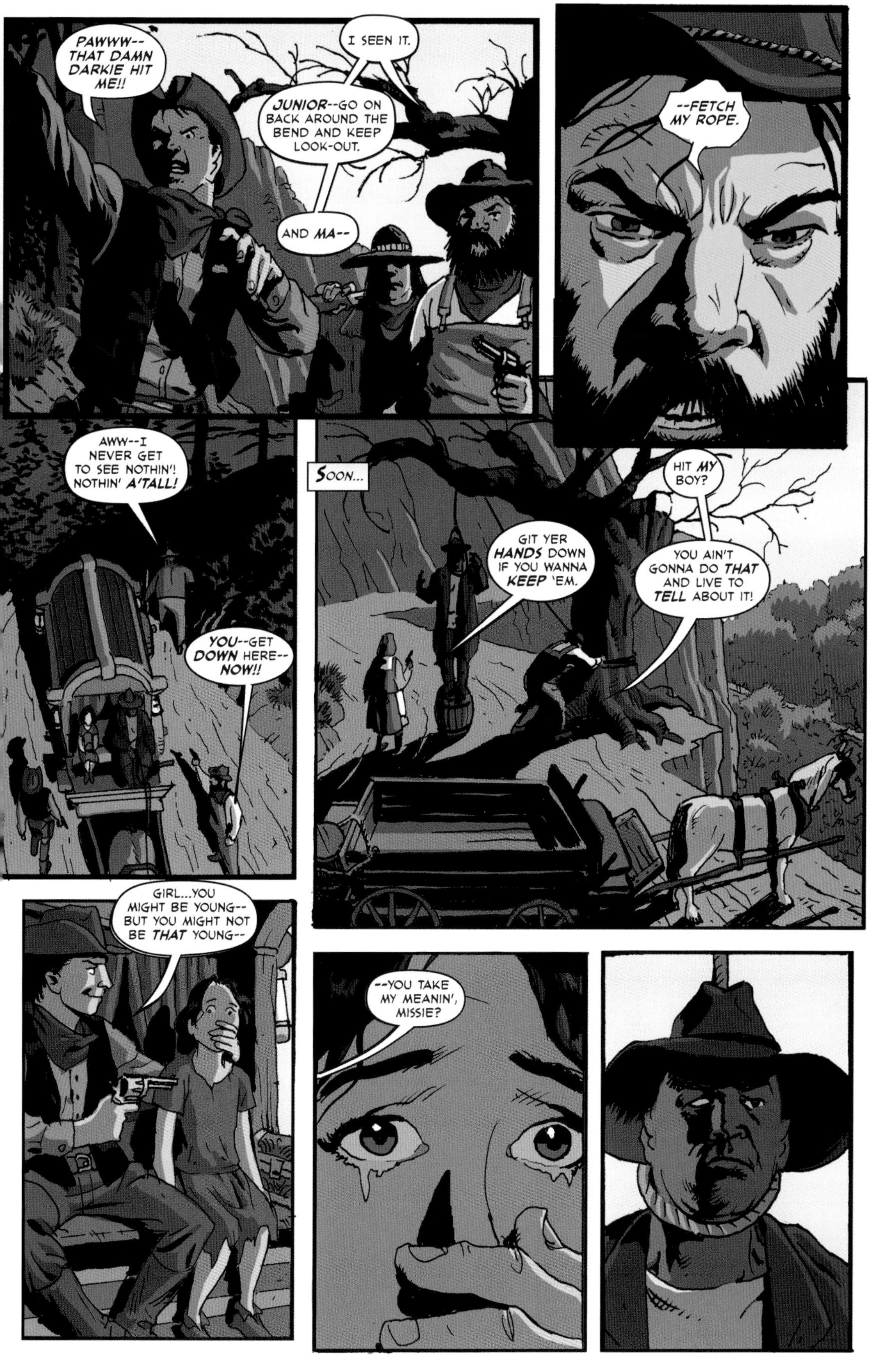
PAWWW--THAT DAMN DARKIE HIT ME!!
I SEEN IT.
JUNIOR--GO ON BACK AROUND THE BEND AND KEEP LOOK-OUT.
AND MA--
--FETCH MY ROPE.
AWW--I NEVER GET TO SEE NOTHIN'! NOTHIN' A'TALL!
YOU--GET DOWN HERE--NOW!!
SOON...
HIT MY BOY?
YOU AIN'T GONNA DO THAT AND LIVE TO TELL ABOUT IT!
GIT YER HANDS DOWN IF YOU WANNA KEEP 'EM.
GIRL...YOU MIGHT BE YOUNG--BUT YOU MIGHT NOT BE THAT YOUNG--
--YOU TAKE MY MEANIN', MISSIE?

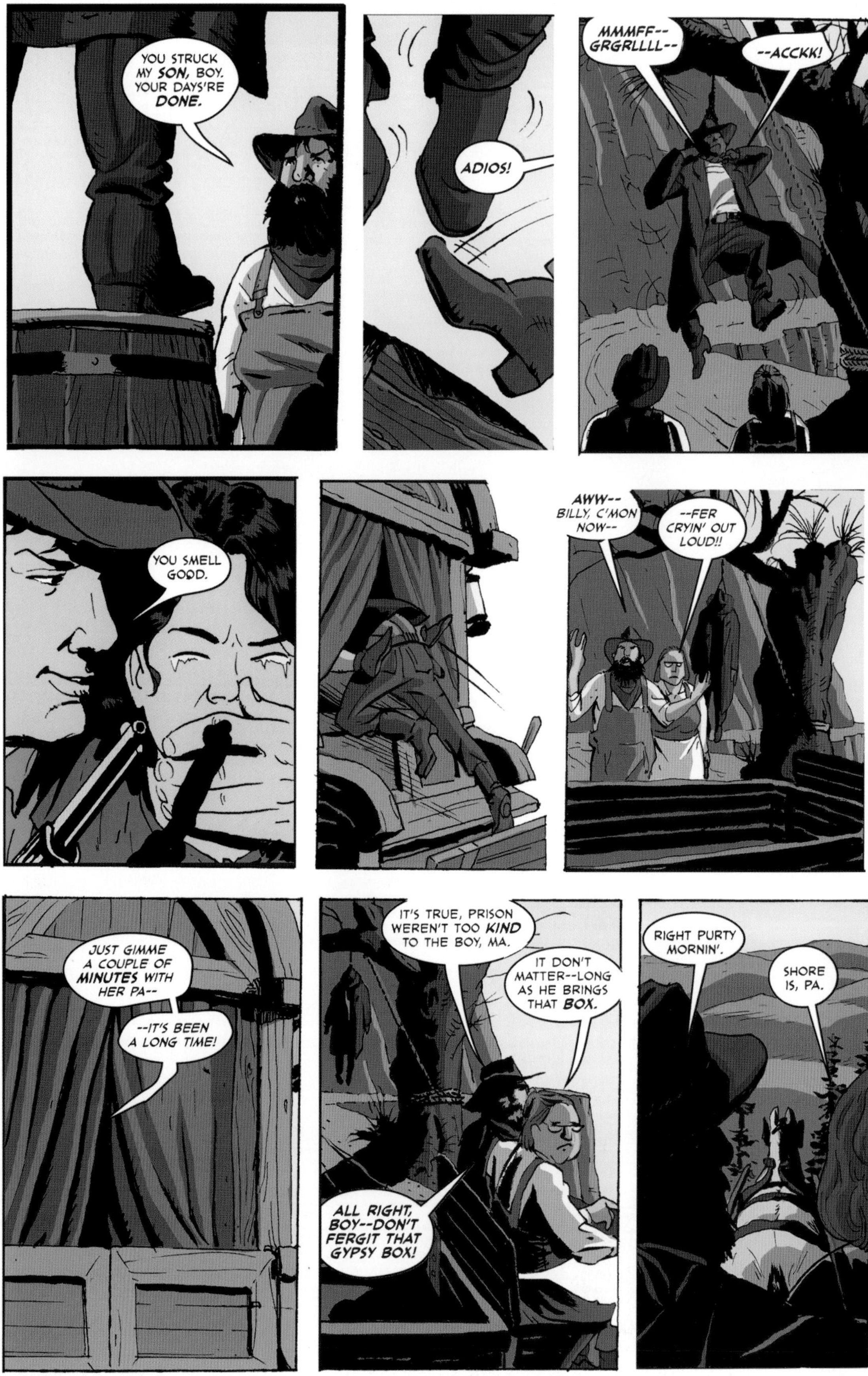

YOU STRUCK MY SON, BOY. YOUR DAYS'RE DONE.
ADIOS!
MMMFF-- GRGRLLLL--
--ACCKK!
YOU SMELL GOOD.
AWW-- BILLY, C'MON NOW--
--FER CRYIN' OUT LOUD!!
JUST GIMME A COUPLE OF MINUTES WITH HER PA--
--IT'S BEEN A LONG TIME!
IT'S TRUE, PRISON WEREN'T TOO KIND TO THE BOY, MA.
IT DON'T MATTER--LONG AS HE BRINGS THAT BOX.
ALL RIGHT, BOY--DON'T FERGIT THAT GYPSY BOX!
RIGHT PURTY MORNIN'.
SHORE IS, PA.

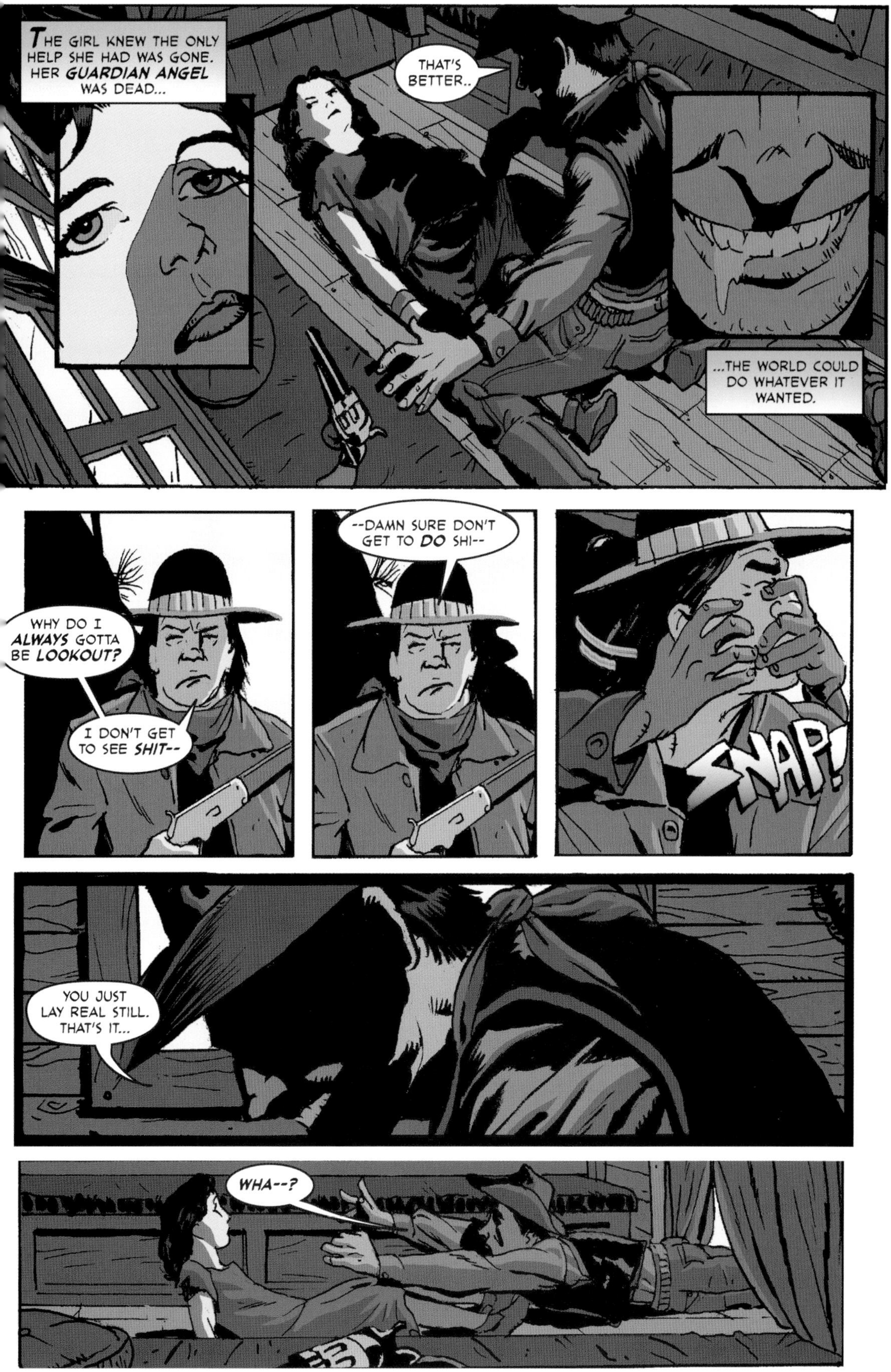
THE GIRL KNEW THE ONLY HELP SHE HAD WAS GONE. HER GUARDIAN ANGEL WAS DEAD...
THAT'S BETTER..
...THE WORLD COULD DO WHATEVER IT WANTED.
WHY DO I ALWAYS GOTTA BE LOOKOUT?
I DON'T GET TO SEE SHIT--
--DAMN SURE DON'T GET TO DO SHI--
SNAP!
YOU JUST LAY REAL STILL. THAT'S IT...
WHA--?

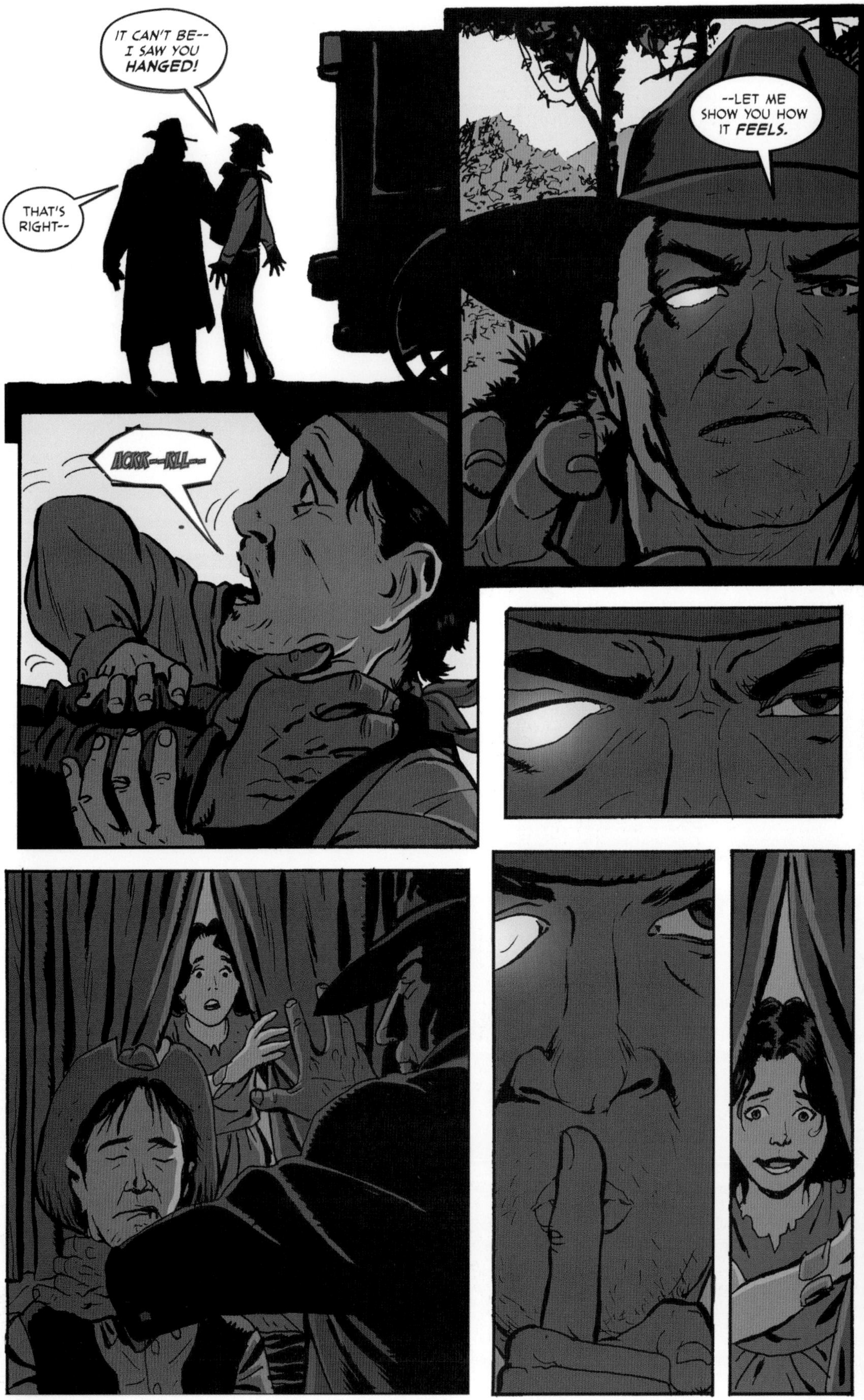
IT CAN'T BE-- I SAW YOU HANGED!
THAT'S RIGHT--
--LET ME SHOW YOU HOW IT FEELS.
ACKK--KLL--

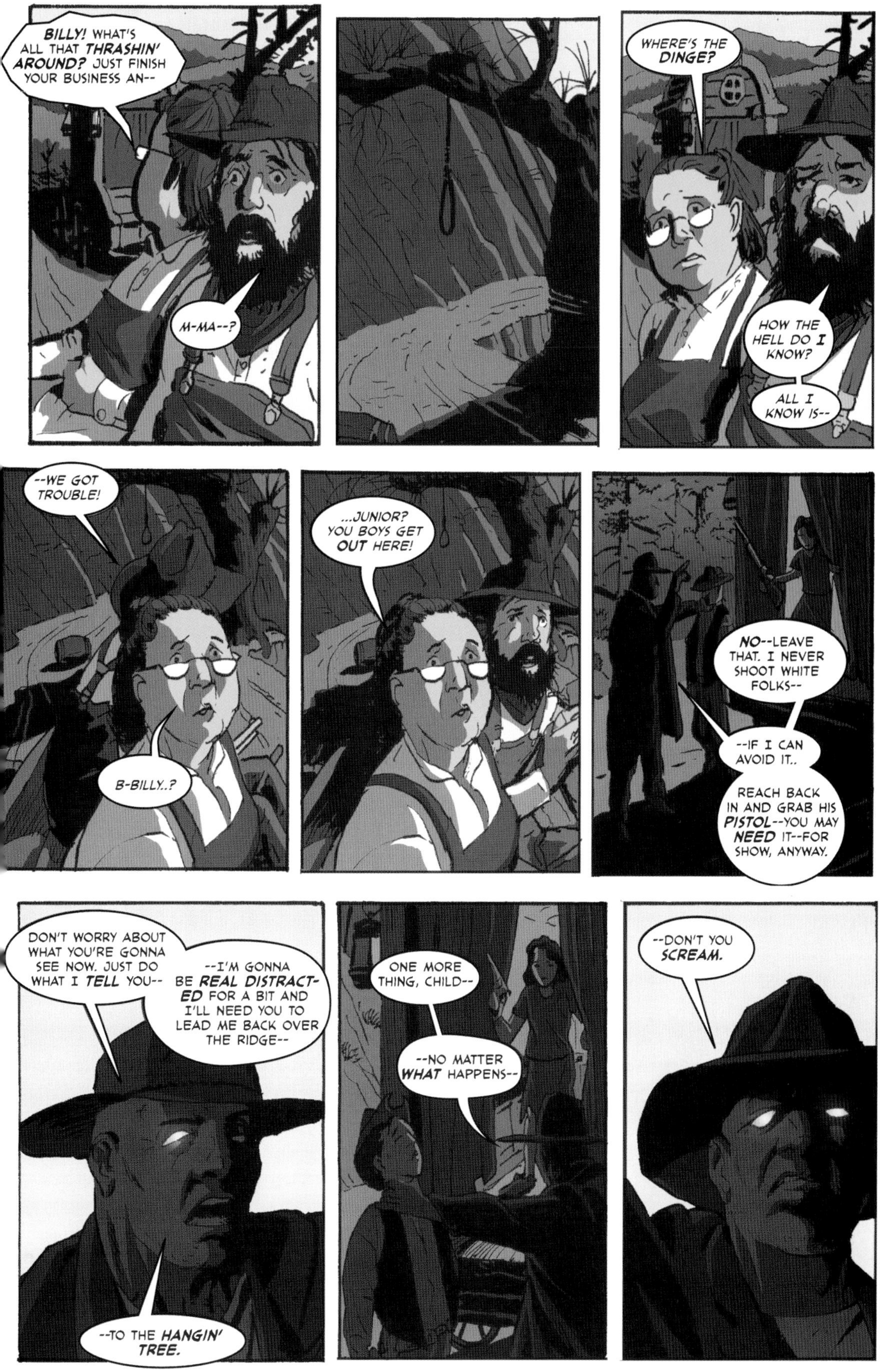
BILLY! WHAT'S ALL THAT THRASHIN' AROUND? JUST FINISH YOUR BUSINESS AN--
M-MA--?
WHERE'S THE DINGE?
HOW THE HELL DO I KNOW?
ALL I KNOW IS--
--WE GOT TROUBLE!
B-BILLY..?
...JUNIOR? YOU BOYS GET OUT HERE!
NO--LEAVE THAT. I NEVER SHOOT WHITE FOLKS--
--IF I CAN AVOID IT..
REACH BACK IN AND GRAB HIS PISTOL--YOU MAY NEED IT--FOR SHOW, ANYWAY.
DON'T WORRY ABOUT WHAT YOU'RE GONNA SEE NOW. JUST DO WHAT I TELL YOU--
--I'M GONNA BE REAL DISTRACT-ED FOR A BIT AND I'LL NEED YOU TO LEAD ME BACK OVER THE RIDGE--
--TO THE HANGIN' TREE.
ONE MORE THING, CHILD--
--NO MATTER WHAT HAPPENS--
--DON'T YOU SCREAM.

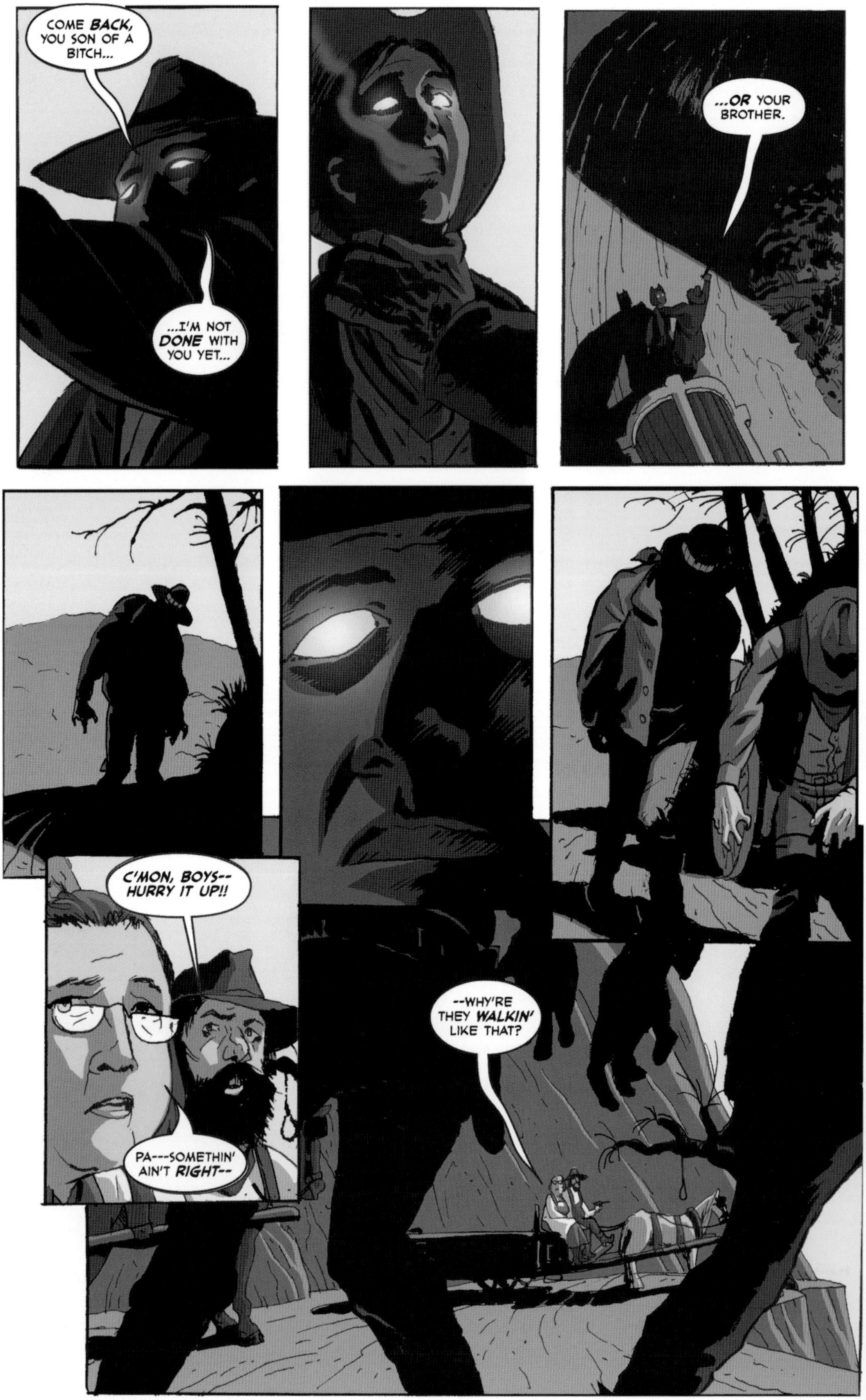
COME BACK, YOU SON OF A BITCH...
...I'M NOT DONE WITH YOU YET...
...OR YOUR BROTHER.
C'MON, BOYS-- HURRY IT UP!!
PA---SOMETHIN' AIN'T RIGHT--
--WHY'RE THEY WALKIN' LIKE THAT?

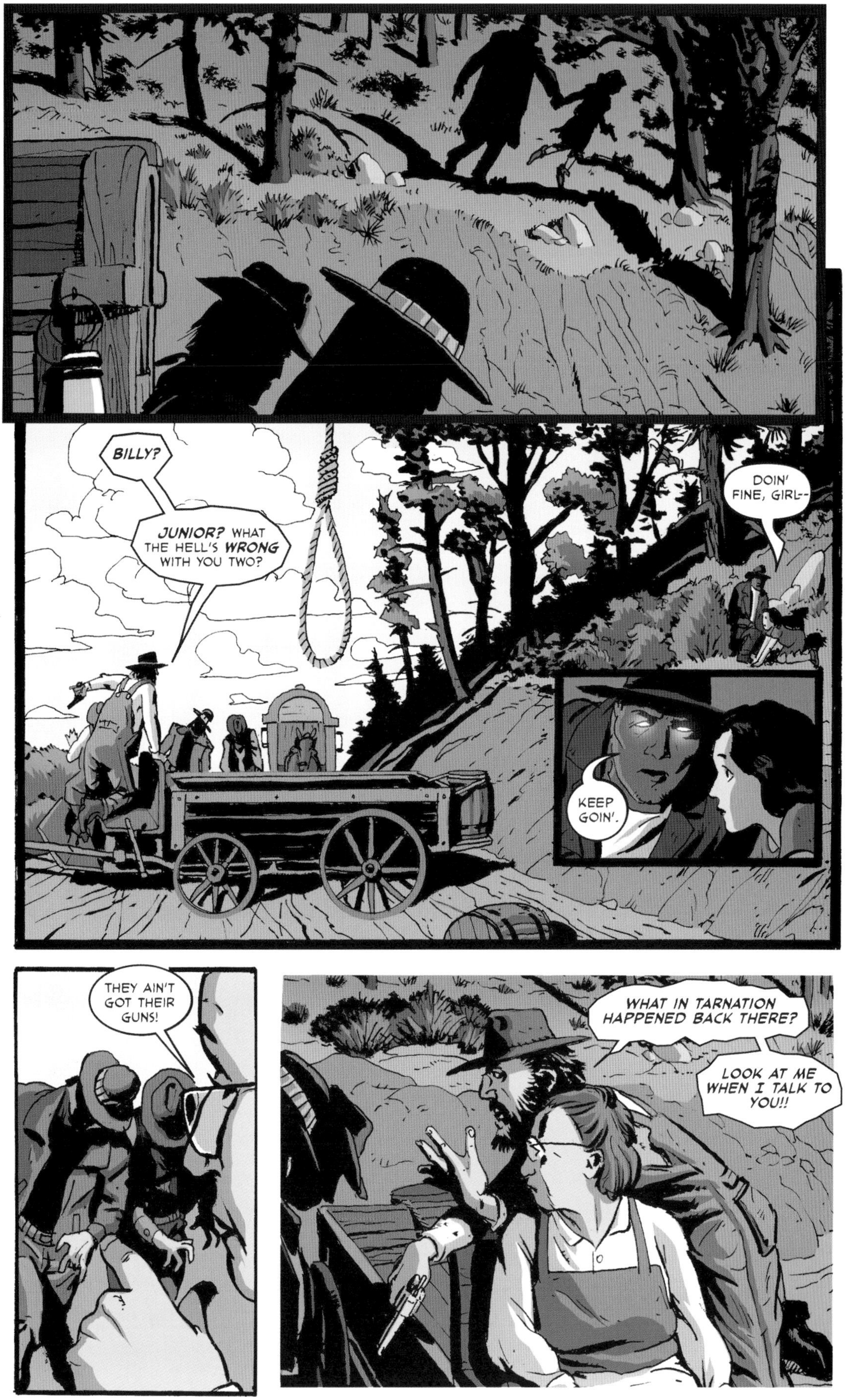
BILLY?
JUNIOR? WHAT THE HELL'S WRONG WITH YOU TWO?
DOIN' FINE, GIRL--
KEEP GOIN'.
THEY AIN'T GOT THEIR GUNS!
WHAT IN TARNATION HAPPENED BACK THERE?
LOOK AT ME WHEN I TALK TO YOU!!

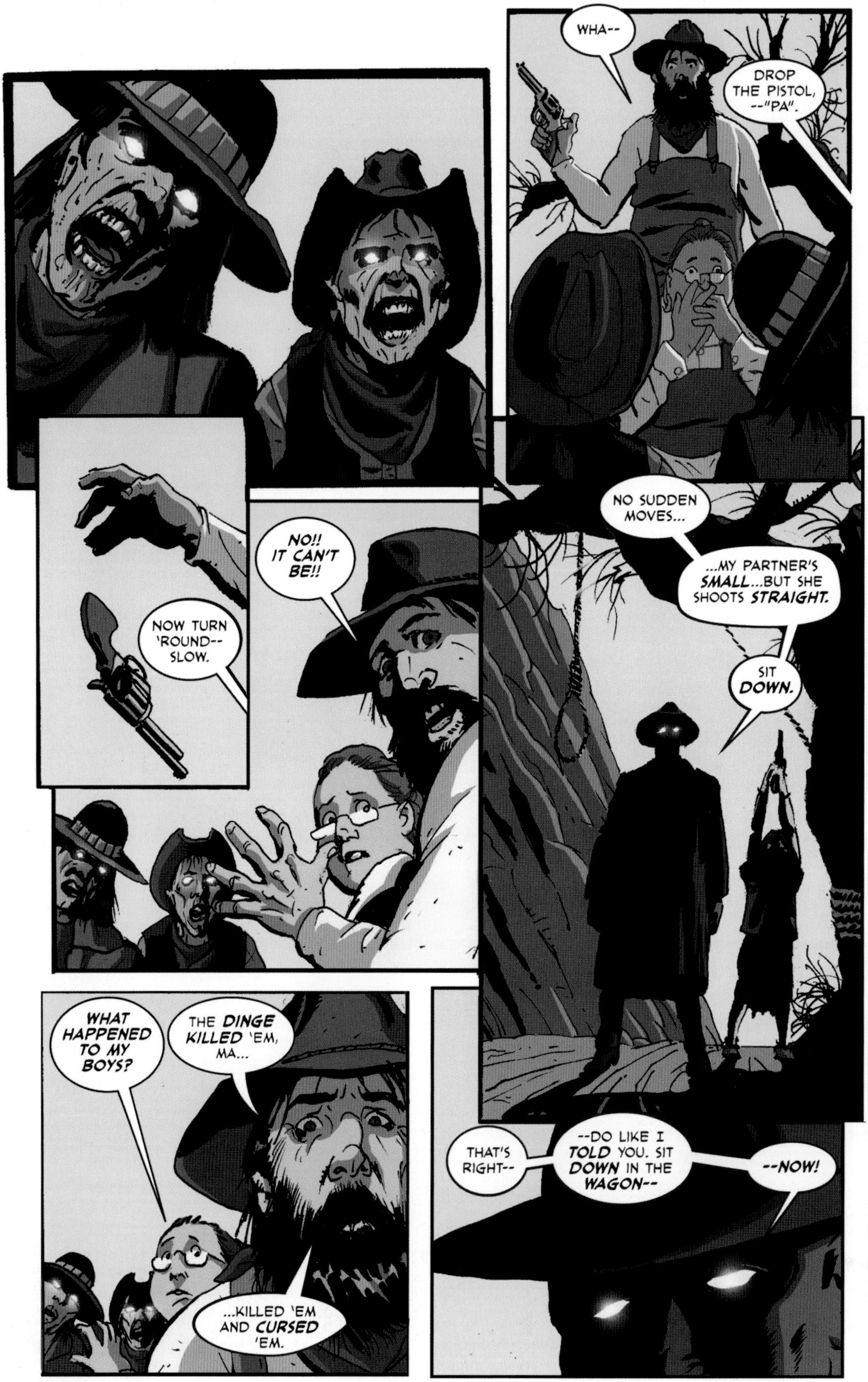
WHA--
DROP THE PISTOL, --"PA".
NOW TURN 'ROUND-- SLOW.
NO!! IT CAN'T BE!!
NO SUDDEN MOVES...
...MY PARTNER'S SMALL...BUT SHE SHOOTS STRAIGHT.
SIT DOWN.
WHAT HAPPENED TO MY BOYS?
THE DINGE KILLED 'EM, MA...
...KILLED 'EM AND CURSED 'EM.
THAT'S RIGHT--
--DO LIKE I TOLD YOU. SIT DOWN IN THE WAGON--
--NOW!

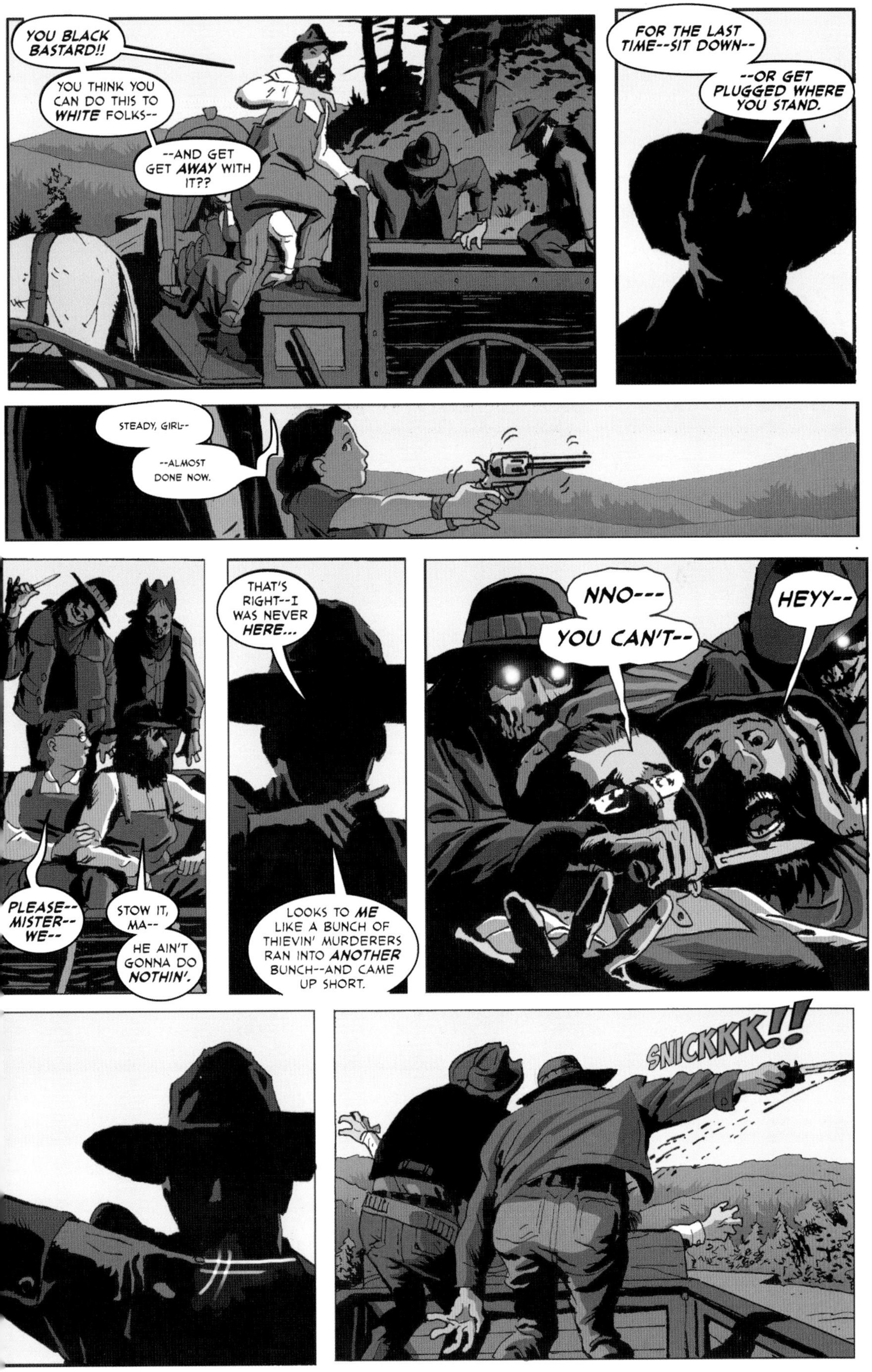
YOU BLACK BASTARD!!
YOU THINK YOU CAN DO THIS TO WHITE FOLKS--
--AND GET GET AWAY WITH IT??
FOR THE LAST TIME--SIT DOWN--
--OR GET PLUGGED WHERE YOU STAND.
STEADY, GIRL--
--ALMOST DONE NOW.
PLEASE--MISTER--WE--
STOW IT, MA--
HE AIN'T GONNA DO NOTHIN'.
THAT'S RIGHT--I WAS NEVER HERE...
LOOKS TO ME LIKE A BUNCH OF THIEVIN' MURDERERS RAN INTO ANOTHER BUNCH--AND CAME UP SHORT.
NNO---
YOU CAN'T--
HEYY--
SNICKKK!!

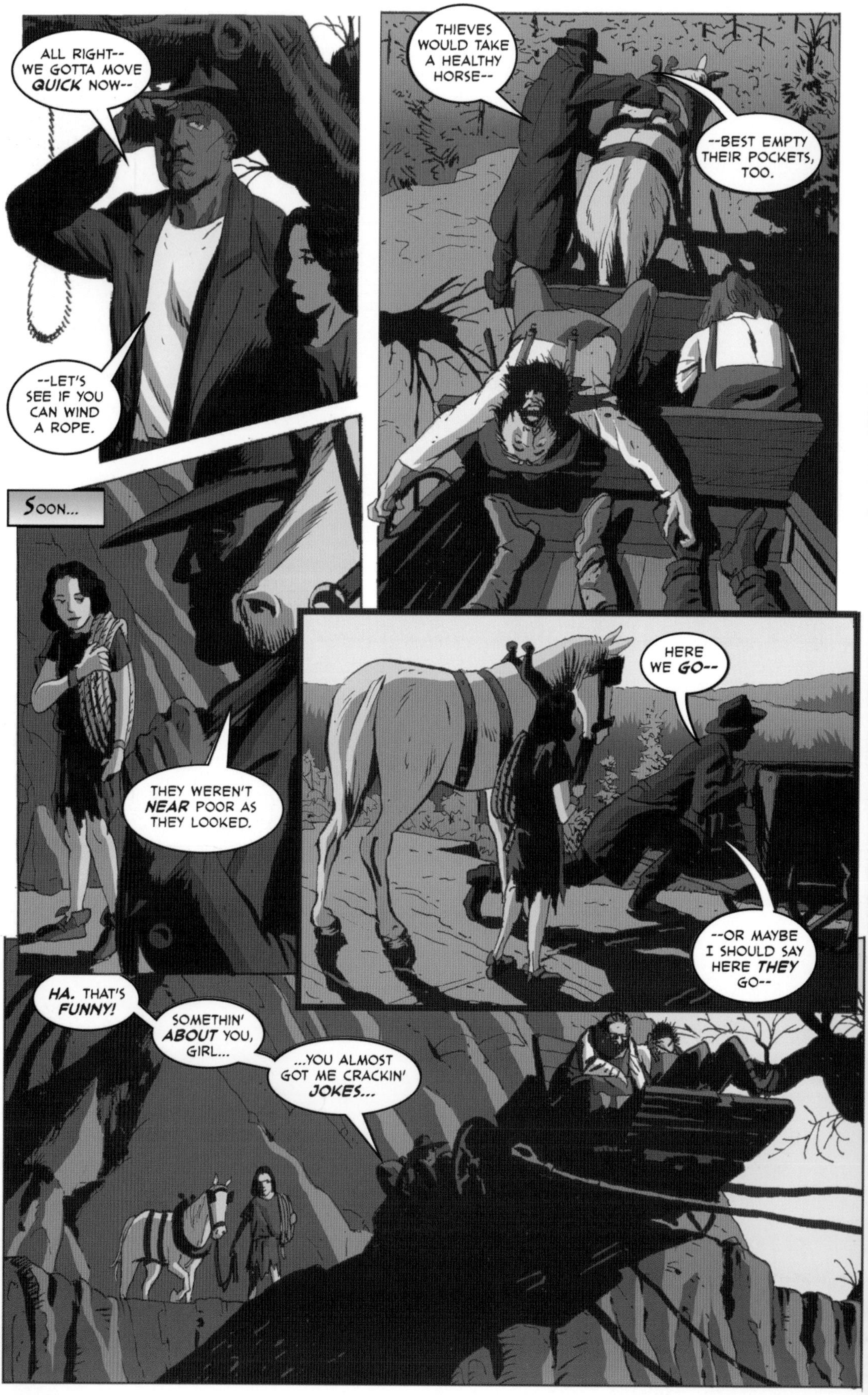
ALL RIGHT-- WE GOTTA MOVE QUICK NOW--
--LET'S SEE IF YOU CAN WIND A ROPE.
THIEVES WOULD TAKE A HEALTHY HORSE--
--BEST EMPTY THEIR POCKETS, TOO.
SOON...
THEY WEREN'T NEAR POOR AS THEY LOOKED.
HERE WE GO--
--OR MAYBE I SHOULD SAY HERE THEY GO--
HA. THAT'S FUNNY!
SOMETHIN' ABOUT YOU, GIRL...
...YOU ALMOST GOT ME CRACKIN' JOKES...

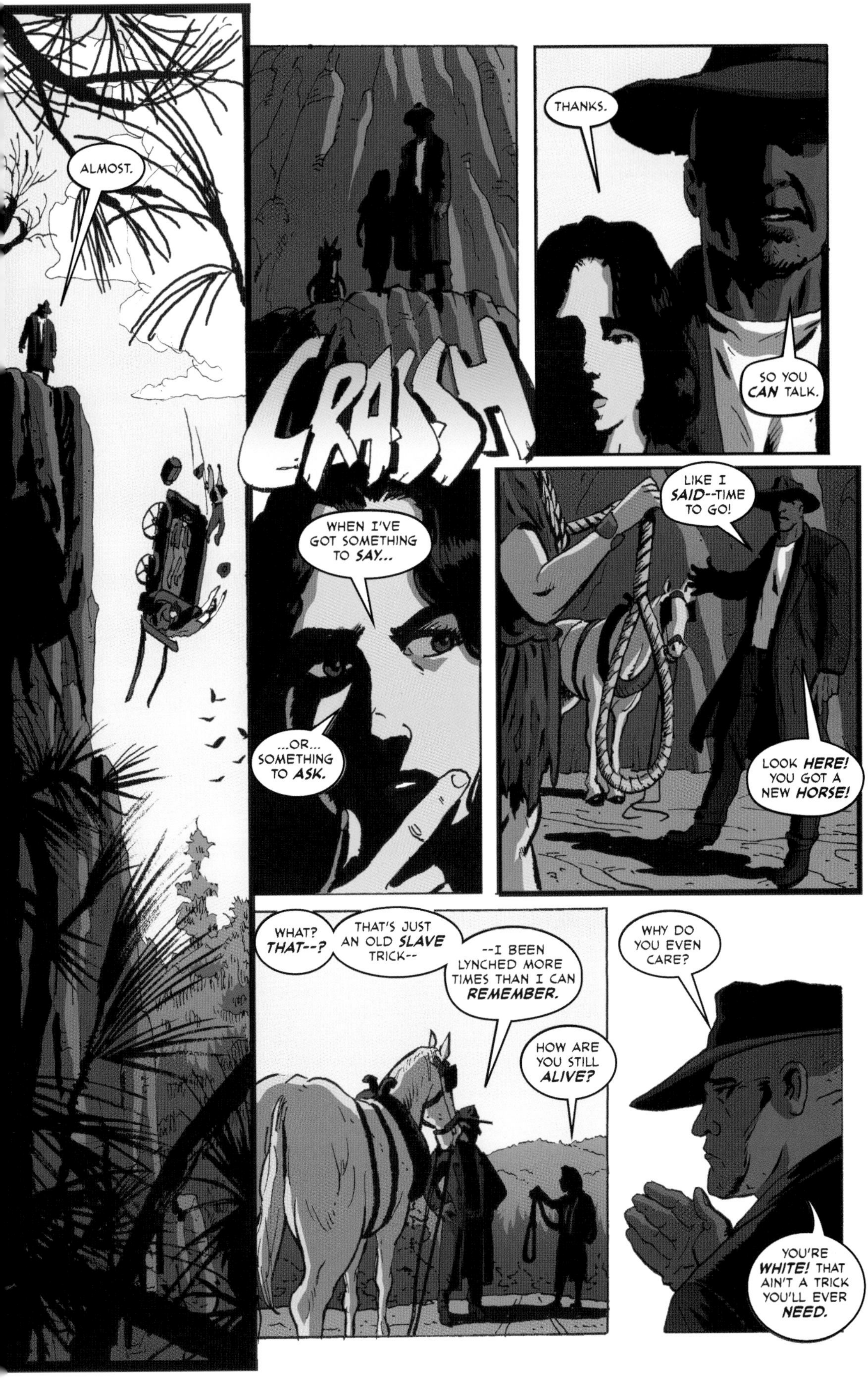
ALMOST.
CRASH
THANKS.
SO YOU CAN TALK.
WHEN I'VE GOT SOMETHING TO SAY...
...OR... SOMETHING TO ASK.
LIKE I SAID--TIME TO GO!
LOOK HERE! YOU GOT A NEW HORSE!
WHAT? THAT--?
THAT'S JUST AN OLD SLAVE TRICK--
--I BEEN LYNCHED MORE TIMES THAN I CAN REMEMBER.
HOW ARE YOU STILL ALIVE?
WHY DO YOU EVEN CARE?
YOU'RE WHITE! THAT AIN'T A TRICK YOU'LL EVER NEED.

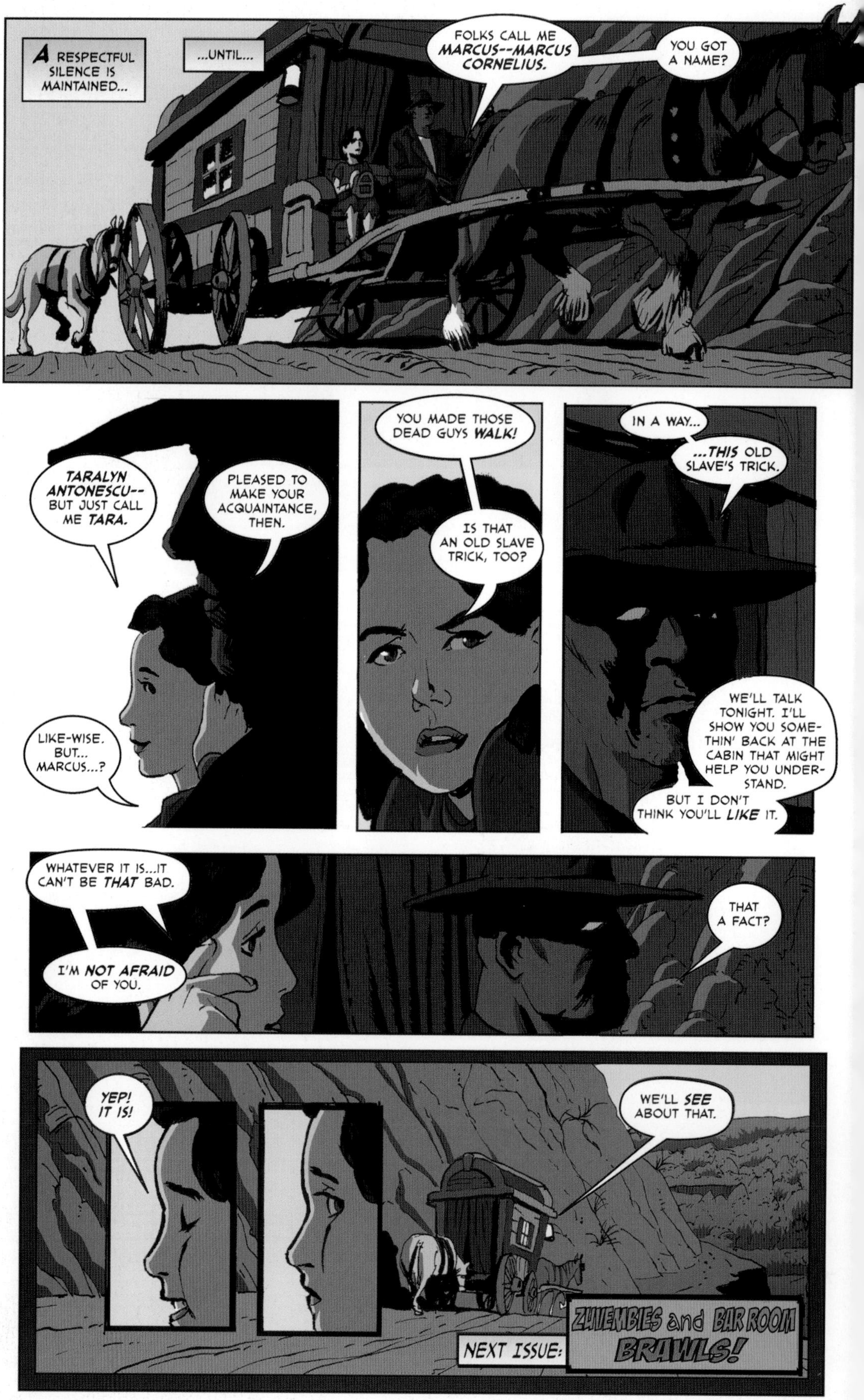
A RESPECTFUL SILENCE IS MAINTAINED...
...UNTIL...
FOLKS CALL ME MARCUS--MARCUS CORNELIUS.
YOU GOT A NAME?
TARALYN ANTONESCU-- BUT JUST CALL ME TARA.
PLEASED TO MAKE YOUR ACQUAINTANCE, THEN.
LIKE-WISE. BUT... MARCUS...?
YOU MADE THOSE DEAD GUYS WALK!
IS THAT AN OLD SLAVE TRICK, TOO?
IN A WAY...
...THIS OLD SLAVE'S TRICK.
WE'LL TALK TONIGHT. I'LL SHOW YOU SOME-THIN' BACK AT THE CABIN THAT MIGHT HELP YOU UNDER-STAND.
BUT I DON'T THINK YOU'LL LIKE IT.
WHATEVER IT IS...IT CAN'T BE THAT BAD.
I'M NOT AFRAID OF YOU.
THAT A FACT?
YEP! IT IS!
WE'LL SEE ABOUT THAT.
NEXT ISSUE:
ZUVEMBIES and BAR ROOM BRAWLS!

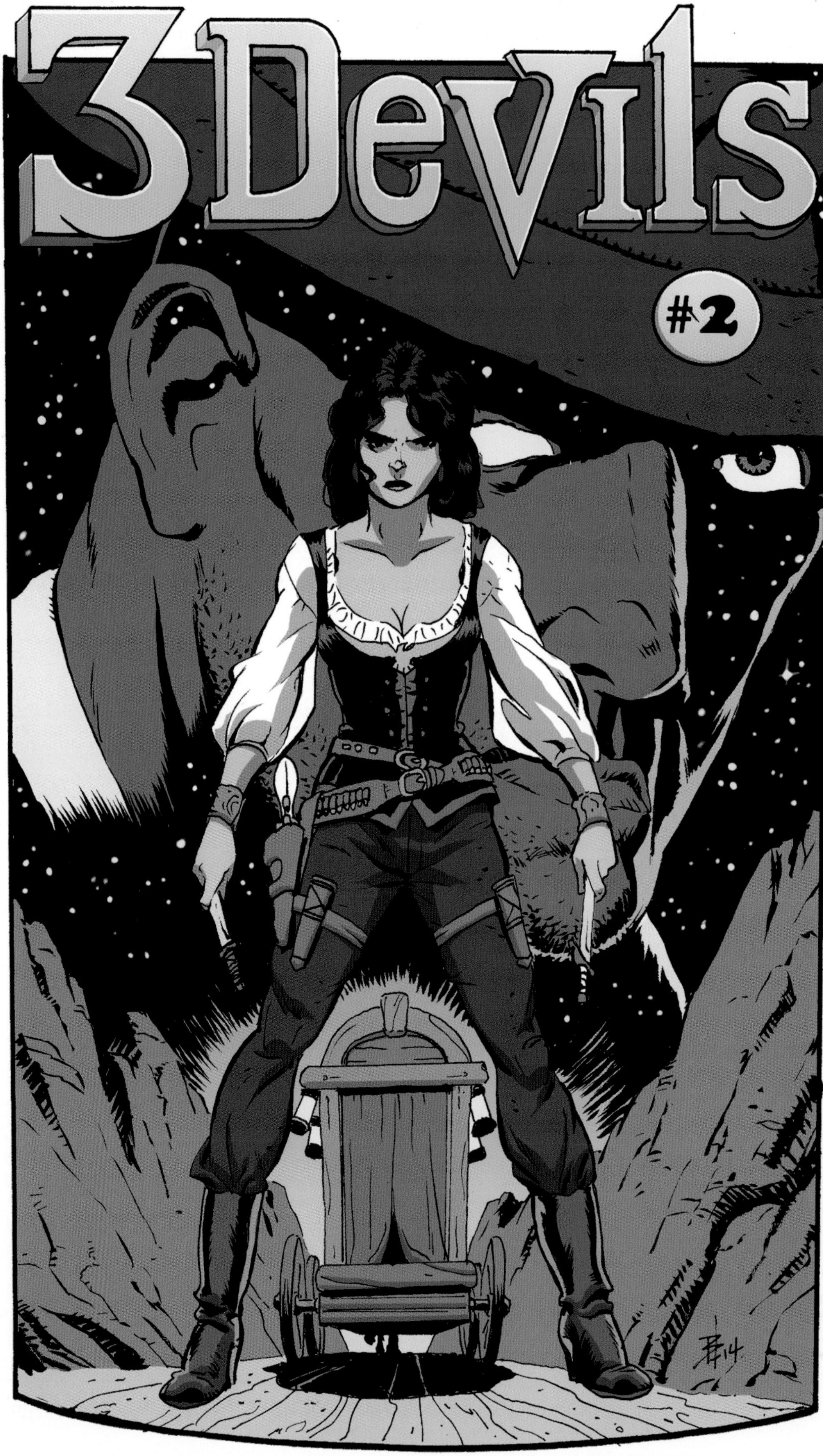
3 Devils
#2

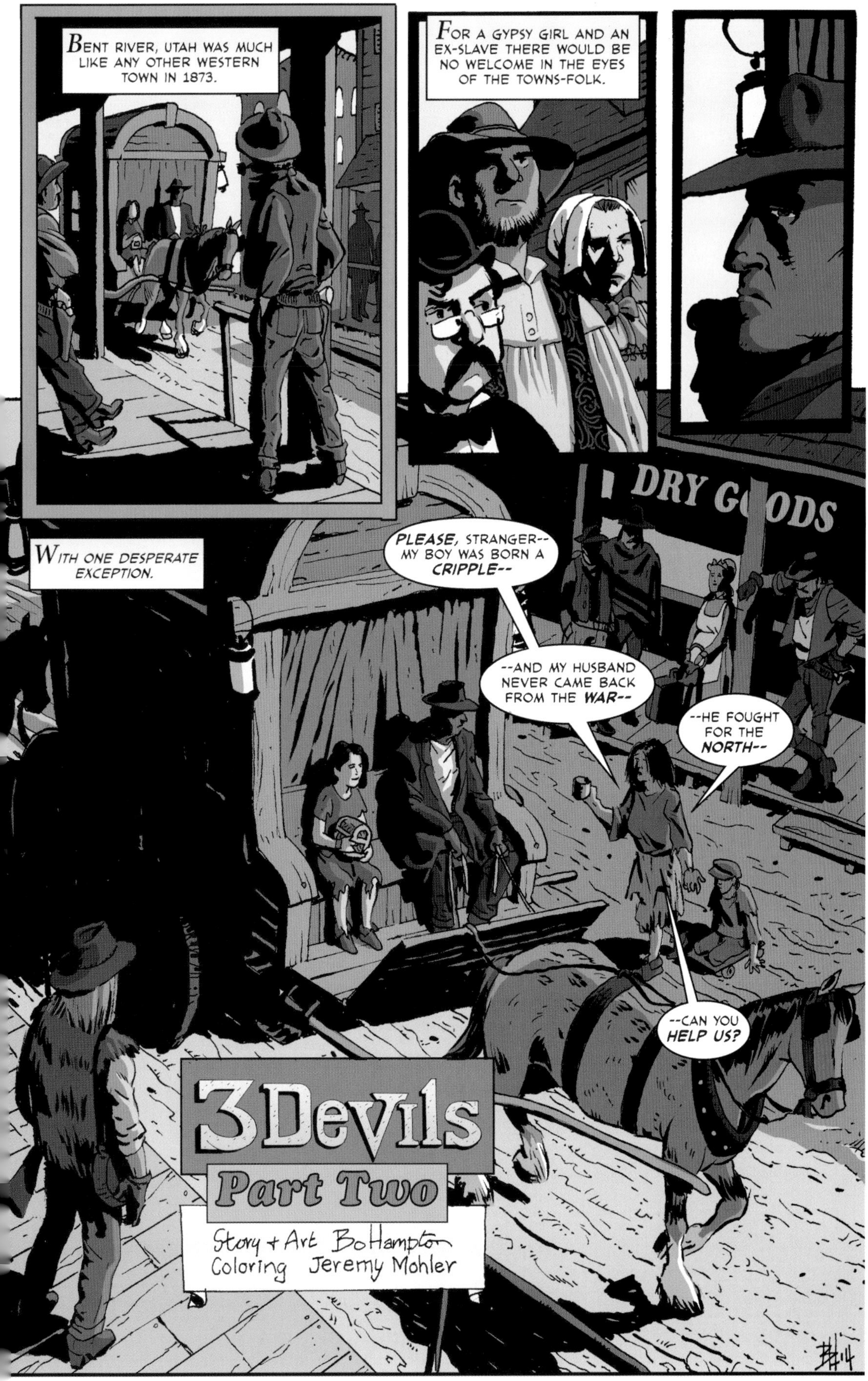
BENT RIVER, UTAH WAS MUCH LIKE ANY OTHER WESTERN TOWN IN 1873.
FOR A GYPSY GIRL AND AN EX-SLAVE THERE WOULD BE NO WELCOME IN THE EYES OF THE TOWNS-FOLK.
DRY GOODS
WITH ONE DESPERATE EXCEPTION.
PLEASE, STRANGER-- MY BOY WAS BORN A CRIPPLE--
--AND MY HUSBAND NEVER CAME BACK FROM THE WAR--
--HE FOUGHT FOR THE NORTH--
--CAN YOU HELP US?
3 Devils
Part Two
Story + Art Bo Hampton
Coloring Jeremy Mohler

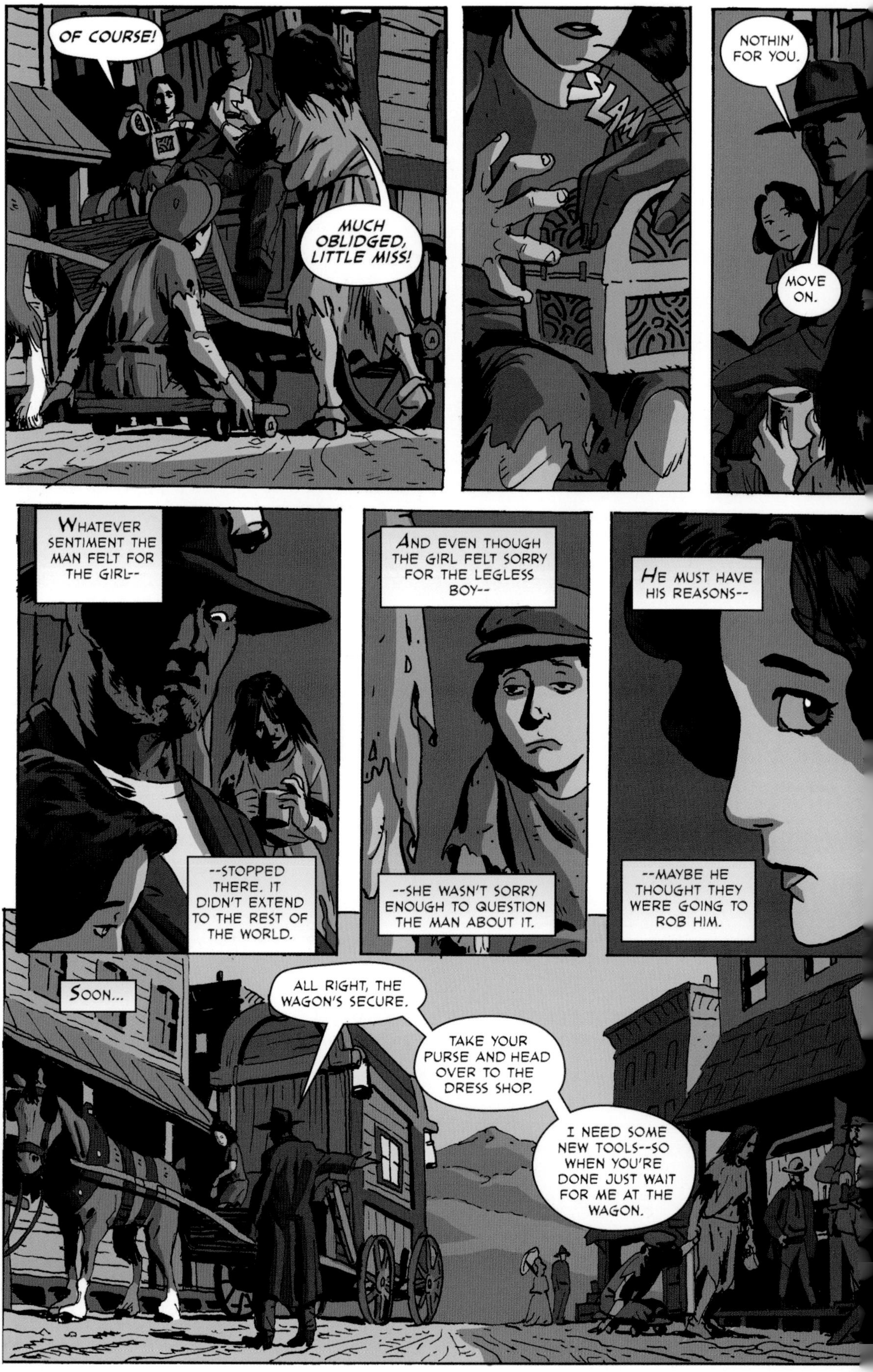
OF COURSE!
MUCH OBLIDGED, LITTLE MISS!
SLAM
NOTHIN' FOR YOU.
MOVE ON.
WHATEVER SENTIMENT THE MAN FELT FOR THE GIRL--
--STOPPED THERE. IT DIDN'T EXTEND TO THE REST OF THE WORLD.
AND EVEN THOUGH THE GIRL FELT SORRY FOR THE LEGLESS BOY--
--SHE WASN'T SORRY ENOUGH TO QUESTION THE MAN ABOUT IT.
HE MUST HAVE HIS REASONS--
--MAYBE HE THOUGHT THEY WERE GOING TO ROB HIM.
SOON...
ALL RIGHT, THE WAGON'S SECURE.
TAKE YOUR PURSE AND HEAD OVER TO THE DRESS SHOP.
I NEED SOME NEW TOOLS--SO WHEN YOU'RE DONE JUST WAIT FOR ME AT THE WAGON.

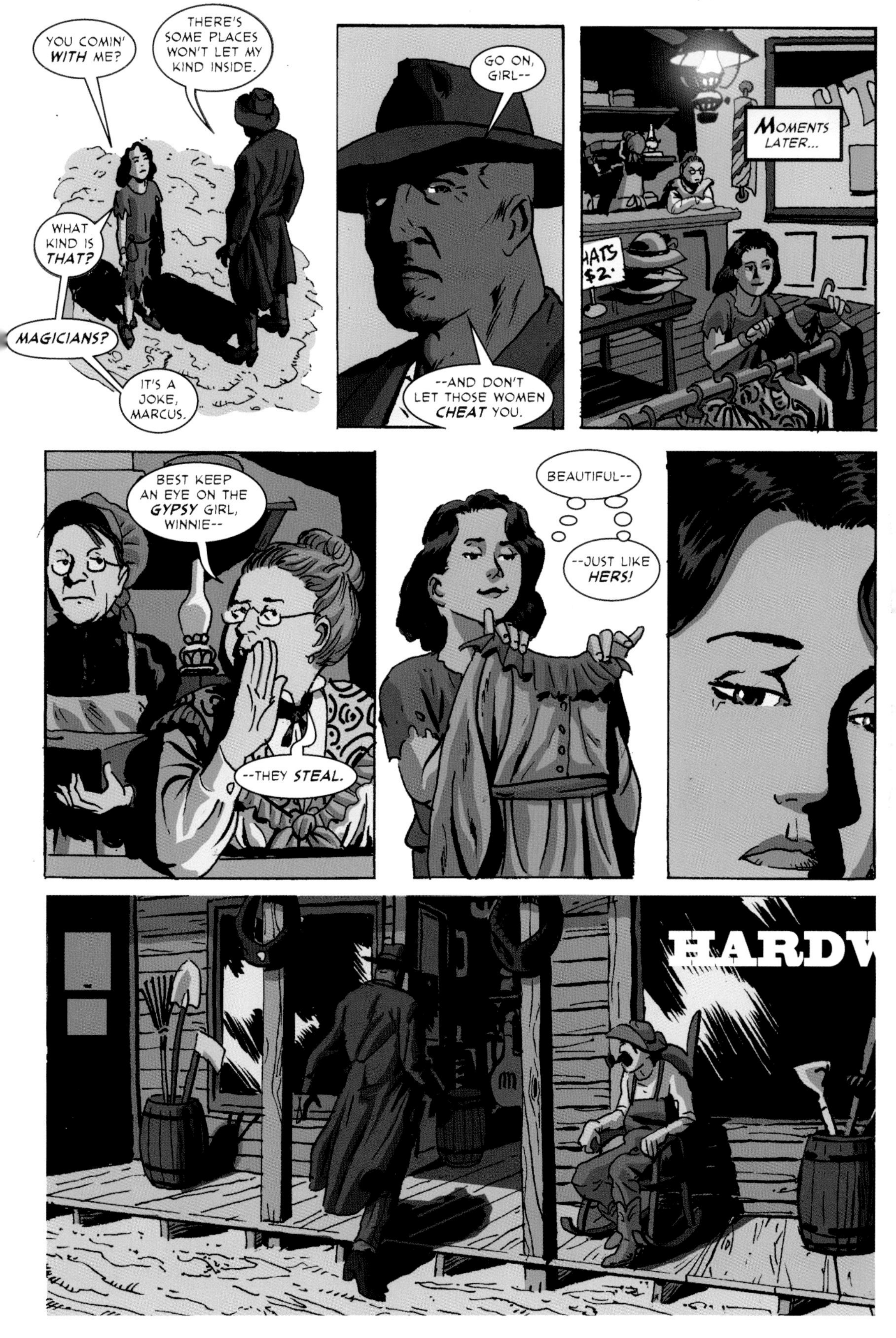
YOU COMIN' WITH ME?
THERE'S SOME PLACES WON'T LET MY KIND INSIDE.
WHAT KIND IS THAT?
MAGICIANS?
IT'S A JOKE, MARCUS.
GO ON, GIRL--
--AND DON'T LET THOSE WOMEN CHEAT YOU.
MOMENTS LATER...
HATS $2.
BEST KEEP AN EYE ON THE GYPSY GIRL, WINNIE--
--THEY STEAL.
BEAUTIFUL--
--JUST LIKE HERS!
HARDW

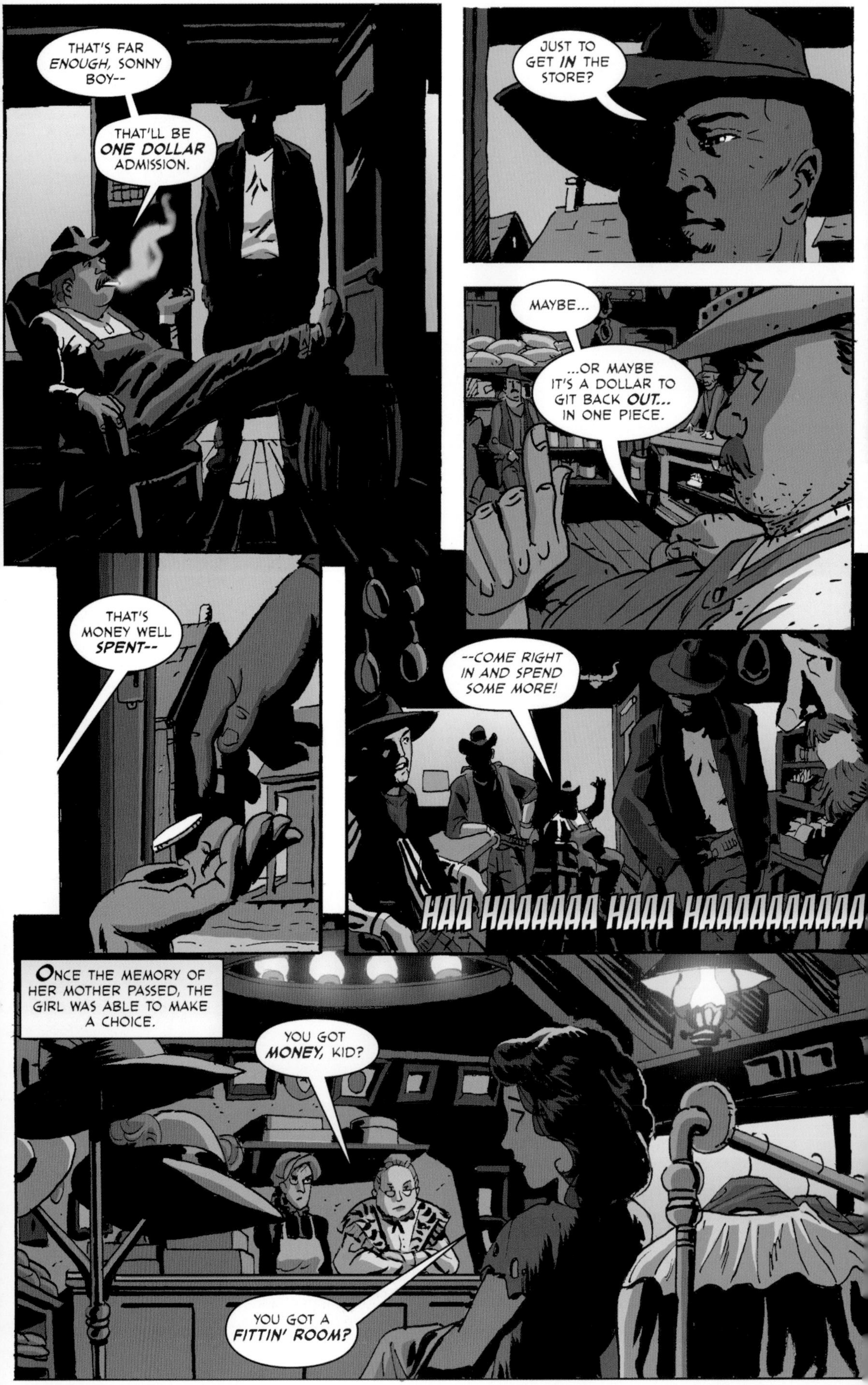
THAT'S FAR ENOUGH, SONNY BOY--
THAT'LL BE ONE DOLLAR ADMISSION.
JUST TO GET IN THE STORE?
MAYBE...
...OR MAYBE IT'S A DOLLAR TO GIT BACK OUT... IN ONE PIECE.
THAT'S MONEY WELL SPENT--
--COME RIGHT IN AND SPEND SOME MORE!
HAA HAAAAAA HAAA HAAAAAAAAAA
ONCE THE MEMORY OF HER MOTHER PASSED, THE GIRL WAS ABLE TO MAKE A CHOICE.
YOU GOT MONEY, KID?
YOU GOT A FITTIN' ROOM?

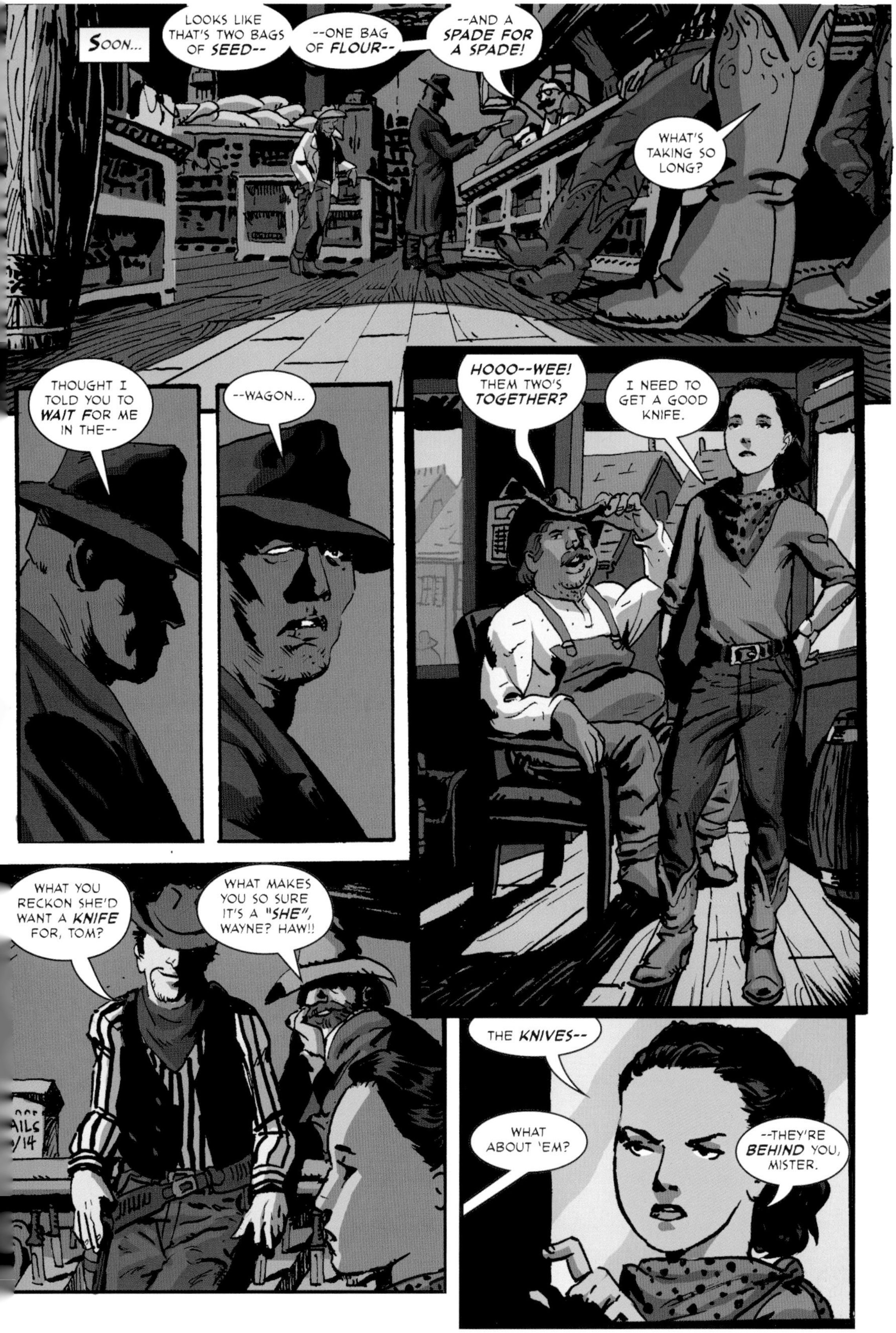
SOON...
LOOKS LIKE THAT'S TWO BAGS OF SEED--
--ONE BAG OF FLOUR--
--AND A SPADE FOR A SPADE!
WHAT'S TAKING SO LONG?
THOUGHT I TOLD YOU TO WAIT FOR ME IN THE--
--WAGON...
HOOO--WEE! THEM TWO'S TOGETHER?
I NEED TO GET A GOOD KNIFE.
WHAT YOU RECKON SHE'D WANT A KNIFE FOR, TOM?
WHAT MAKES YOU SO SURE IT'S A "SHE", WAYNE? HAW!!
THE KNIVES--
WHAT ABOUT 'EM?
--THEY'RE BEHIND YOU, MISTER.

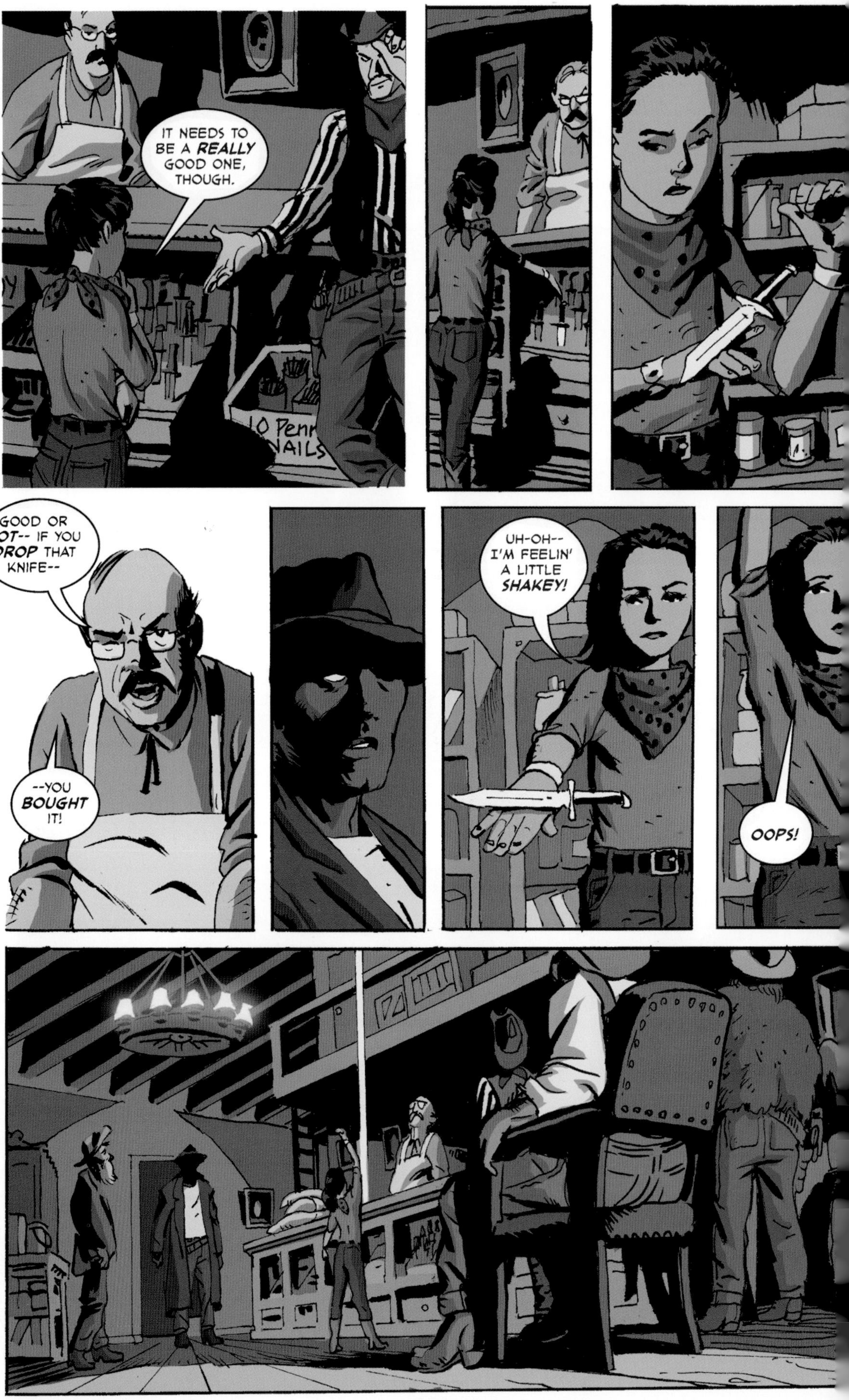
IT NEEDS TO BE A REALLY GOOD ONE, THOUGH.
10 Penny NAILS
GOOD OR NOT-- IF YOU DROP THAT KNIFE--
--YOU BOUGHT IT!
UH-OH-- I'M FEELIN' A LITTLE SHAKEY!
OOPS!

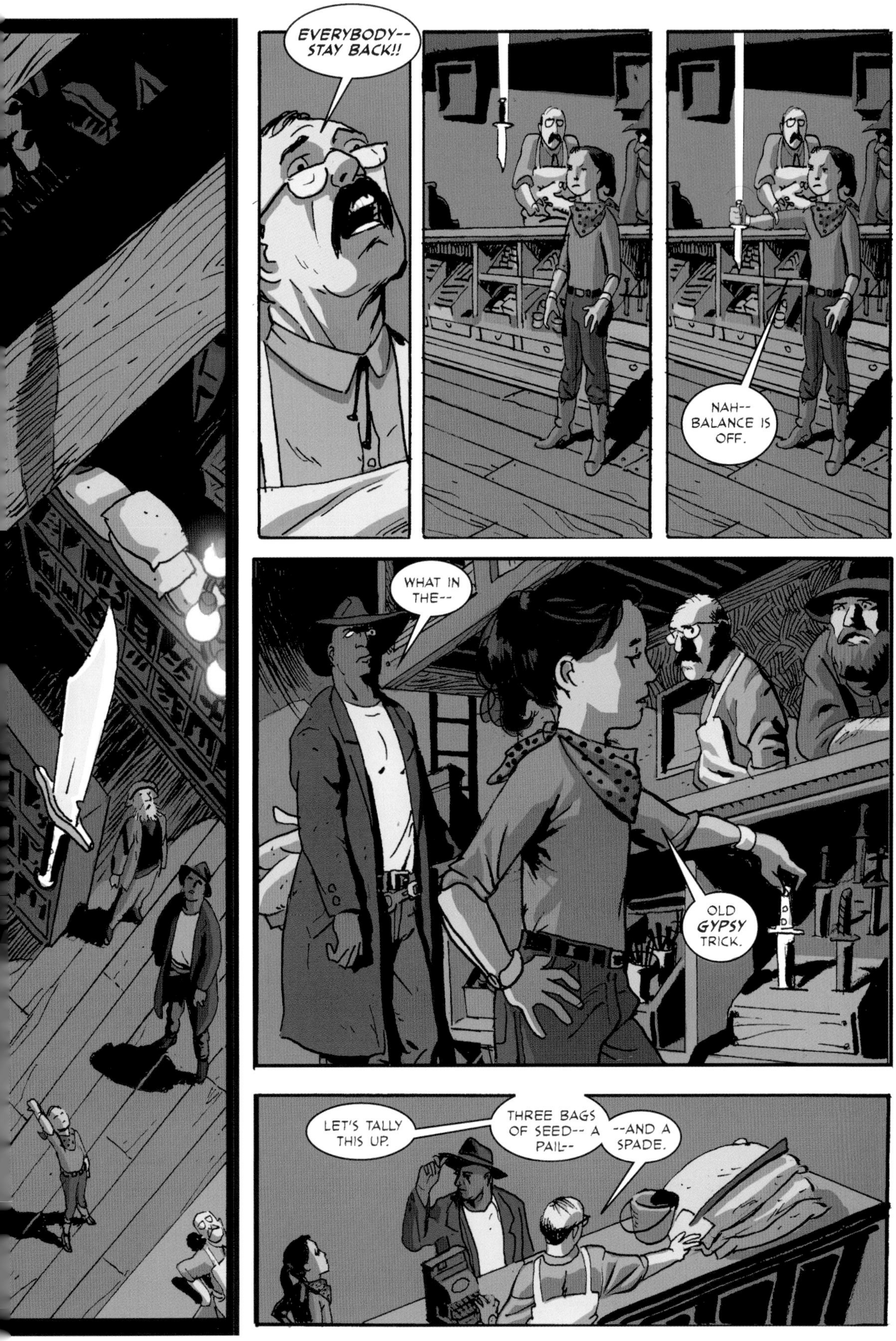
EVERYBODY-- STAY BACK!!
NAH-- BALANCE IS OFF.
WHAT IN THE--
OLD GYPSY TRICK.
LET'S TALLY THIS UP.
THREE BAGS OF SEED-- A PAIL--
--AND A SPADE.

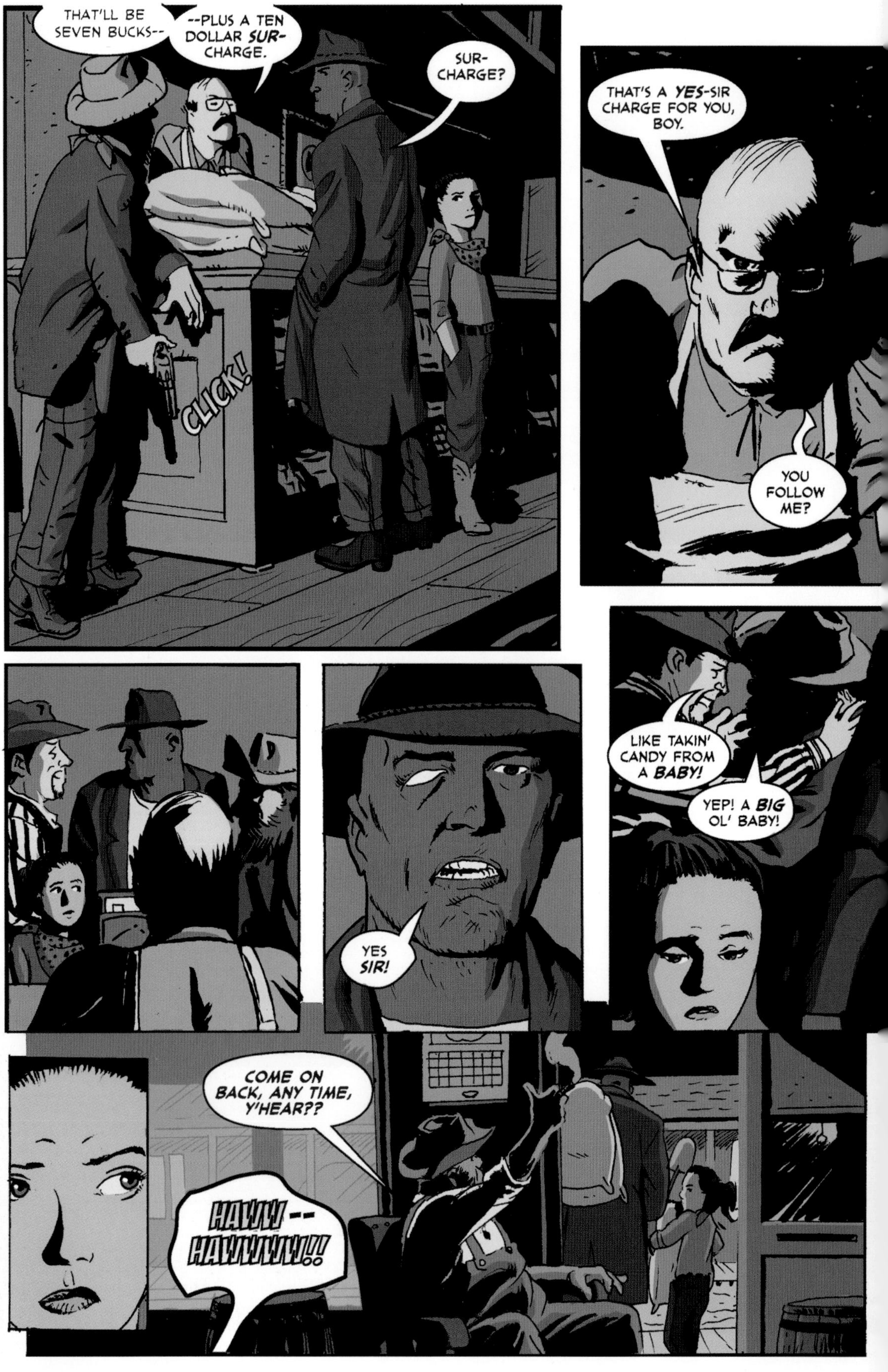
THAT'LL BE SEVEN BUCKS--
--PLUS A TEN DOLLAR SUR-CHARGE.
SUR-CHARGE?
CLICK!
THAT'S A YES-SIR CHARGE FOR YOU, BOY.
YOU FOLLOW ME?
YES SIR!
LIKE TAKIN' CANDY FROM A BABY!
YEP! A BIG OL' BABY!
COME ON BACK, ANY TIME, Y'HEAR??
HAWW-- HAWWWW!!

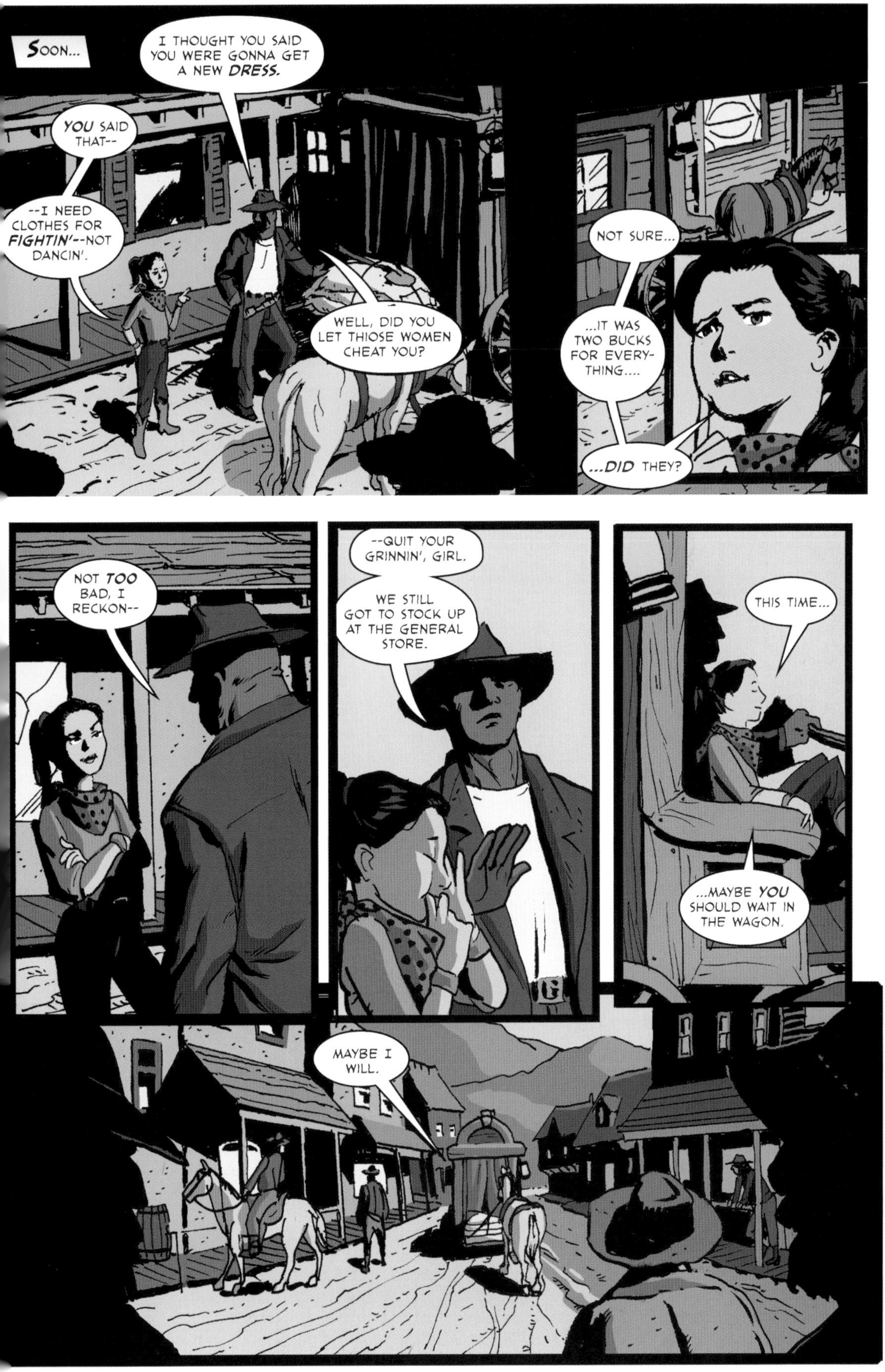

Soon...
I THOUGHT YOU SAID YOU WERE GONNA GET A NEW DRESS.
YOU SAID THAT--
--I NEED CLOTHES FOR FIGHTIN'--NOT DANCIN'.
WELL, DID YOU LET THIOSE WOMEN CHEAT YOU?
NOT SURE...
...IT WAS TWO BUCKS FOR EVERY-THING....
...DID THEY?
NOT TOO BAD, I RECKON--
--QUIT YOUR GRINNIN', GIRL.
WE STILL GOT TO STOCK UP AT THE GENERAL STORE.
THIS TIME...
...MAYBE YOU SHOULD WAIT IN THE WAGON.
MAYBE I WILL.

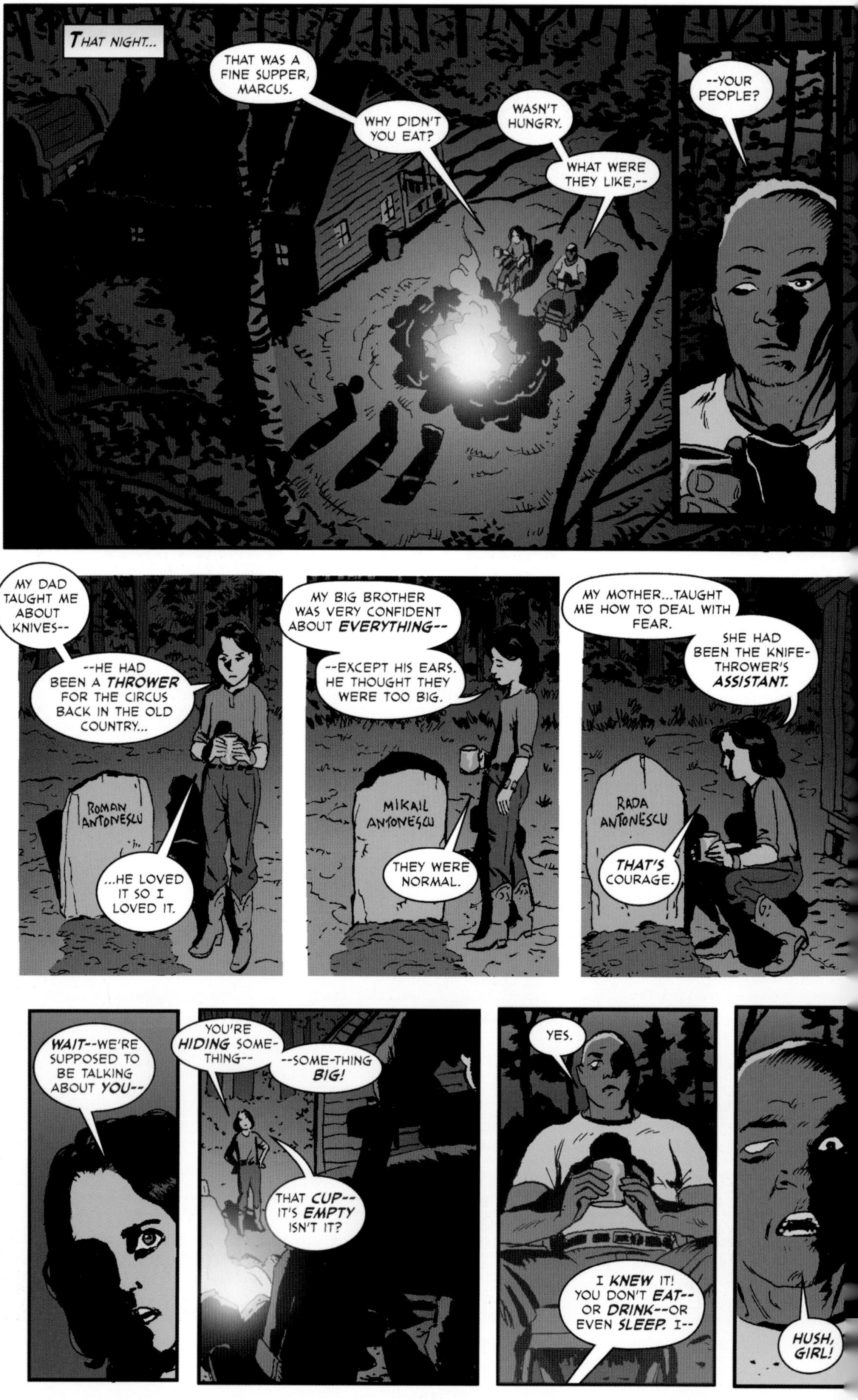
THAT NIGHT...
THAT WAS A FINE SUPPER, MARCUS.
WHY DIDN'T YOU EAT?
WASN'T HUNGRY.
WHAT WERE THEY LIKE,--
--YOUR PEOPLE?
MY DAD TAUGHT ME ABOUT KNIVES--
--HE HAD BEEN A THROWER FOR THE CIRCUS BACK IN THE OLD COUNTRY...
ROMAN ANTONESCU
...HE LOVED IT SO I LOVED IT.
MY BIG BROTHER WAS VERY CONFIDENT ABOUT EVERYTHING--
--EXCEPT HIS EARS. HE THOUGHT THEY WERE TOO BIG.
MIKAIL ANTONESCU
THEY WERE NORMAL.
MY MOTHER...TAUGHT ME HOW TO DEAL WITH FEAR.
SHE HAD BEEN THE KNIFE-THROWER'S ASSISTANT.
RADA ANTONESCU
THAT'S COURAGE.
WAIT--WE'RE SUPPOSED TO BE TALKING ABOUT YOU--
YOU'RE HIDING SOME-THING--
--SOME-THING BIG!
THAT CUP-- IT'S EMPTY ISN'T IT?
YES.
I KNEW IT! YOU DON'T EAT-- OR DRINK--OR EVEN SLEEP. I--
HUSH, GIRL!

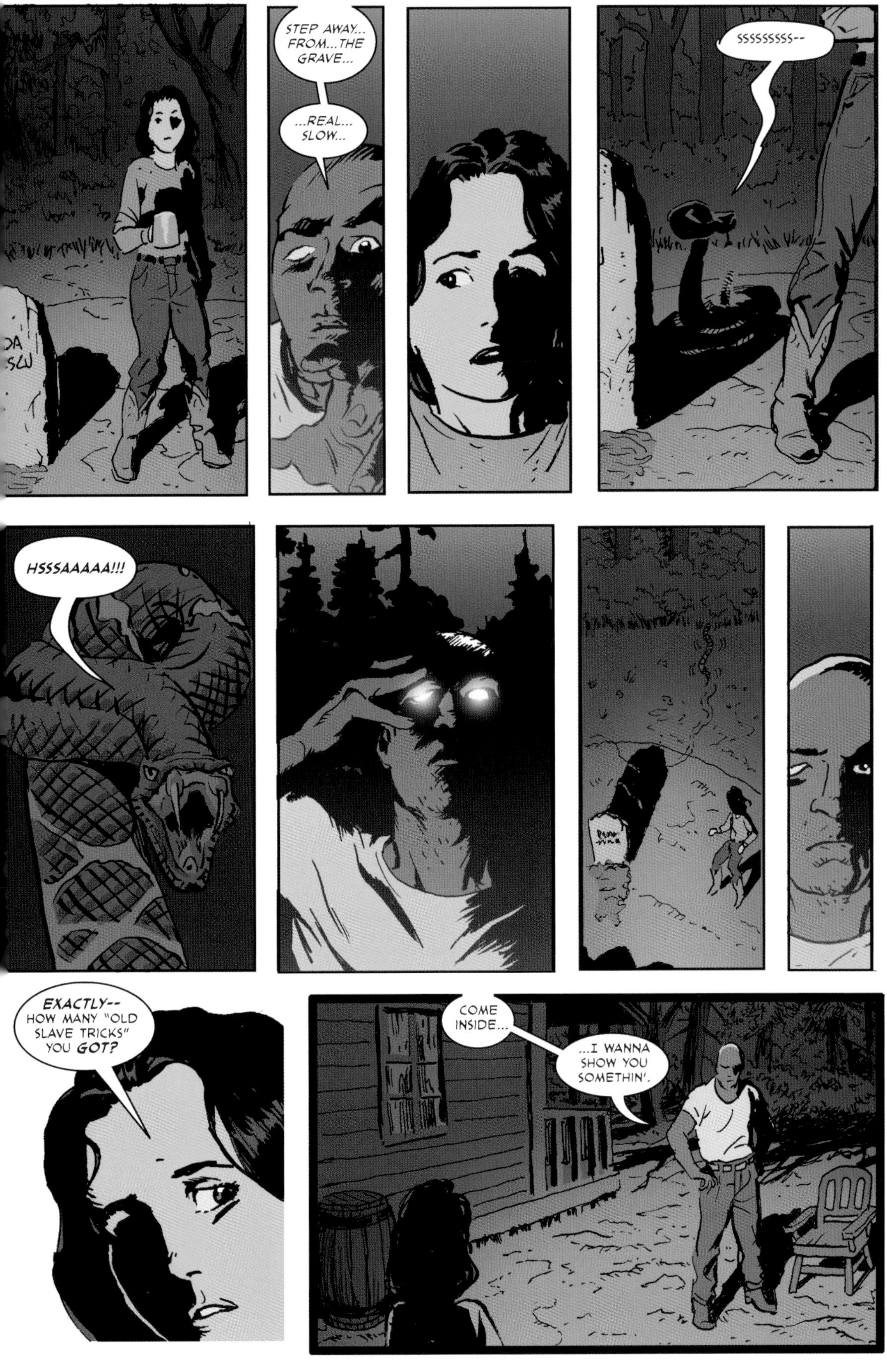
STEP AWAY... FROM...THE GRAVE...
...REAL... SLOW...
SSSSSSSSS--
HSSSAAAAA!!!
EXACTLY-- HOW MANY "OLD SLAVE TRICKS" YOU GOT?
COME INSIDE...
...I WANNA SHOW YOU SOMETHIN'.

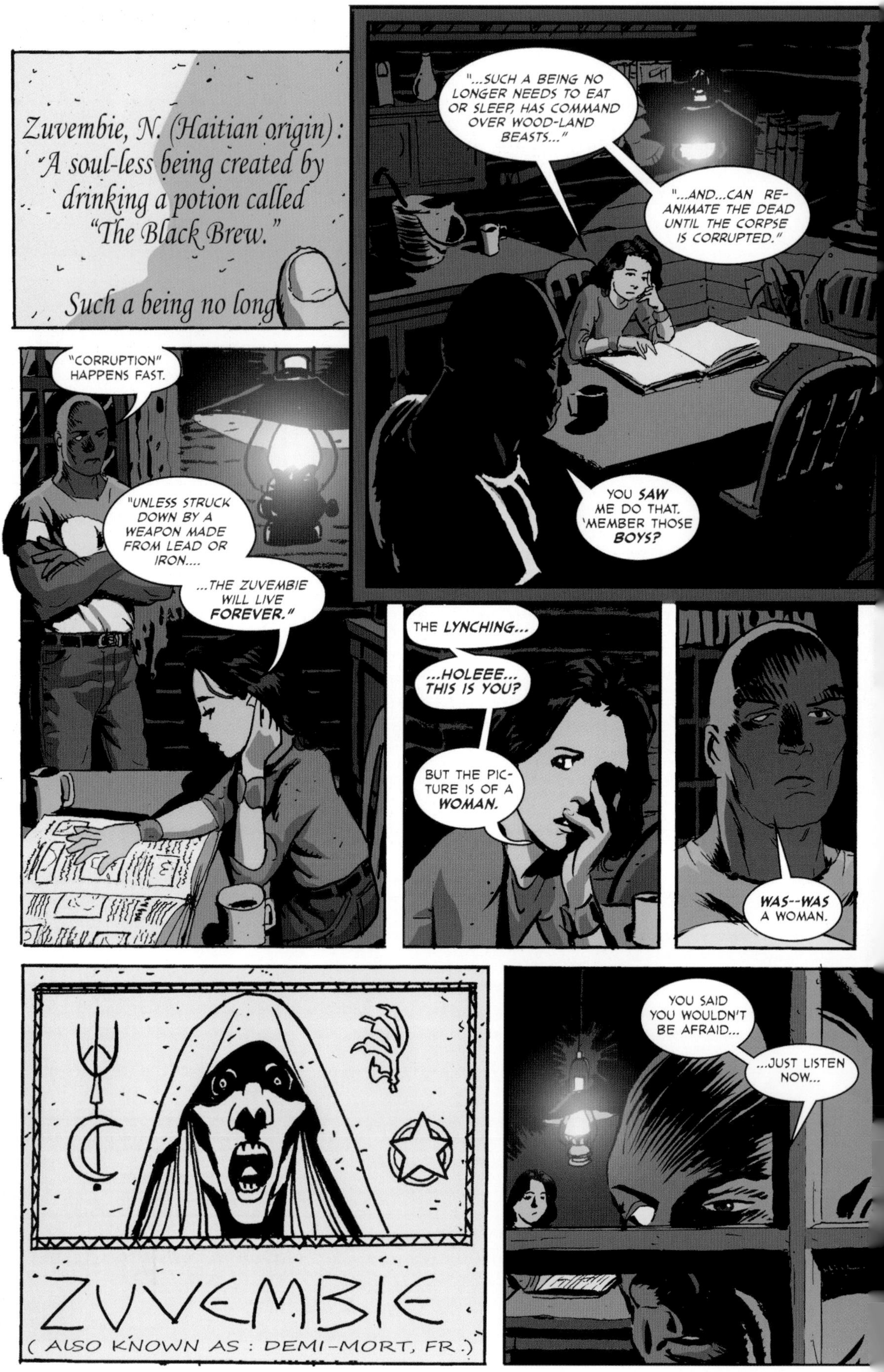
Zuvembie, N. (Haitian origin): "A soul-less being created by drinking a potion called "The Black Brew."
Such a being no long
"...SUCH A BEING NO LONGER NEEDS TO EAT OR SLEEP, HAS COMMAND OVER WOOD-LAND BEASTS..."
"...AND...CAN RE-ANIMATE THE DEAD UNTIL THE CORPSE IS CORRUPTED."
YOU SAW ME DO THAT. 'MEMBER THOSE BOYS?
"CORRUPTION" HAPPENS FAST.
"UNLESS STRUCK DOWN BY A WEAPON MADE FROM LEAD OR IRON....
...THE ZUVEMBIE WILL LIVE FOREVER."
THE LYNCHING...
...HOLEEE... THIS IS YOU?
BUT THE PICTURE IS OF A WOMAN.
WAS--WAS A WOMAN.
ZUVEMBIE
(ALSO KNOWN AS : DEMI-MORT, FR.)
YOU SAID YOU WOULDN'T BE AFRAID...
...JUST LISTEN NOW...

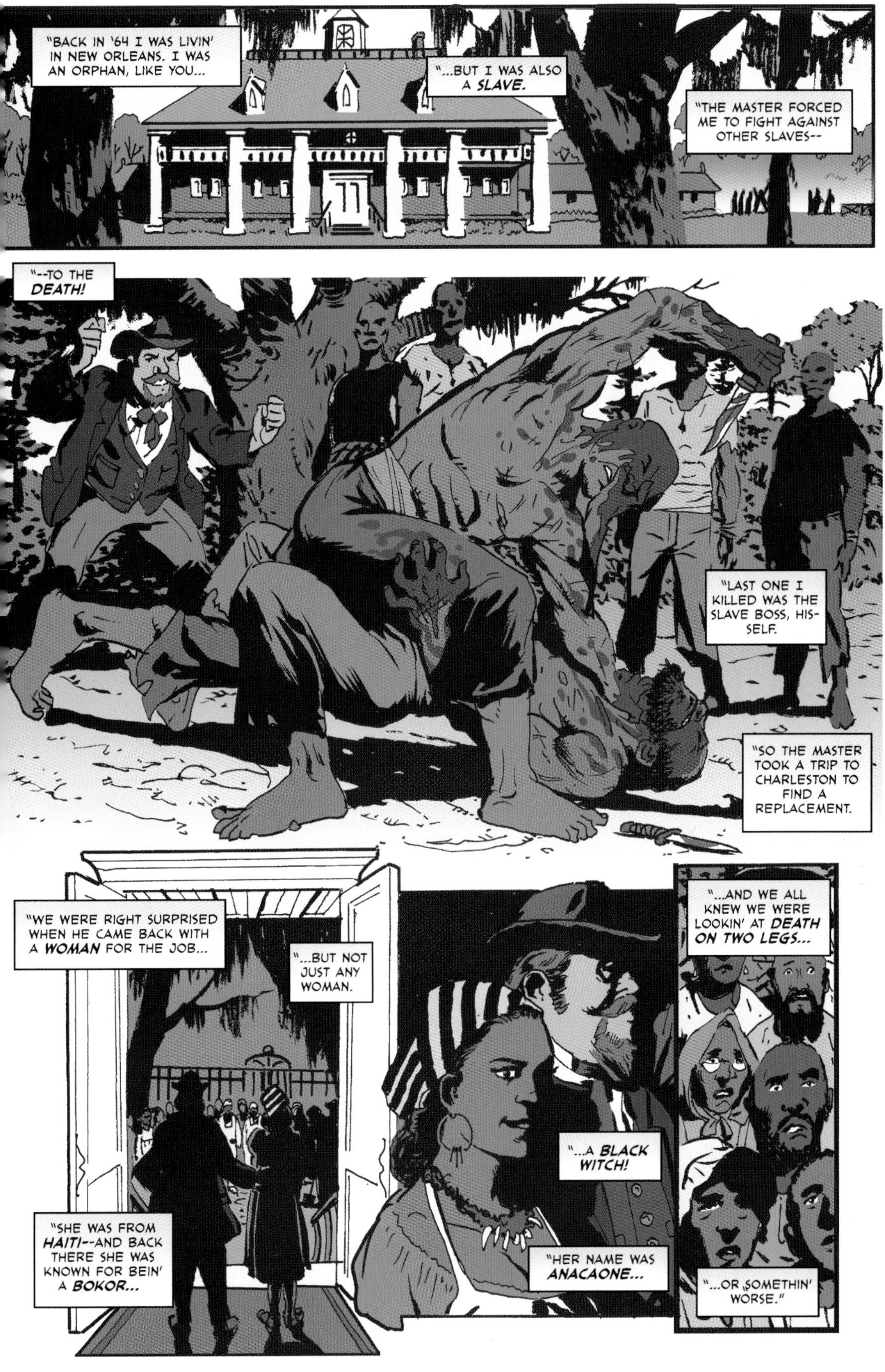
"BACK IN '64 I WAS LIVIN' IN NEW ORLEANS. I WAS AN ORPHAN, LIKE YOU...
"...BUT I WAS ALSO A *SLAVE.*
"THE MASTER FORCED ME TO FIGHT AGAINST OTHER SLAVES--
"--TO THE *DEATH!*
"LAST ONE I KILLED WAS THE SLAVE BOSS, HIS-SELF.
"SO THE MASTER TOOK A TRIP TO CHARLESTON TO FIND A REPLACEMENT.
"WE WERE RIGHT SURPRISED WHEN HE CAME BACK WITH A *WOMAN* FOR THE JOB...
"...BUT NOT JUST ANY WOMAN.
"SHE WAS FROM *HAITI*--AND BACK THERE SHE WAS KNOWN FOR BEIN' A *BOKOR...*
"...A *BLACK WITCH!*
"HER NAME WAS *ANACAONE...*
"...AND WE ALL KNEW WE WERE LOOKIN' AT *DEATH ON TWO LEGS...*
"...OR SOMETHIN' WORSE."

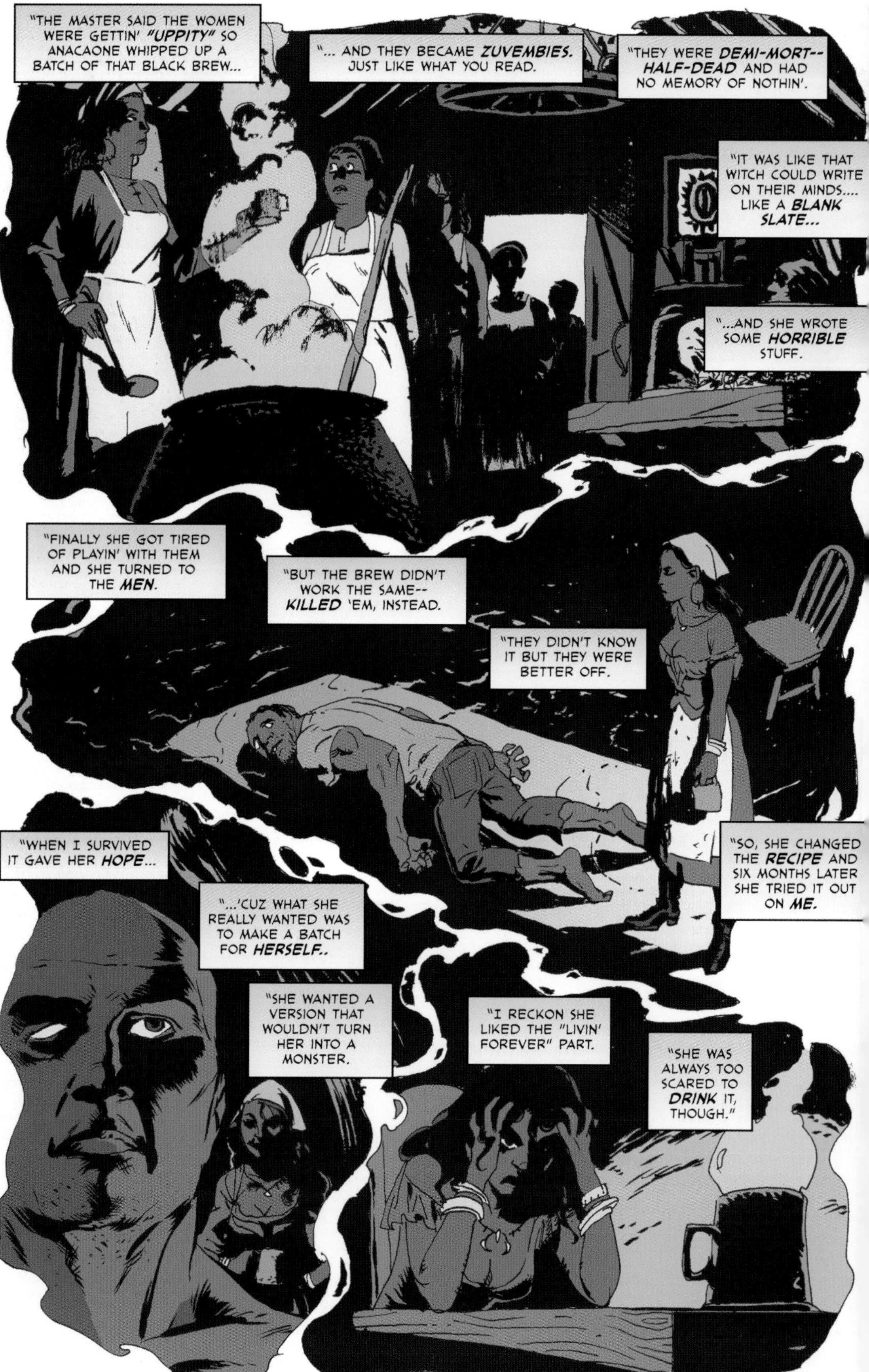
"THE MASTER SAID THE WOMEN WERE GETTIN' "UPPITY" SO ANACAONE WHIPPED UP A BATCH OF THAT BLACK BREW...
"... AND THEY BECAME ZUVEMBIES. JUST LIKE WHAT YOU READ.
"THEY WERE DEMI-MORT-- HALF-DEAD AND HAD NO MEMORY OF NOTHIN'.
"IT WAS LIKE THAT WITCH COULD WRITE ON THEIR MINDS.... LIKE A BLANK SLATE...
"...AND SHE WROTE SOME HORRIBLE STUFF.
"FINALLY SHE GOT TIRED OF PLAYIN' WITH THEM AND SHE TURNED TO THE MEN.
"BUT THE BREW DIDN'T WORK THE SAME-- KILLED 'EM, INSTEAD.
"THEY DIDN'T KNOW IT BUT THEY WERE BETTER OFF.
"WHEN I SURVIVED IT GAVE HER HOPE...
"...'CUZ WHAT SHE REALLY WANTED WAS TO MAKE A BATCH FOR HERSELF..
"SO, SHE CHANGED THE RECIPE AND SIX MONTHS LATER SHE TRIED IT OUT ON ME.
"SHE WANTED A VERSION THAT WOULDN'T TURN HER INTO A MONSTER.
"I RECKON SHE LIKED THE "LIVIN' FOREVER" PART.
"SHE WAS ALWAYS TOO SCARED TO DRINK IT, THOUGH."

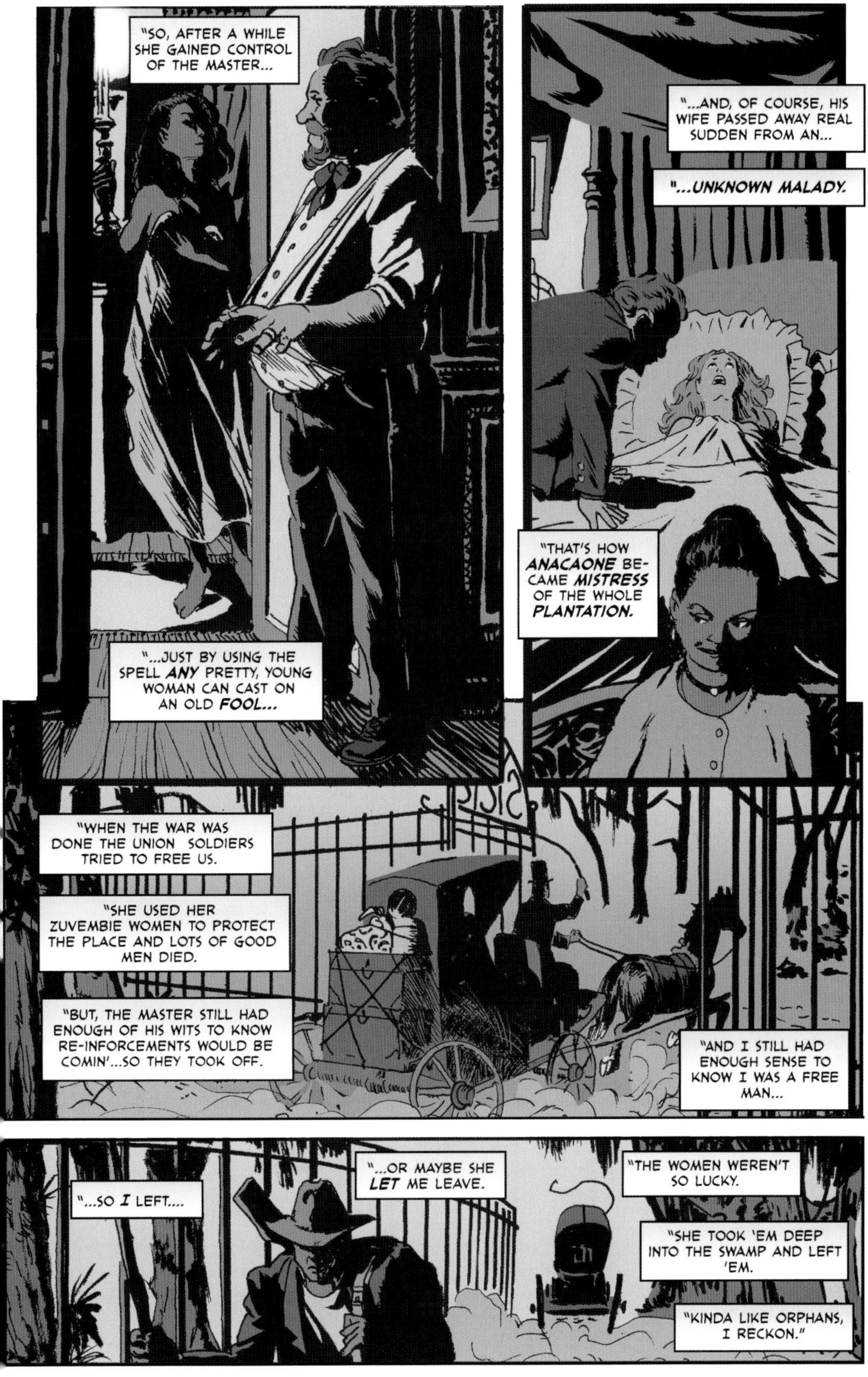
"SO, AFTER A WHILE SHE GAINED CONTROL OF THE MASTER...
"...JUST BY USING THE SPELL ANY PRETTY, YOUNG WOMAN CAN CAST ON AN OLD FOOL...
"...AND, OF COURSE, HIS WIFE PASSED AWAY REAL SUDDEN FROM AN...
"...UNKNOWN MALADY.
"THAT'S HOW ANACAONE BECAME MISTRESS OF THE WHOLE PLANTATION.
"WHEN THE WAR WAS DONE THE UNION SOLDIERS TRIED TO FREE US.
"SHE USED HER ZUVEMBIE WOMEN TO PROTECT THE PLACE AND LOTS OF GOOD MEN DIED.
"BUT, THE MASTER STILL HAD ENOUGH OF HIS WITS TO KNOW RE-INFORCEMENTS WOULD BE COMIN'...SO THEY TOOK OFF.
"AND I STILL HAD ENOUGH SENSE TO KNOW I WAS A FREE MAN...
"...SO I LEFT....
"...OR MAYBE SHE LET ME LEAVE.
"THE WOMEN WEREN'T SO LUCKY.
"SHE TOOK 'EM DEEP INTO THE SWAMP AND LEFT 'EM.
"KINDA LIKE ORPHANS, I RECKON."

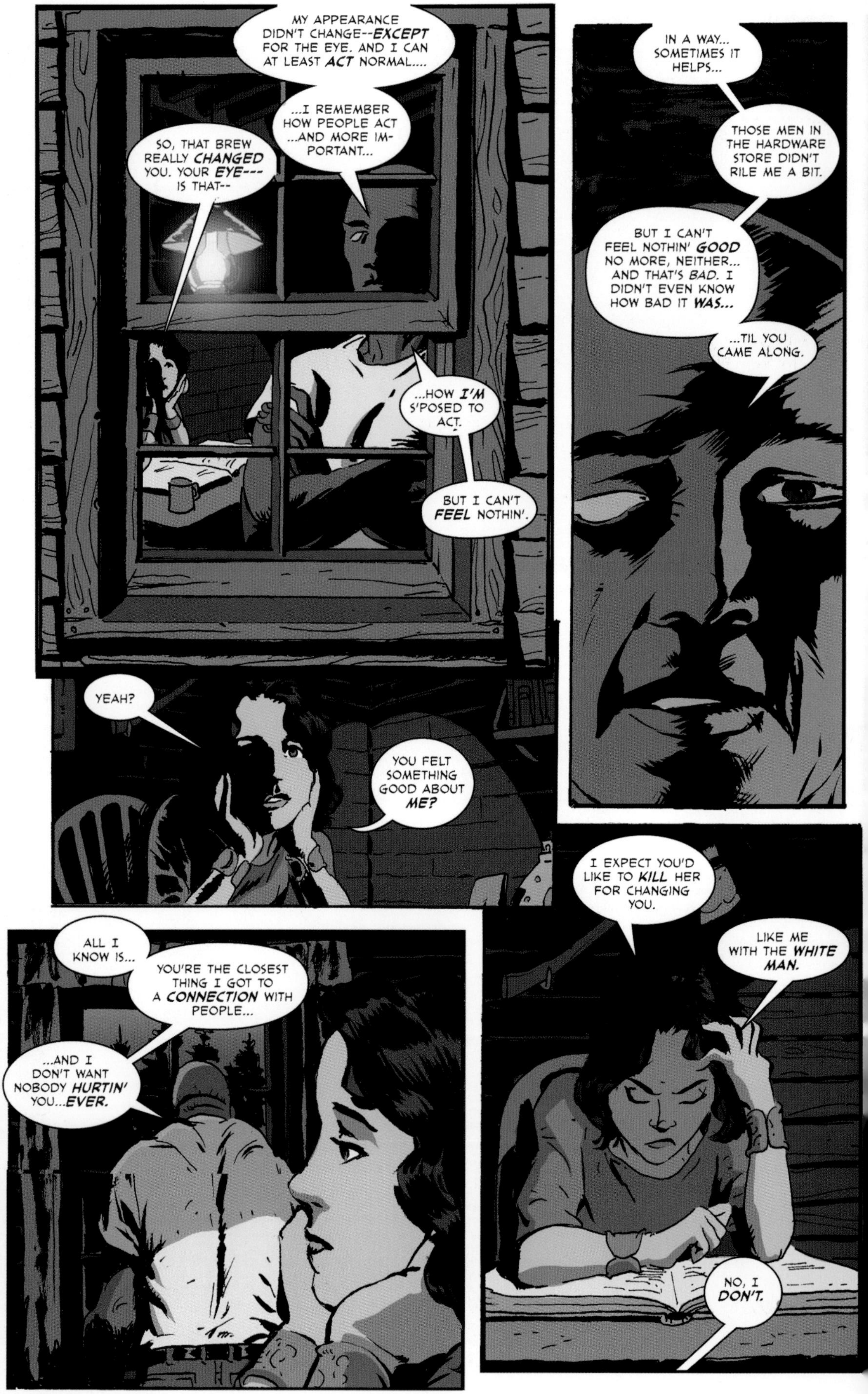
MY APPEARANCE DIDN'T CHANGE--*EXCEPT* FOR THE EYE. AND I CAN AT LEAST *ACT* NORMAL....
SO, THAT BREW REALLY *CHANGED* YOU. YOUR *EYE*--- IS THAT--
...I REMEMBER HOW PEOPLE ACT ...AND MORE IMPORTANT...
...HOW *I'M* S'POSED TO ACT.
BUT I CAN'T *FEEL* NOTHIN'.
IN A WAY... SOMETIMES IT HELPS...
THOSE MEN IN THE HARDWARE STORE DIDN'T RILE ME A BIT.
BUT I CAN'T FEEL NOTHIN' *GOOD* NO MORE, NEITHER... AND THAT'S *BAD*. I DIDN'T EVEN KNOW HOW BAD IT *WAS...*
...TIL YOU CAME ALONG.
YEAH?
YOU FELT SOMETHING GOOD ABOUT *ME?*
ALL I KNOW IS...
YOU'RE THE CLOSEST THING I GOT TO A *CONNECTION* WITH PEOPLE...
...AND I DON'T WANT NOBODY *HURTIN'* YOU...*EVER.*
I EXPECT YOU'D LIKE TO *KILL* HER FOR CHANGING YOU.
LIKE ME WITH THE *WHITE MAN.*
NO, I *DON'T.*

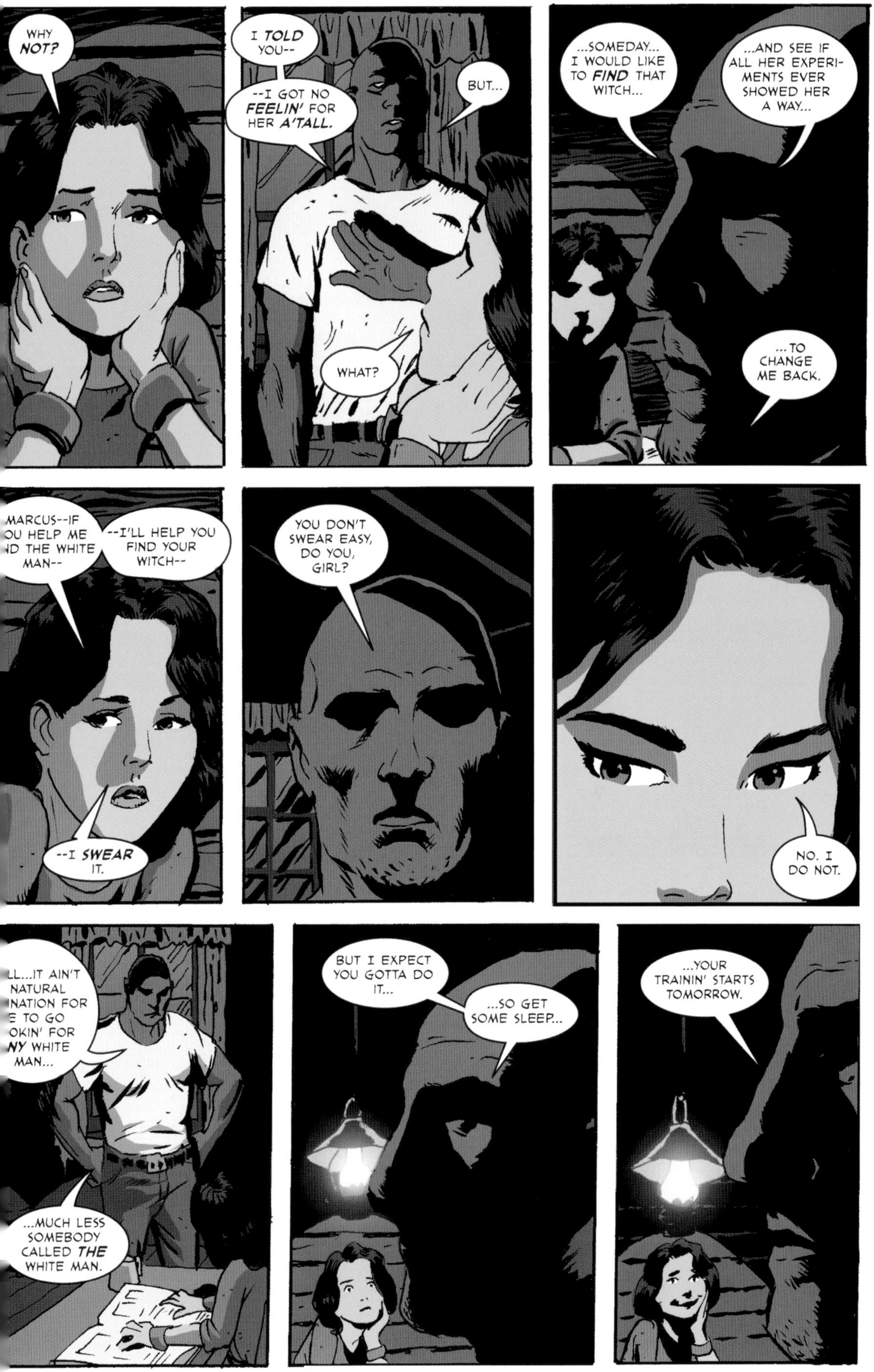
WHY NOT?
I TOLD YOU--
--I GOT NO FEELIN' FOR HER A'TALL.
BUT...
WHAT?
...SOMEDAY... I WOULD LIKE TO FIND THAT WITCH...
...AND SEE IF ALL HER EXPERIMENTS EVER SHOWED HER A WAY...
...TO CHANGE ME BACK.
MARCUS--IF OU HELP ME ID THE WHITE MAN--
--I'LL HELP YOU FIND YOUR WITCH--
--I SWEAR IT.
YOU DON'T SWEAR EASY, DO YOU, GIRL?
NO. I DO NOT.
LL...IT AIN'T NATURAL NATION FOR E TO GO OKIN' FOR NY WHITE MAN...
...MUCH LESS SOMEBODY CALLED THE WHITE MAN.
BUT I EXPECT YOU GOTTA DO IT...
...SO GET SOME SLEEP...
...YOUR TRAININ' STARTS TOMORROW.

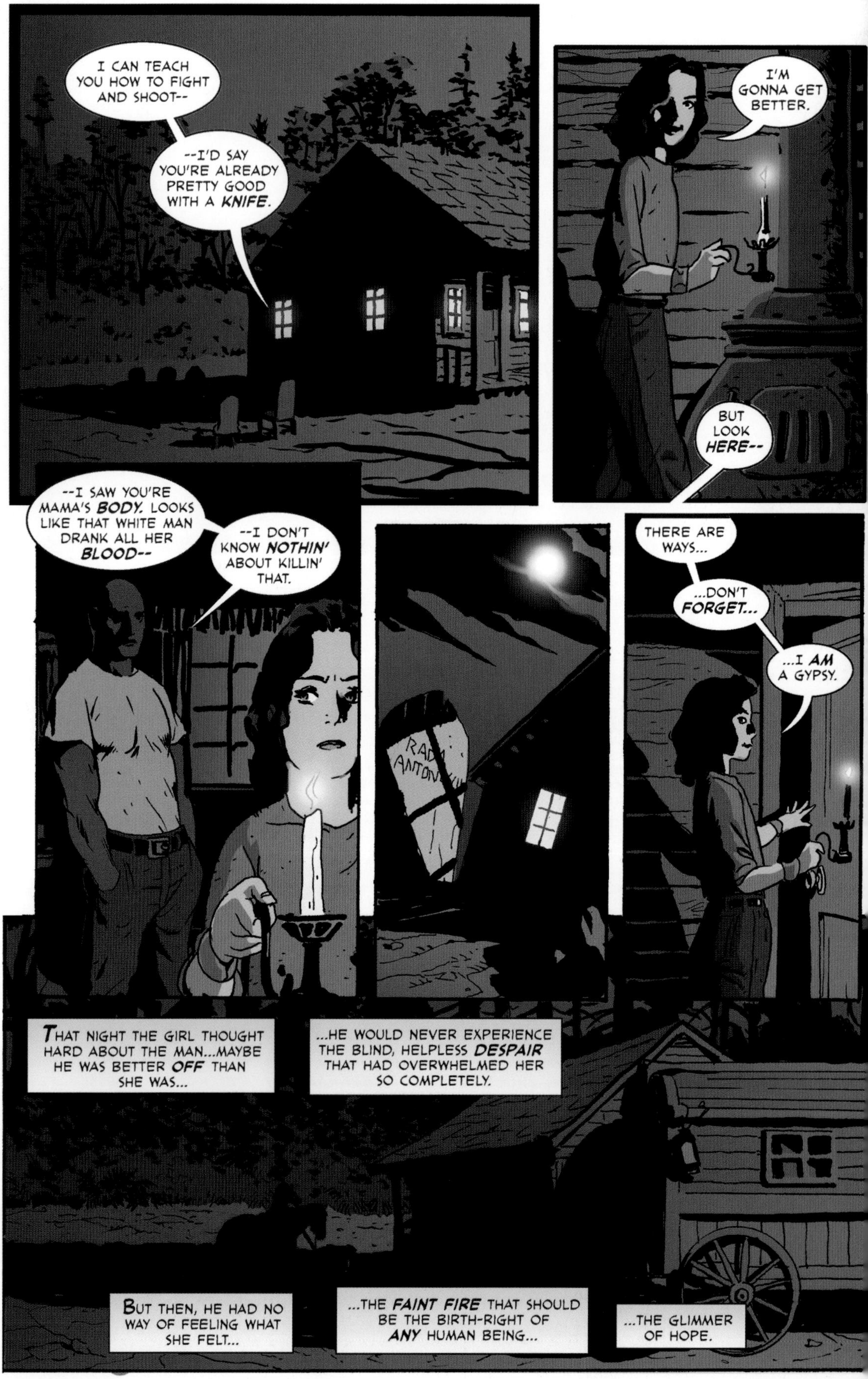

I CAN TEACH YOU HOW TO FIGHT AND SHOOT--
--I'D SAY YOU'RE ALREADY PRETTY GOOD WITH A *KNIFE*.
I'M GONNA GET BETTER.
BUT LOOK *HERE--*
--I SAW YOU'RE MAMA'S *BODY.* LOOKS LIKE THAT WHITE MAN DRANK ALL HER *BLOOD--*
--I DON'T KNOW *NOTHIN'* ABOUT KILLIN' THAT.
RADU ANTON
THERE ARE WAYS...
...DON'T *FORGET...*
...I *AM* A GYPSY.
THAT NIGHT THE GIRL THOUGHT HARD ABOUT THE MAN...MAYBE HE WAS BETTER *OFF* THAN SHE WAS...
...HE WOULD NEVER EXPERIENCE THE BLIND, HELPLESS *DESPAIR* THAT HAD OVERWHELMED HER SO COMPLETELY.
BUT THEN, HE HAD NO WAY OF FEELING WHAT SHE FELT...
...THE *FAINT FIRE* THAT SHOULD BE THE BIRTH-RIGHT OF *ANY* HUMAN BEING...
...THE GLIMMER OF HOPE.

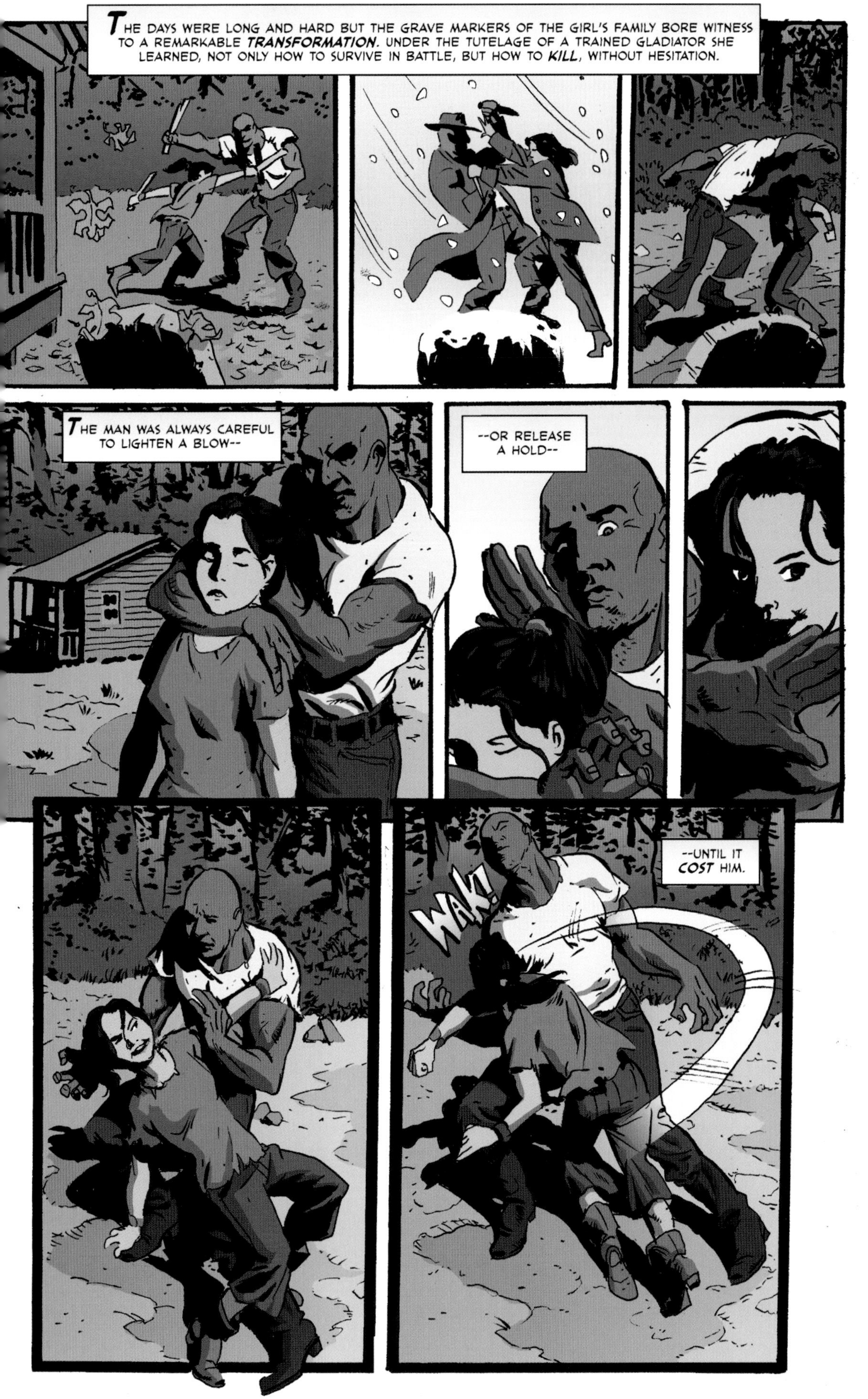
THE DAYS WERE LONG AND HARD BUT THE GRAVE MARKERS OF THE GIRL'S FAMILY BORE WITNESS TO A REMARKABLE TRANSFORMATION. UNDER THE TUTELAGE OF A TRAINED GLADIATOR SHE LEARNED, NOT ONLY HOW TO SURVIVE IN BATTLE, BUT HOW TO KILL, WITHOUT HESITATION.
THE MAN WAS ALWAYS CAREFUL TO LIGHTEN A BLOW--
--OR RELEASE A HOLD--
--UNTIL IT COST HIM.
WAK!

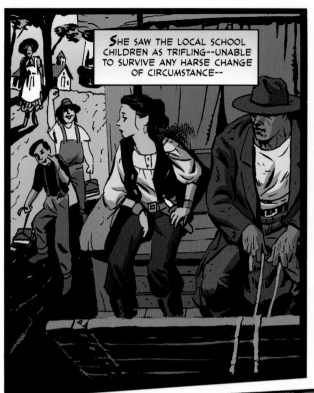

SHE SAW THE LOCAL SCHOOL CHILDREN AS TRIFLING--UNABLE TO SURVIVE ANY HARSE CHANGE OF CIRCUMSTANCE--

--NAIVE IN TERMS OF THE WORLD--

--UNACQUAINTED WITH THE BRUTALITY--THE *HORROR.*

STILL, SHE KNEW ENOUGH TO KNOW WHAT SHE DIDN'T KNOW.

IGNORANCE WOULD ONLY WORK AGAINST HER--

--AND SHE NEVER KNEW WHAT ROLES MIGHT BE REQUIRED--

--IN THE DARK SCENARIOS OF *REVENGE* CONSTANTLY BEING MOUNTED IN HER MIND.

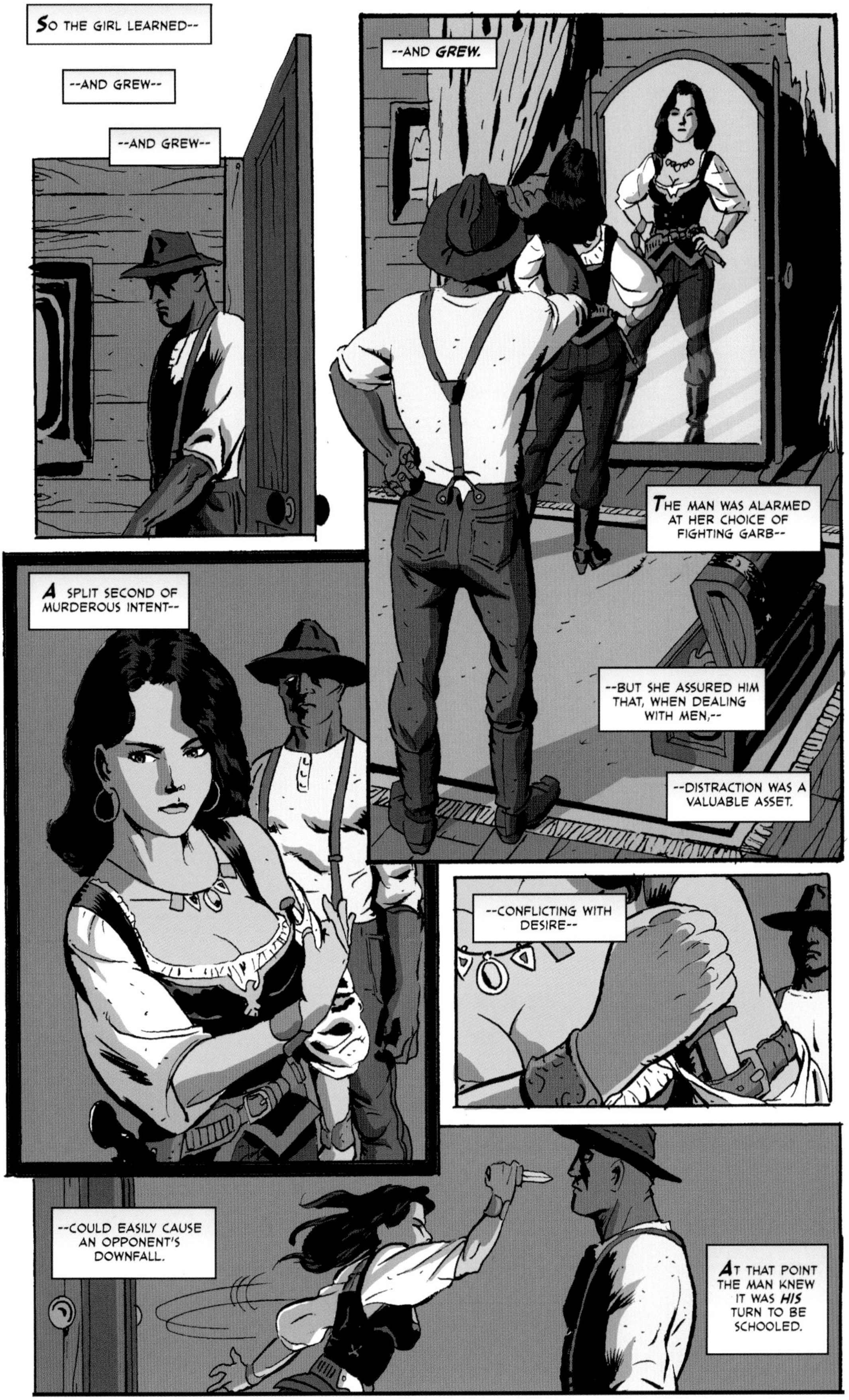
So the girl learned--
--and grew--
--and grew--
--and GREW.
The man was alarmed at her choice of fighting garb--
--but she assured him that, when dealing with men,--
--distraction was a valuable asset.
A split second of murderous intent--
--conflicting with desire--
--could easily cause an opponent's downfall.
At that point the man knew it was HIS turn to be schooled.

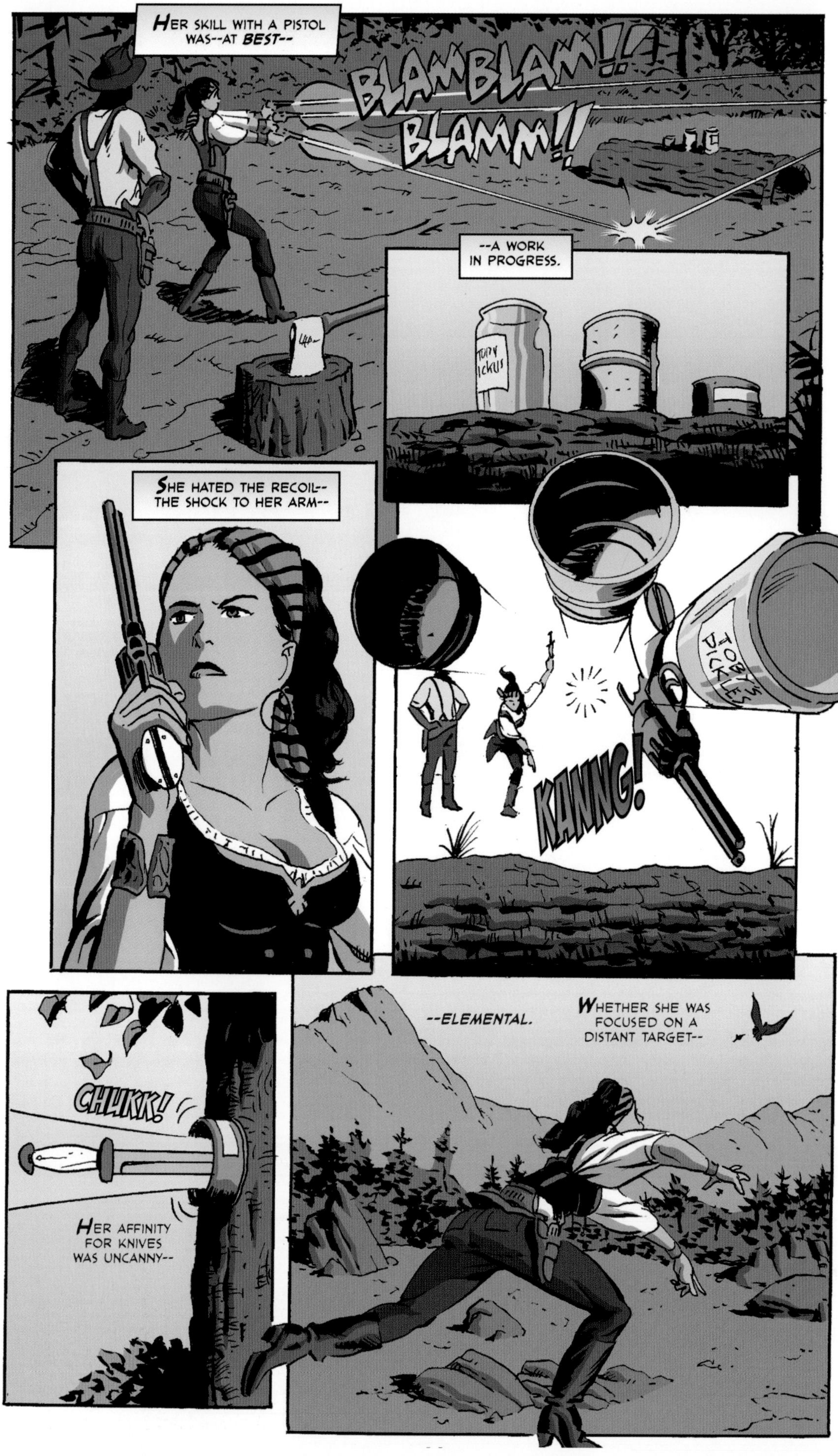
HER SKILL WITH A PISTOL WAS--AT BEST--
BLAMBLAM!!
BLAMM!!
--A WORK IN PROGRESS.
SHE HATED THE RECOIL-- THE SHOCK TO HER ARM--
KANNG!
CHUKK!
HER AFFINITY FOR KNIVES WAS UNCANNY--
--ELEMENTAL.
WHETHER SHE WAS FOCUSED ON A DISTANT TARGET--

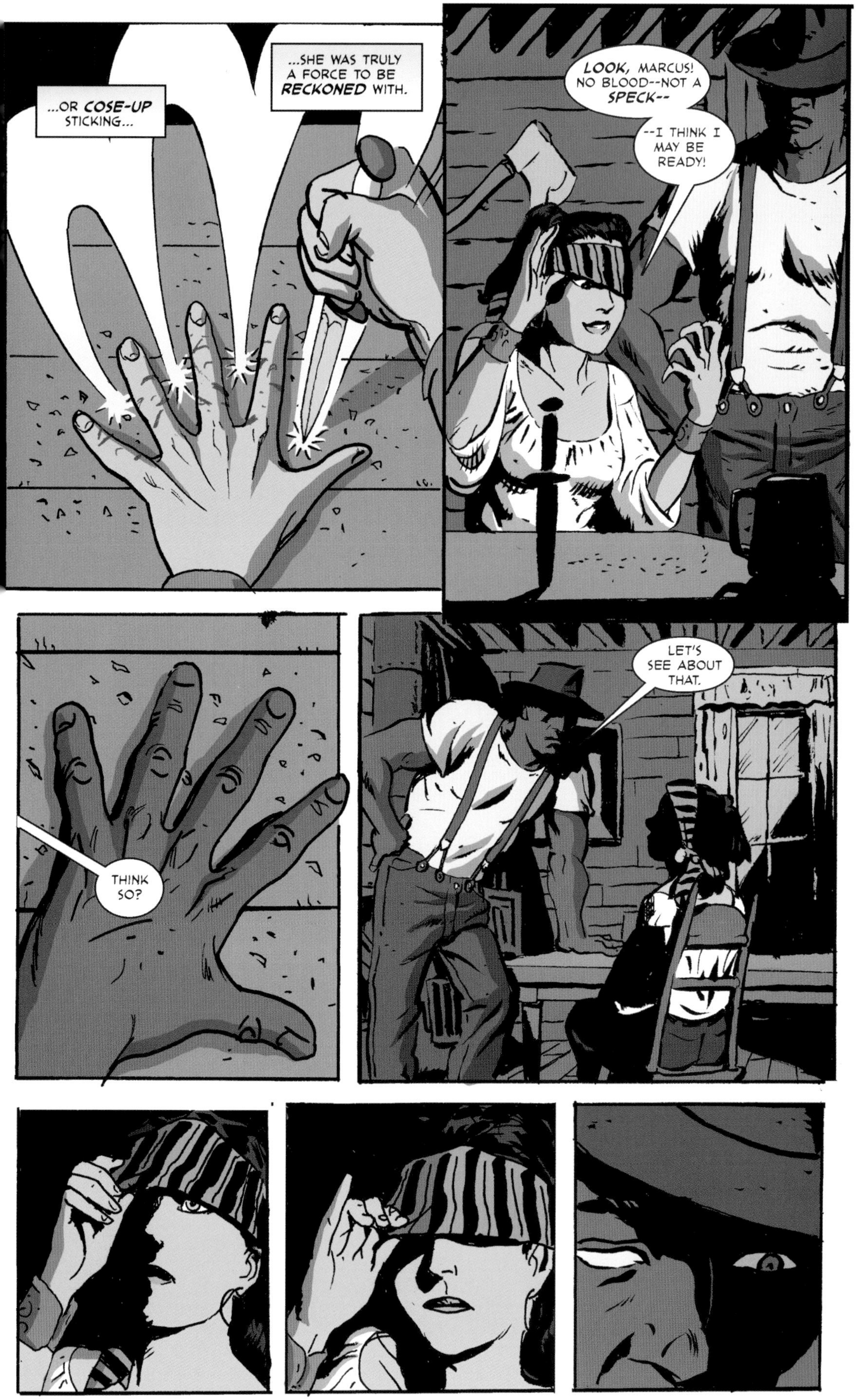
...OR COSE-UP STICKING...
...SHE WAS TRULY A FORCE TO BE RECKONED WITH.
LOOK, MARCUS! NO BLOOD--NOT A SPECK--
--I THINK I MAY BE READY!
THINK SO?
LET'S SEE ABOUT THAT.

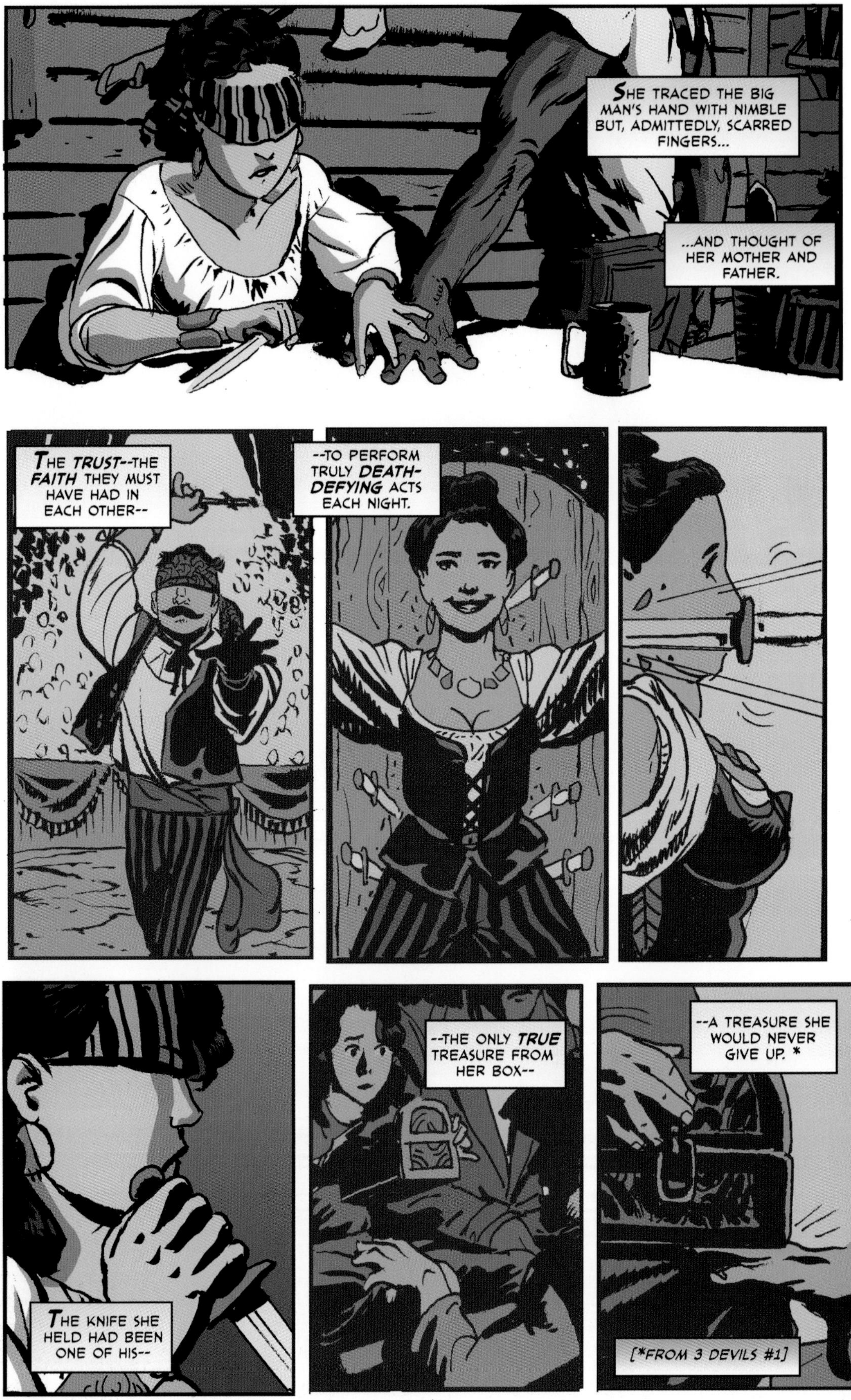
SHE TRACED THE BIG MAN'S HAND WITH NIMBLE BUT, ADMITTEDLY, SCARRED FINGERS...
...AND THOUGHT OF HER MOTHER AND FATHER.
THE TRUST--THE FAITH THEY MUST HAVE HAD IN EACH OTHER--
--TO PERFORM TRULY DEATH-DEFYING ACTS EACH NIGHT.
THE KNIFE SHE HELD HAD BEEN ONE OF HIS--
--THE ONLY TRUE TREASURE FROM HER BOX--
--A TREASURE SHE WOULD NEVER GIVE UP. *
[*FROM 3 DEVILS #1]

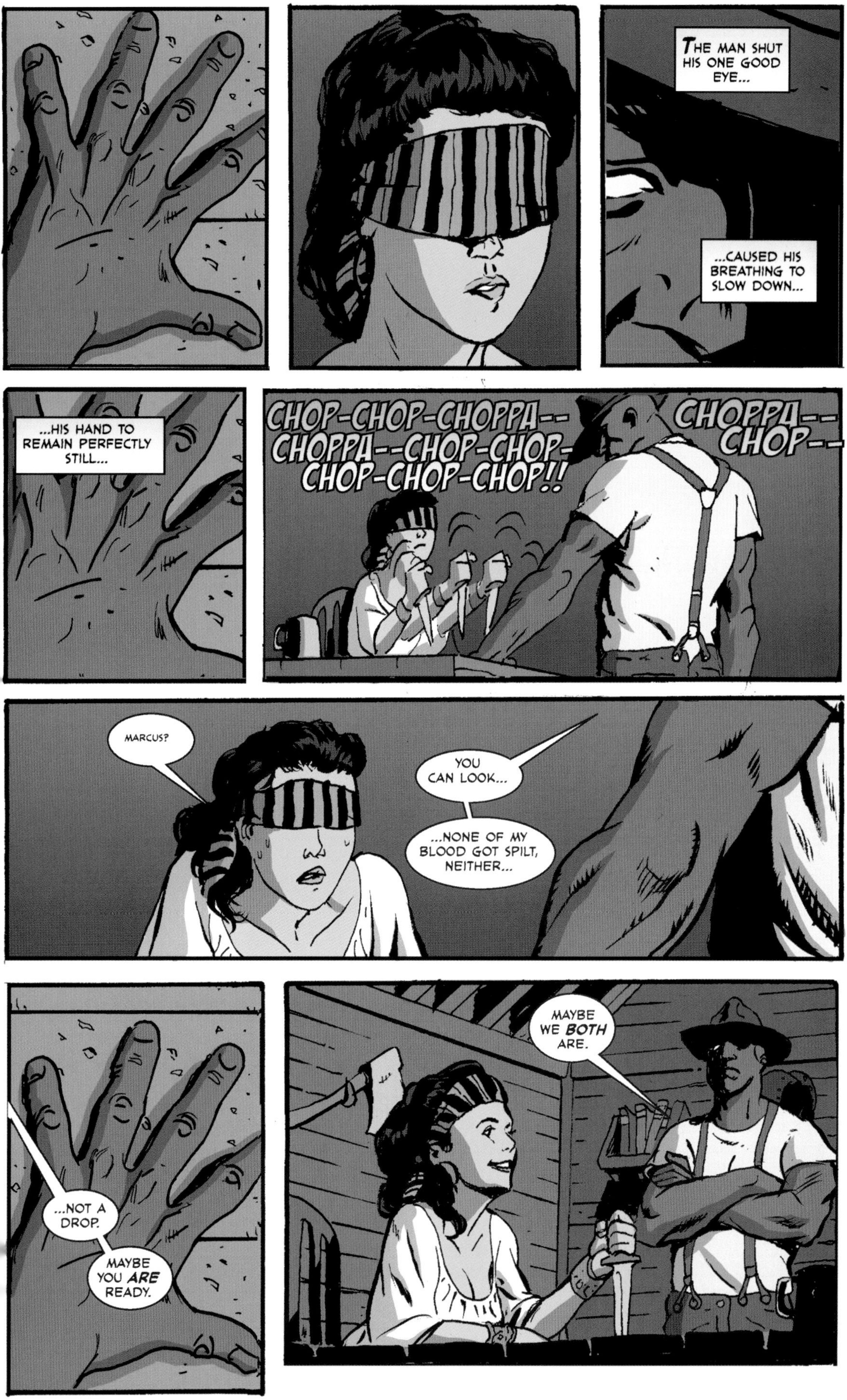
THE MAN SHUT HIS ONE GOOD EYE...
...CAUSED HIS BREATHING TO SLOW DOWN...
...HIS HAND TO REMAIN PERFECTLY STILL...
CHOP-CHOP-CHOPPA--CHOPPA--CHOP-CHOP-CHOP-CHOP-CHOP!!
CHOPPA--CHOP--
MARCUS?
YOU CAN LOOK...
...NONE OF MY BLOOD GOT SPILT, NEITHER...
...NOT A DROP.
MAYBE YOU ARE READY.
MAYBE WE BOTH ARE.

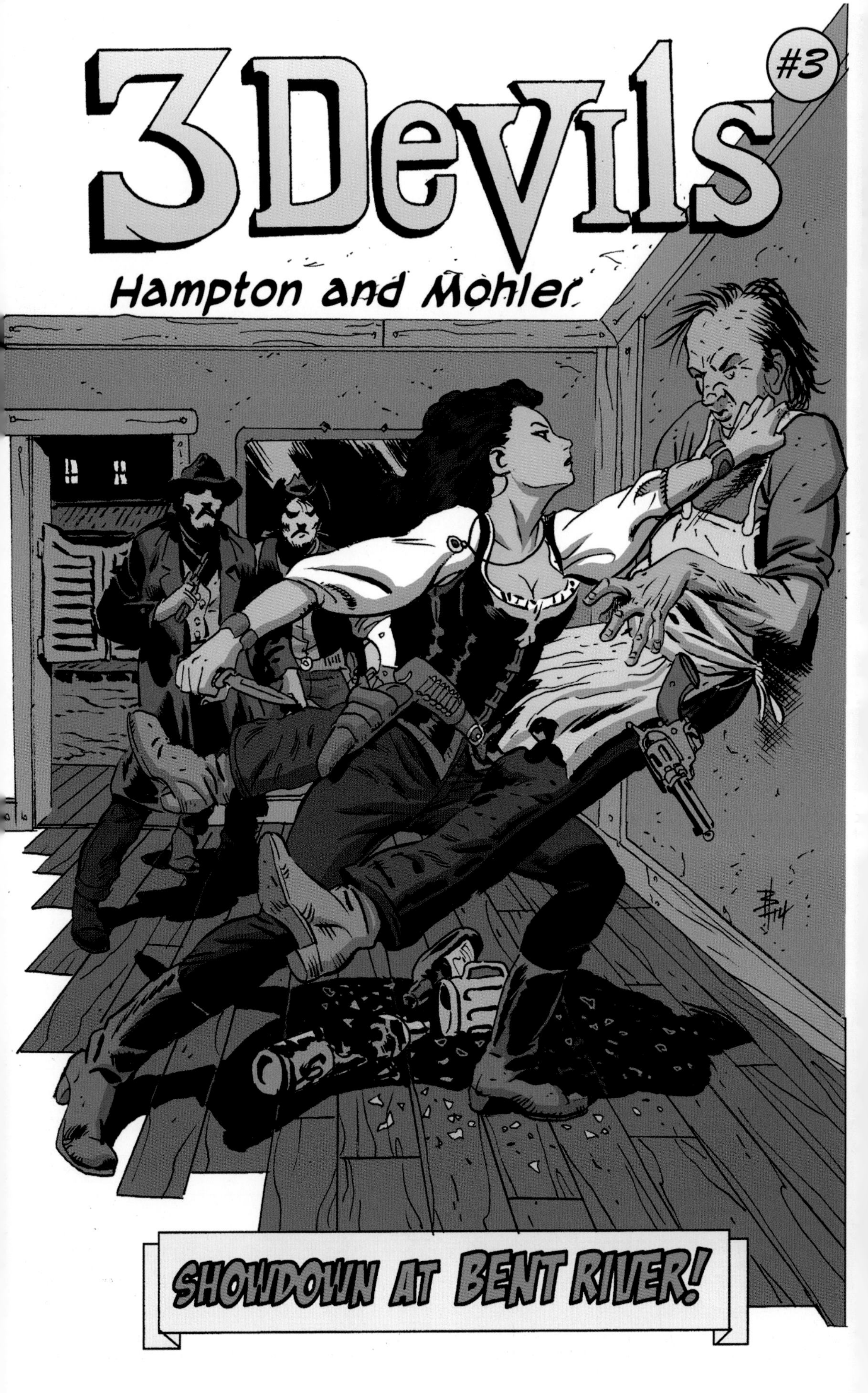
3 Devils
#3
Hampton and Mohler
SHOWDOWN AT BENT RIVER!

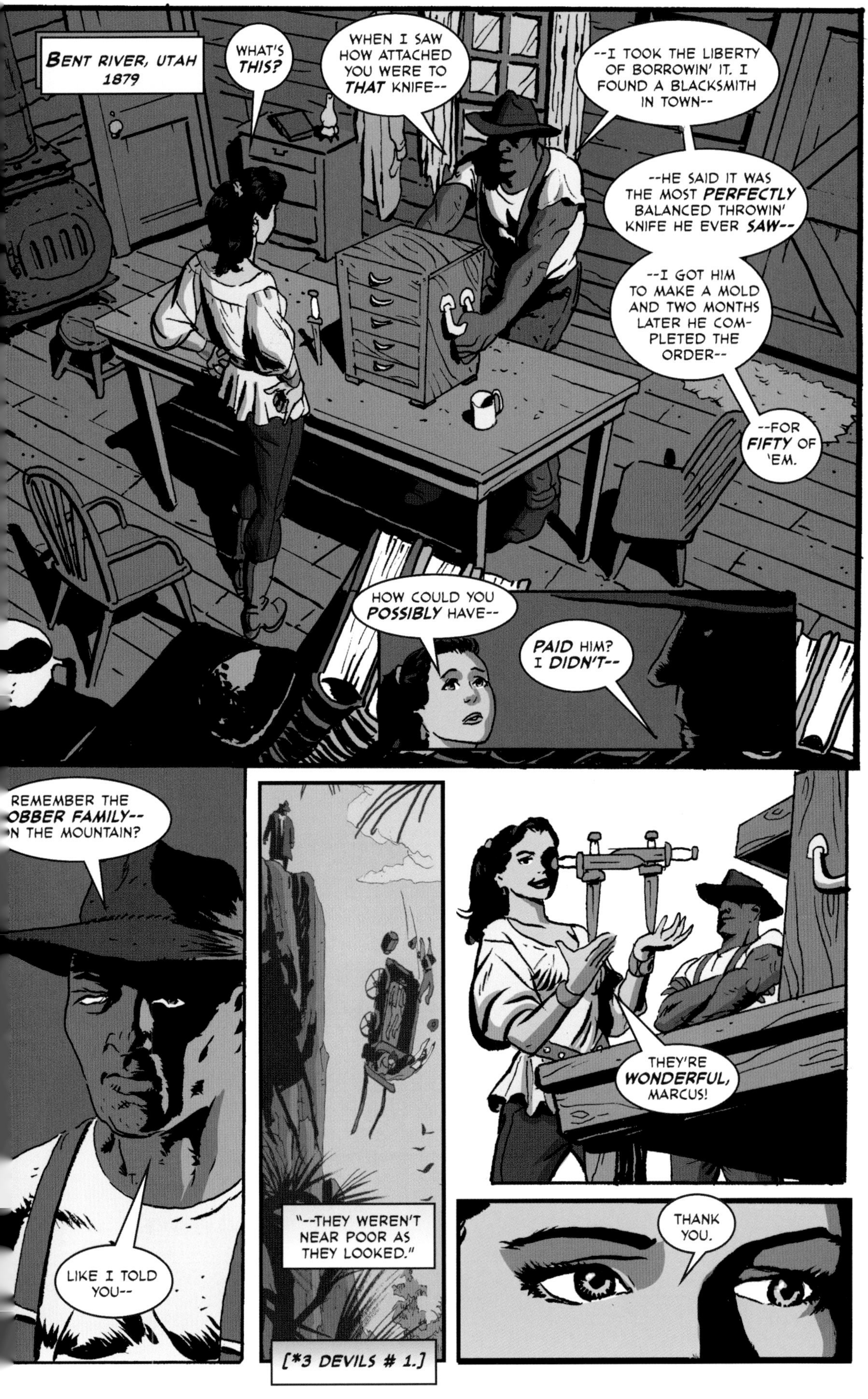
BENT RIVER, UTAH
1879
WHAT'S THIS?
WHEN I SAW HOW ATTACHED YOU WERE TO THAT KNIFE--
--I TOOK THE LIBERTY OF BORROWIN' IT. I FOUND A BLACKSMITH IN TOWN--
--HE SAID IT WAS THE MOST PERFECTLY BALANCED THROWIN' KNIFE HE EVER SAW--
--I GOT HIM TO MAKE A MOLD AND TWO MONTHS LATER HE COM-PLETED THE ORDER--
--FOR FIFTY OF 'EM.
HOW COULD YOU POSSIBLY HAVE--
PAID HIM? I DIDN'T--
REMEMBER THE OBBER FAMILY-- N THE MOUNTAIN?
LIKE I TOLD YOU--
"--THEY WEREN'T NEAR POOR AS THEY LOOKED."
[*3 DEVILS # 1.]
THEY'RE WONDERFUL, MARCUS!
THANK YOU.

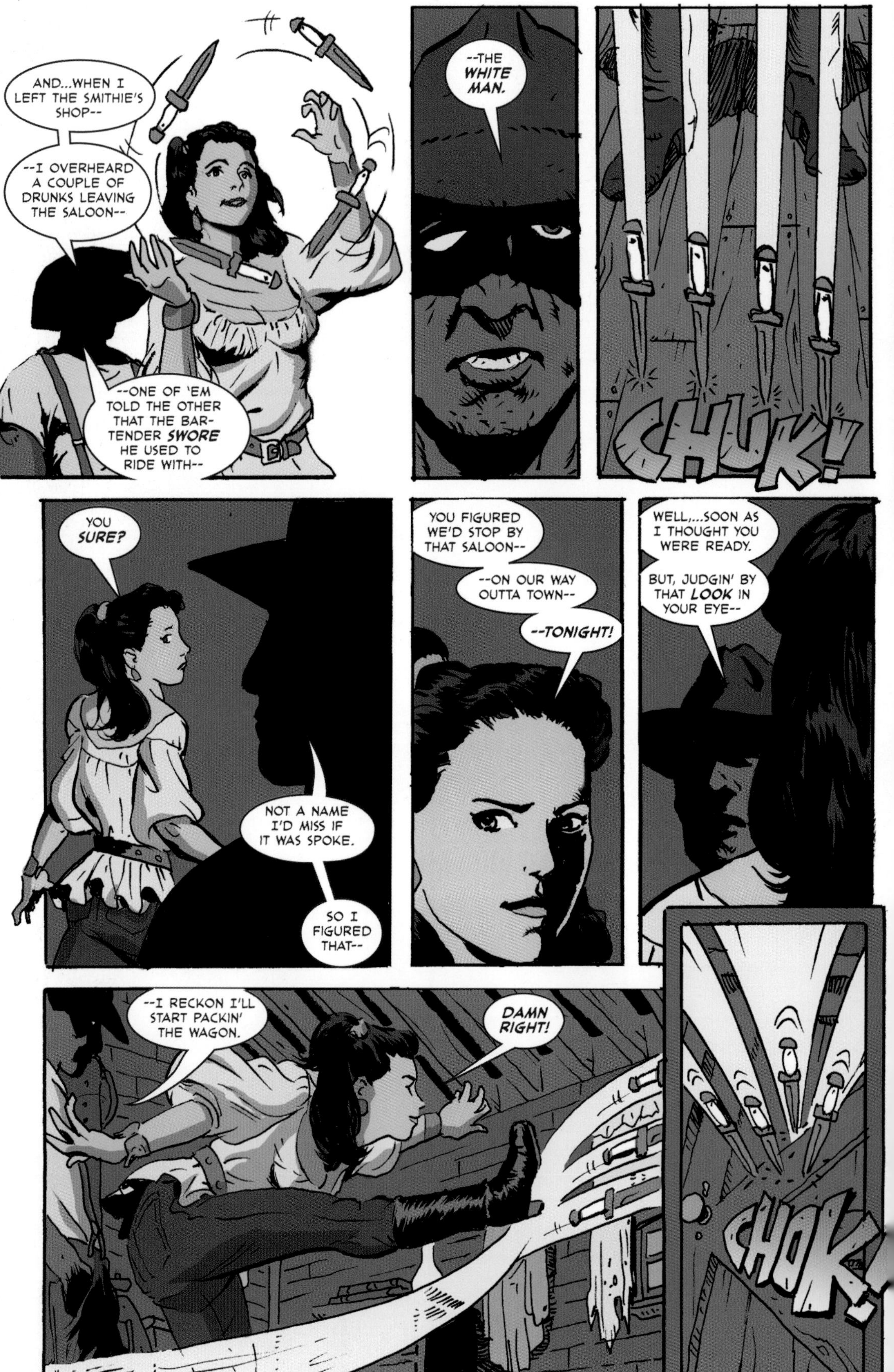
AND...WHEN I LEFT THE SMITHIE'S SHOP--
--I OVERHEARD A COUPLE OF DRUNKS LEAVING THE SALOON--
--ONE OF 'EM TOLD THE OTHER THAT THE BAR-TENDER SWORE HE USED TO RIDE WITH--
--THE WHITE MAN.
CHUK!
YOU SURE?
NOT A NAME I'D MISS IF IT WAS SPOKE.
SO I FIGURED THAT--
YOU FIGURED WE'D STOP BY THAT SALOON--
--ON OUR WAY OUTTA TOWN--
--TONIGHT!
WELL,...SOON AS I THOUGHT YOU WERE READY.
BUT, JUDGIN' BY THAT LOOK IN YOUR EYE--
--I RECKON I'LL START PACKIN' THE WAGON.
DAMN RIGHT!
CHOK!

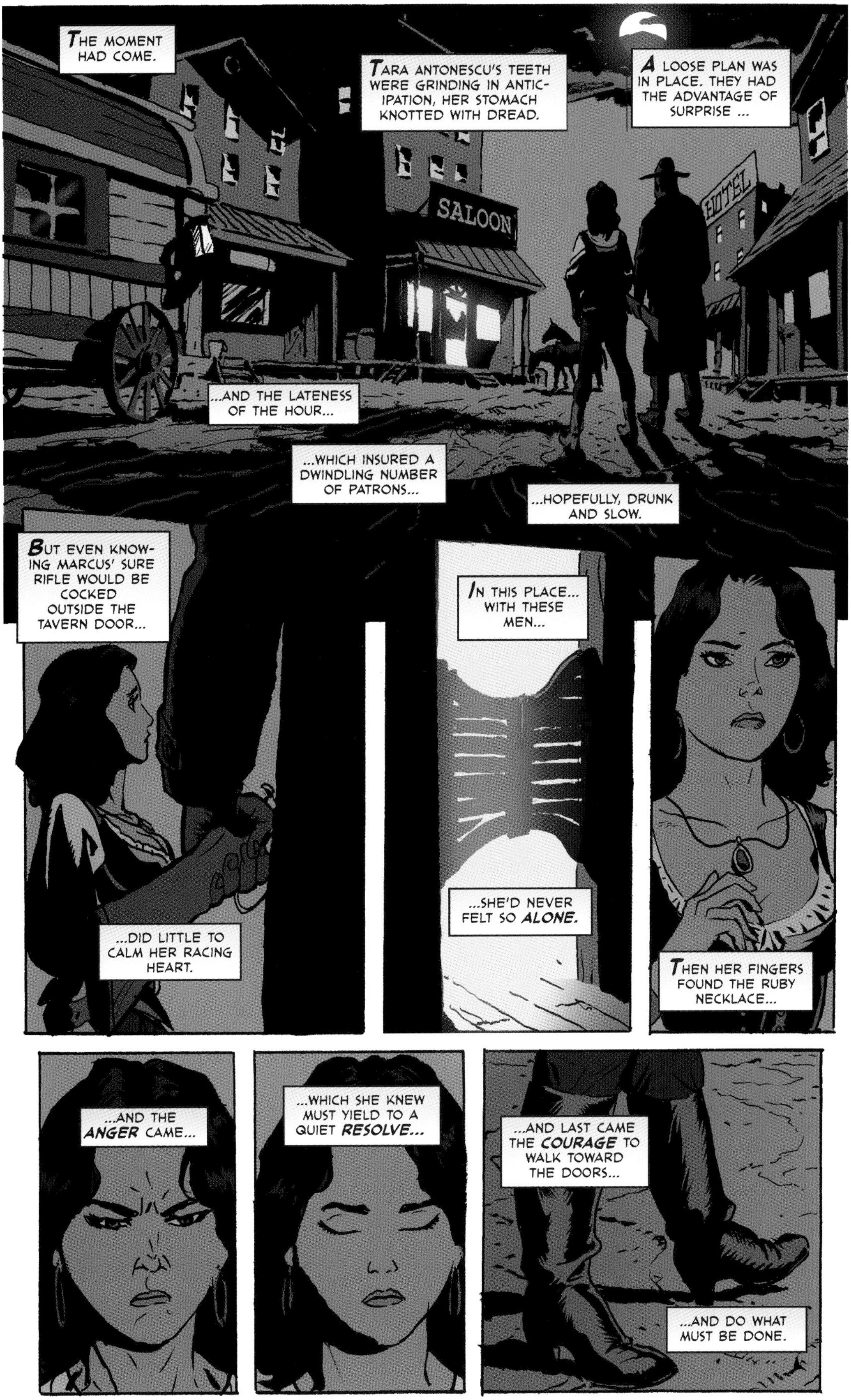
THE MOMENT HAD COME.
TARA ANTONESCU'S TEETH WERE GRINDING IN ANTIC-IPATION, HER STOMACH KNOTTED WITH DREAD.
A LOOSE PLAN WAS IN PLACE. THEY HAD THE ADVANTAGE OF SURPRISE ...
SALOON
HOTEL
...AND THE LATENESS OF THE HOUR...
...WHICH INSURED A DWINDLING NUMBER OF PATRONS...
...HOPEFULLY, DRUNK AND SLOW.
BUT EVEN KNOW-ING MARCUS' SURE RIFLE WOULD BE COCKED OUTSIDE THE TAVERN DOOR...
...DID LITTLE TO CALM HER RACING HEART.
IN THIS PLACE... WITH THESE MEN...
...SHE'D NEVER FELT SO ALONE.
THEN HER FINGERS FOUND THE RUBY NECKLACE...
...AND THE ANGER CAME...
...WHICH SHE KNEW MUST YIELD TO A QUIET RESOLVE...
...AND LAST CAME THE COURAGE TO WALK TOWARD THE DOORS...
...AND DO WHAT MUST BE DONE.

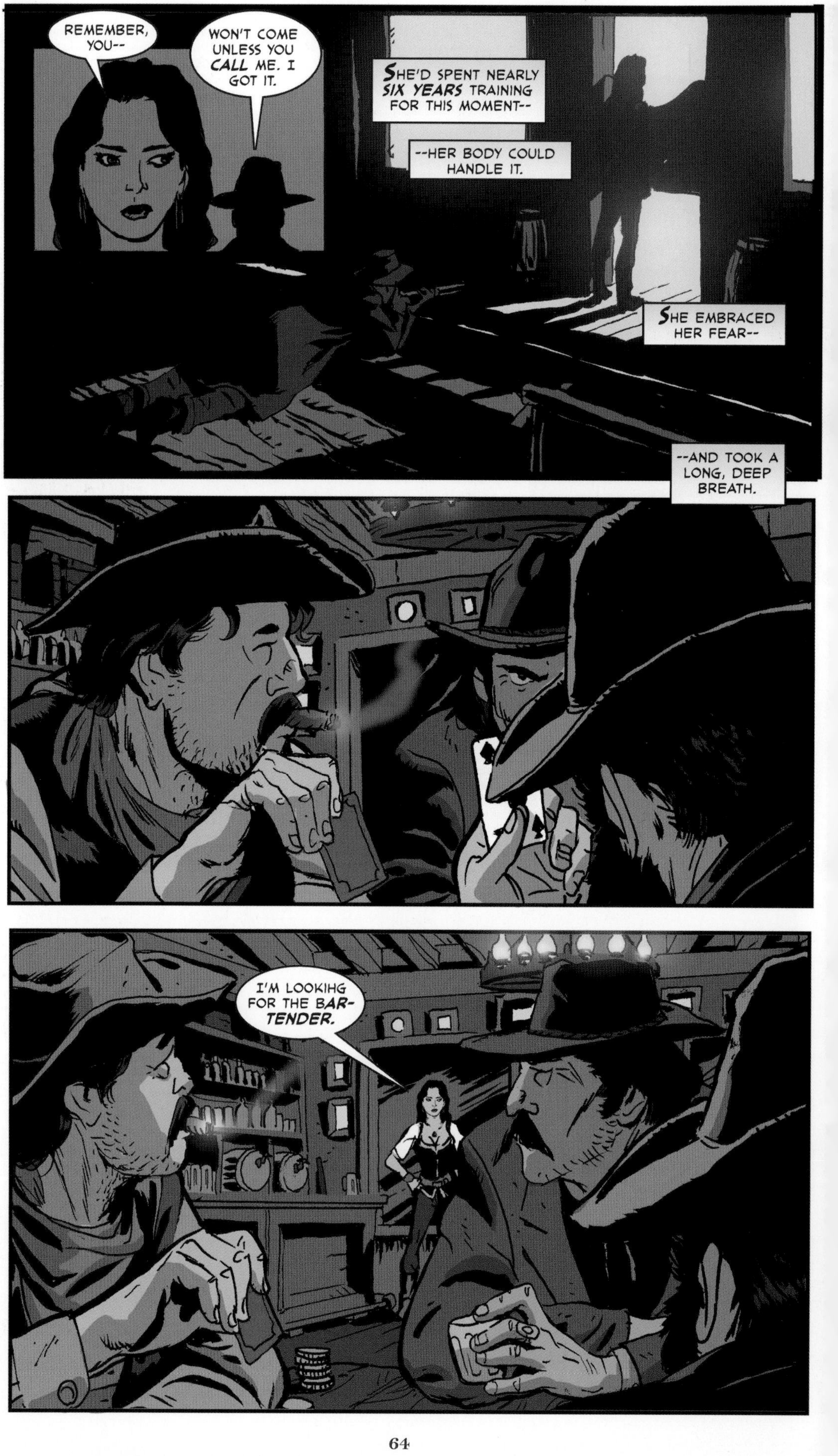
REMEMBER, YOU--
WON'T COME UNLESS YOU CALL ME. I GOT IT.
SHE'D SPENT NEARLY SIX YEARS TRAINING FOR THIS MOMENT--
--HER BODY COULD HANDLE IT.
SHE EMBRACED HER FEAR--
--AND TOOK A LONG, DEEP BREATH.
I'M LOOKIHG FOR THE BAR-TENDER.

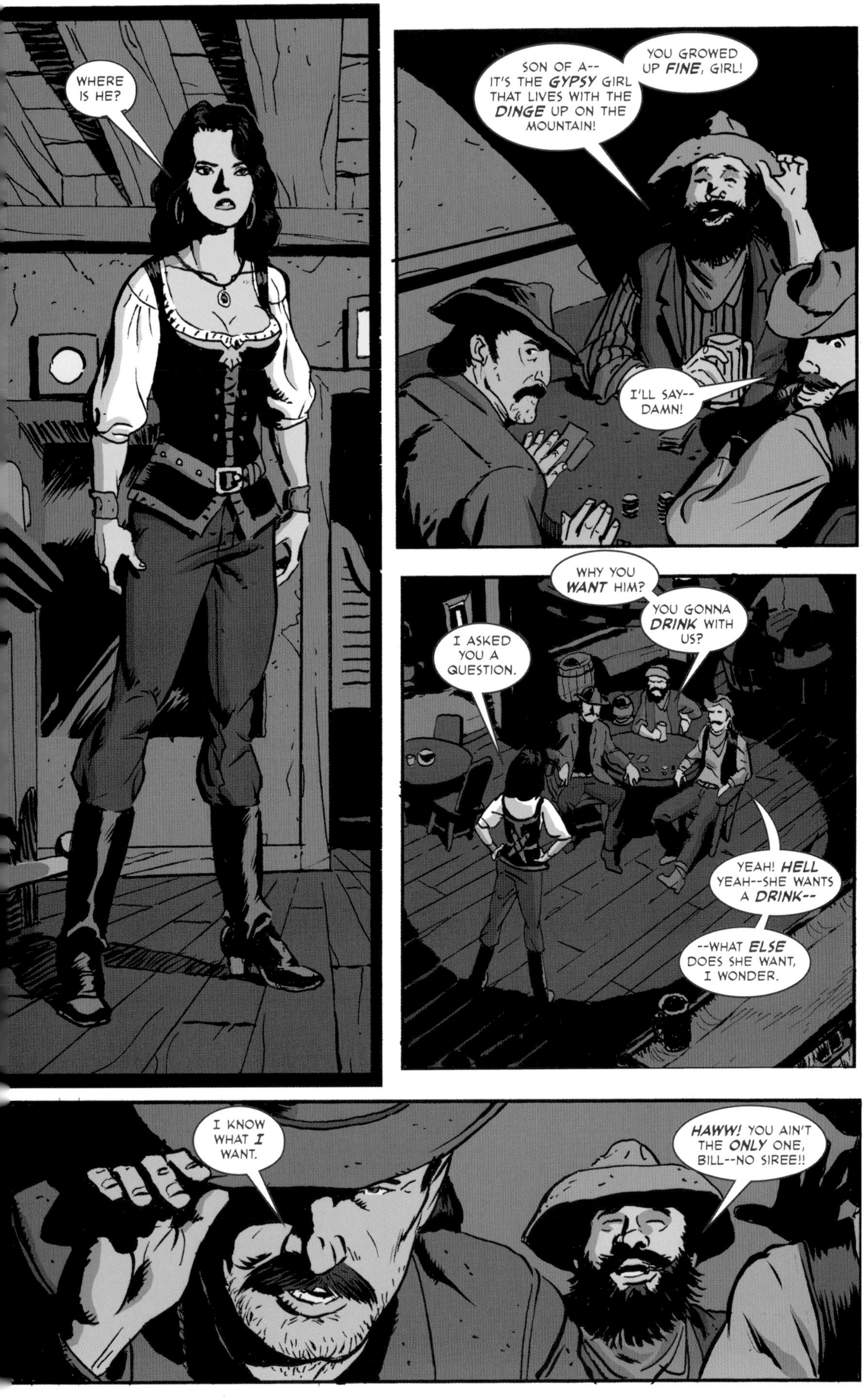
WHERE IS HE?
SON OF A-- IT'S THE GYPSY GIRL THAT LIVES WITH THE DINGE UP ON THE MOUNTAIN!
YOU GROWED UP FINE, GIRL!
I'LL SAY-- DAMN!
WHY YOU WANT HIM?
YOU GONNA DRINK WITH US?
I ASKED YOU A QUESTION.
YEAH! HELL YEAH--SHE WANTS A DRINK--
--WHAT ELSE DOES SHE WANT, I WONDER.
I KNOW WHAT I WANT.
HAWW! YOU AIN'T THE ONLY ONE, BILL--NO SIREE!!

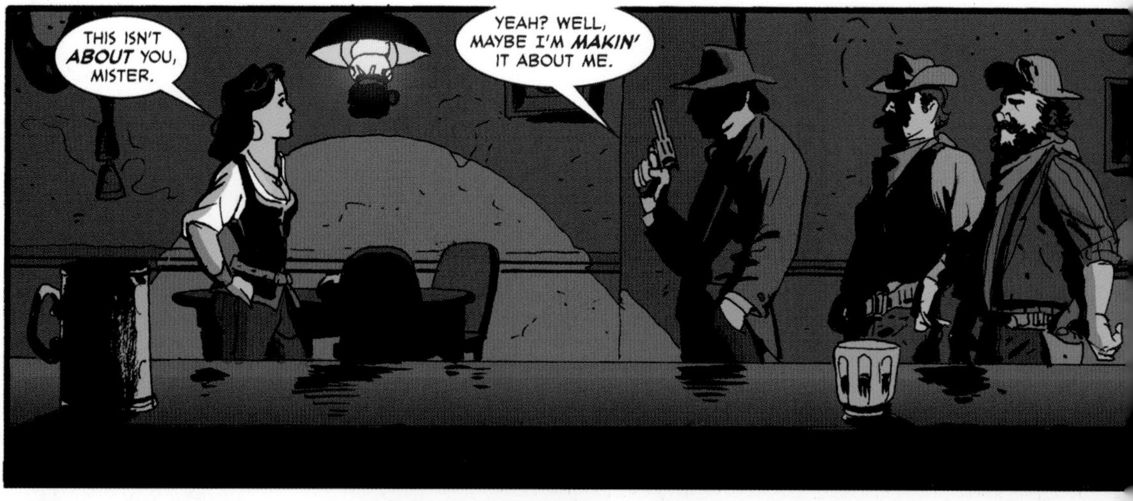
THIS ISN'T ABOUT YOU, MISTER.
YEAH? WELL, MAYBE I'M MAKIN' IT ABOUT ME.

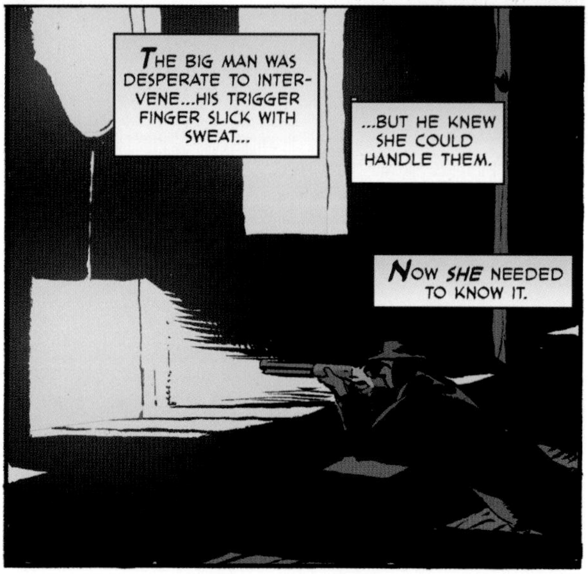
THE BIG MAN WAS DESPERATE TO INTER-VENE...HIS TRIGGER FINGER SLICK WITH SWEAT...
...BUT HE KNEW SHE COULD HANDLE THEM.
NOW SHE NEEDED TO KNOW IT.

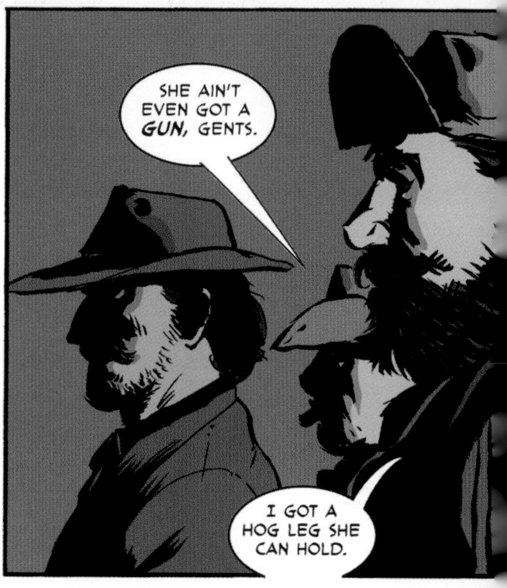
SHE AIN'T EVEN GOT A GUN, GENTS.
I GOT A HOG LEG SHE CAN HOLD.

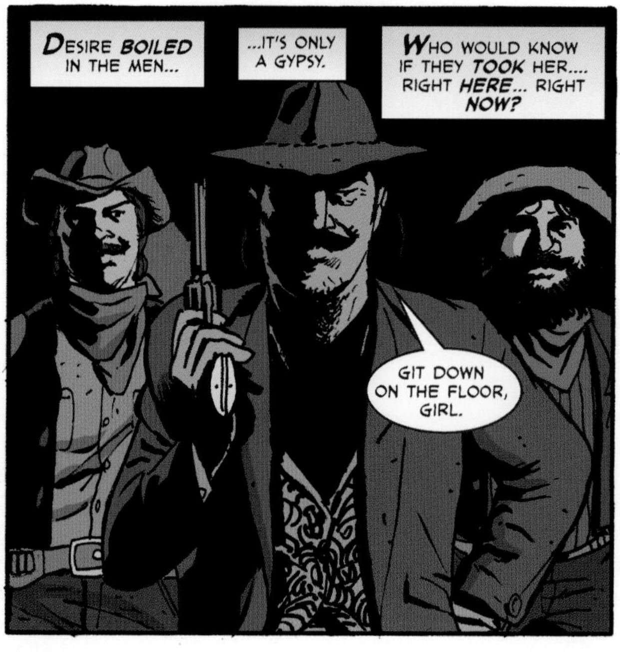
DESIRE BOILED IN THE MEN...
...IT'S ONLY A GYPSY.
WHO WOULD KNOW IF THEY TOOK HER.... RIGHT HERE... RIGHT NOW?
GIT DOWN ON THE FLOOR, GIRL.

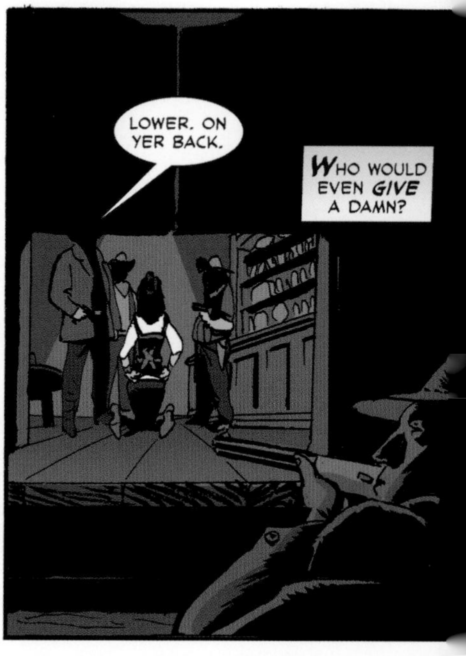
LOWER. ON YER BACK.
WHO WOULD EVEN GIVE A DAMN?

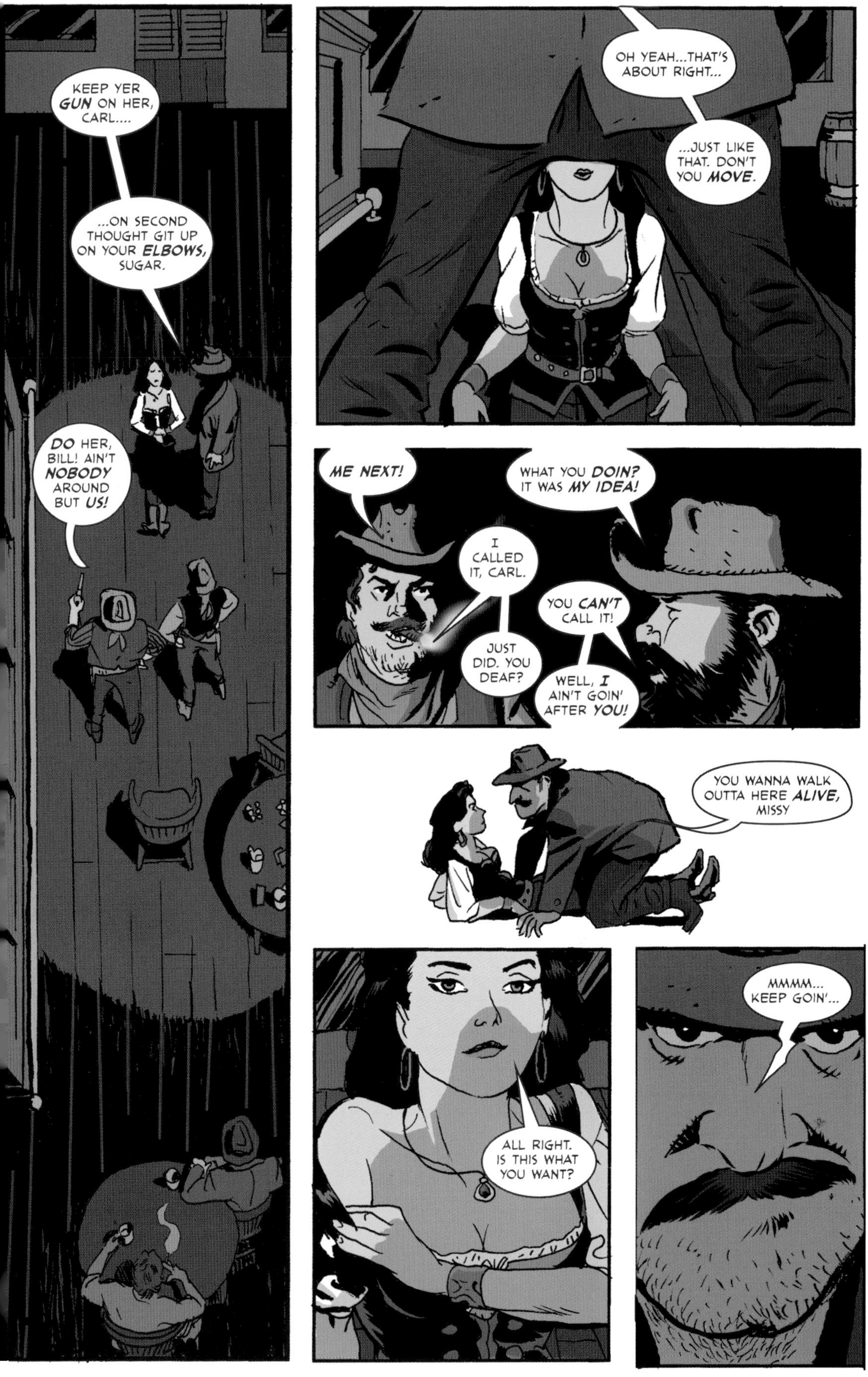
KEEP YER GUN ON HER, CARL....
...ON SECOND THOUGHT GIT UP ON YOUR ELBOWS, SUGAR.
DO HER, BILL! AIN'T NOBODY AROUND BUT US!
OH YEAH...THAT'S ABOUT RIGHT...
...JUST LIKE THAT. DON'T YOU MOVE.
ME NEXT!
WHAT YOU DOIN? IT WAS MY IDEA!
I CALLED IT, CARL.
YOU CAN'T CALL IT!
JUST DID. YOU DEAF?
WELL, I AIN'T GOIN' AFTER YOU!
YOU WANNA WALK OUTTA HERE ALIVE, MISSY
ALL RIGHT. IS THIS WHAT YOU WANT?
MMMM... KEEP GOIN'...

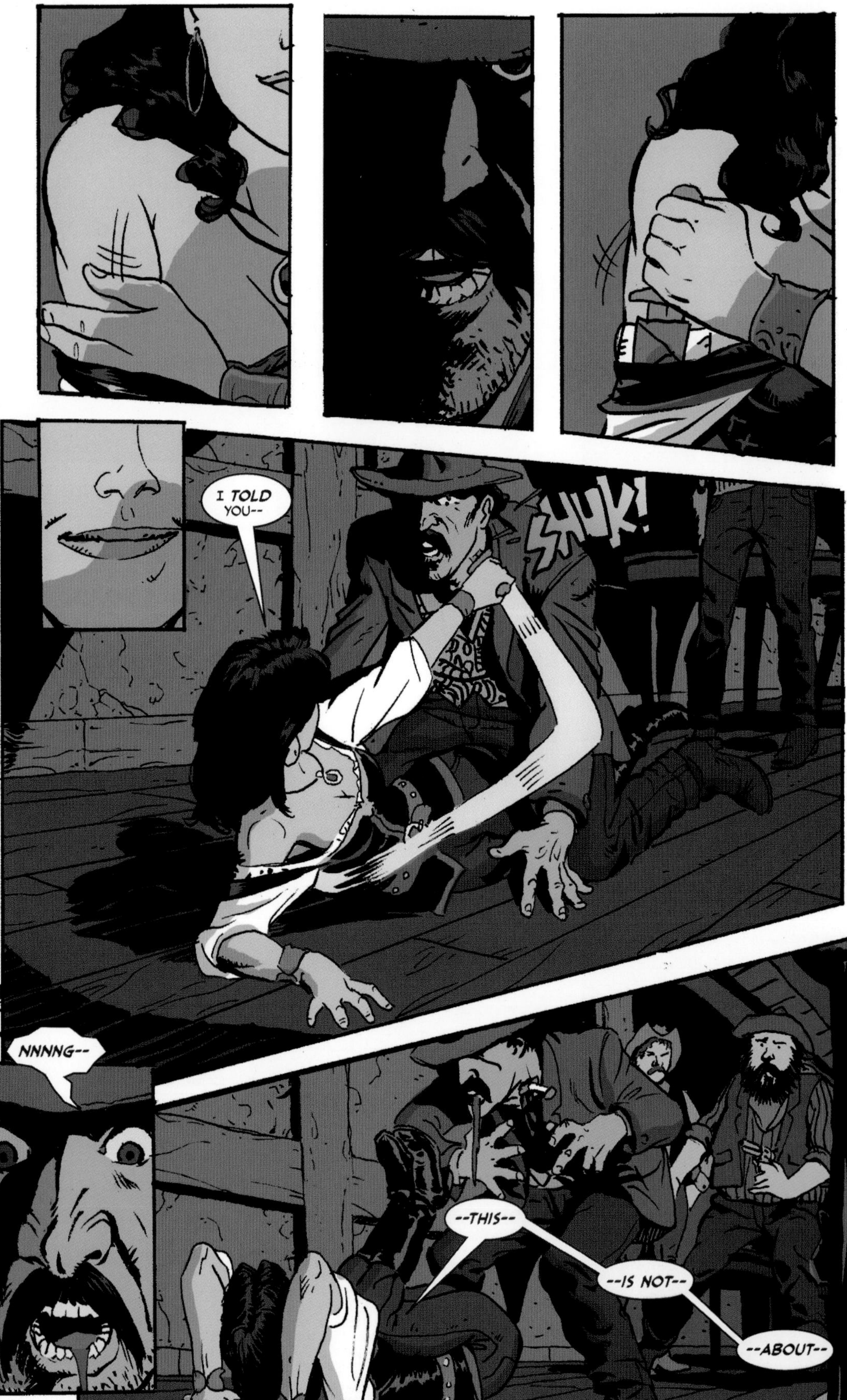
I TOLD YOU--
SHUK!
NNNNG--
--THIS--
--IS NOT--
--ABOUT--

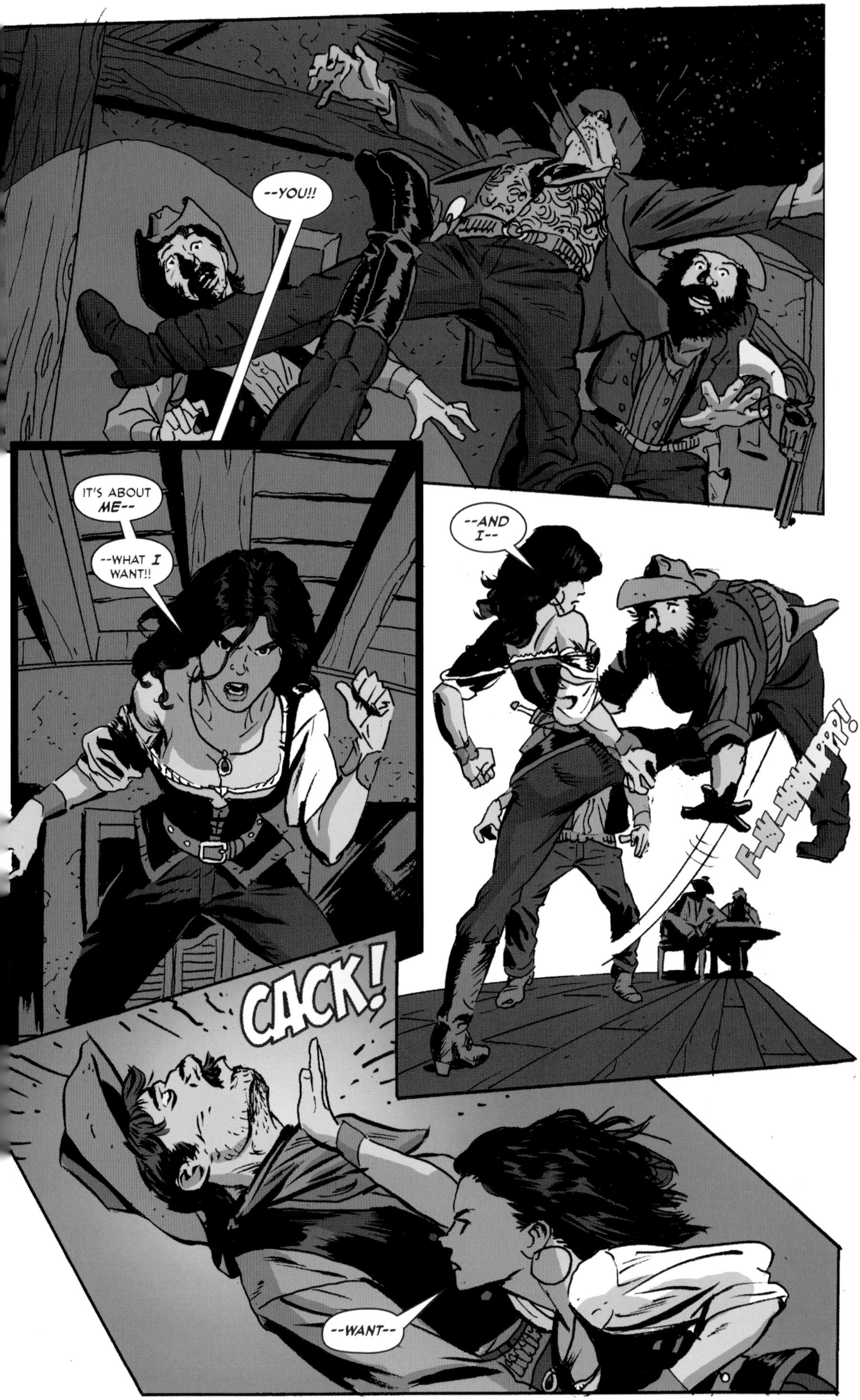
--YOU!!
IT'S ABOUT ME--
--WHAT I WANT!!
--AND I--
CACK!
--WANT--

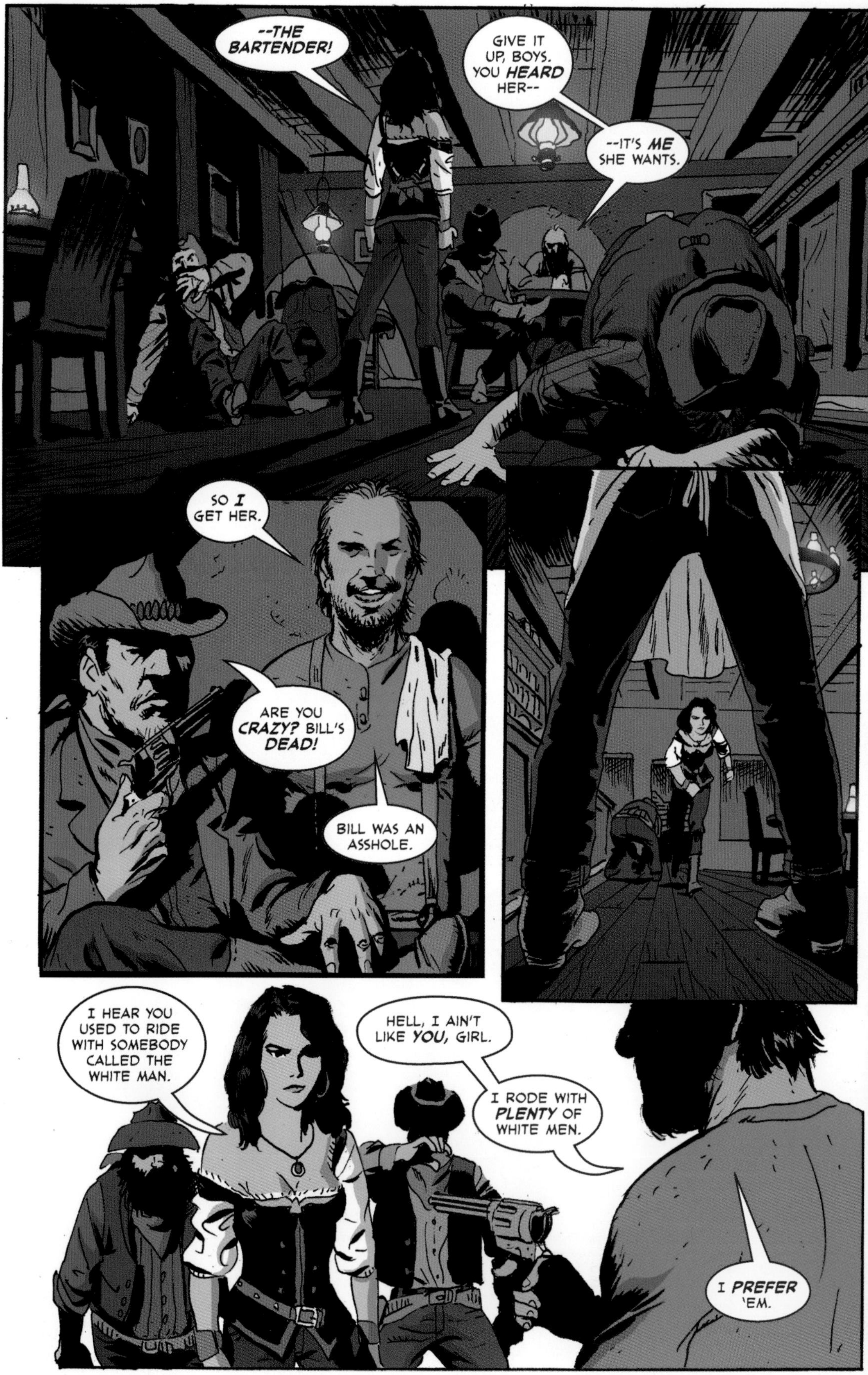
--THE BARTENDER!
GIVE IT UP, BOYS. YOU HEARD HER--
--IT'S ME SHE WANTS.
SO I GET HER.
ARE YOU CRAZY? BILL'S DEAD!
BILL WAS AN ASSHOLE.
I HEAR YOU USED TO RIDE WITH SOMEBODY CALLED THE WHITE MAN.
HELL, I AIN'T LIKE YOU, GIRL.
I RODE WITH PLENTY OF WHITE MEN.
I PREFER 'EM.

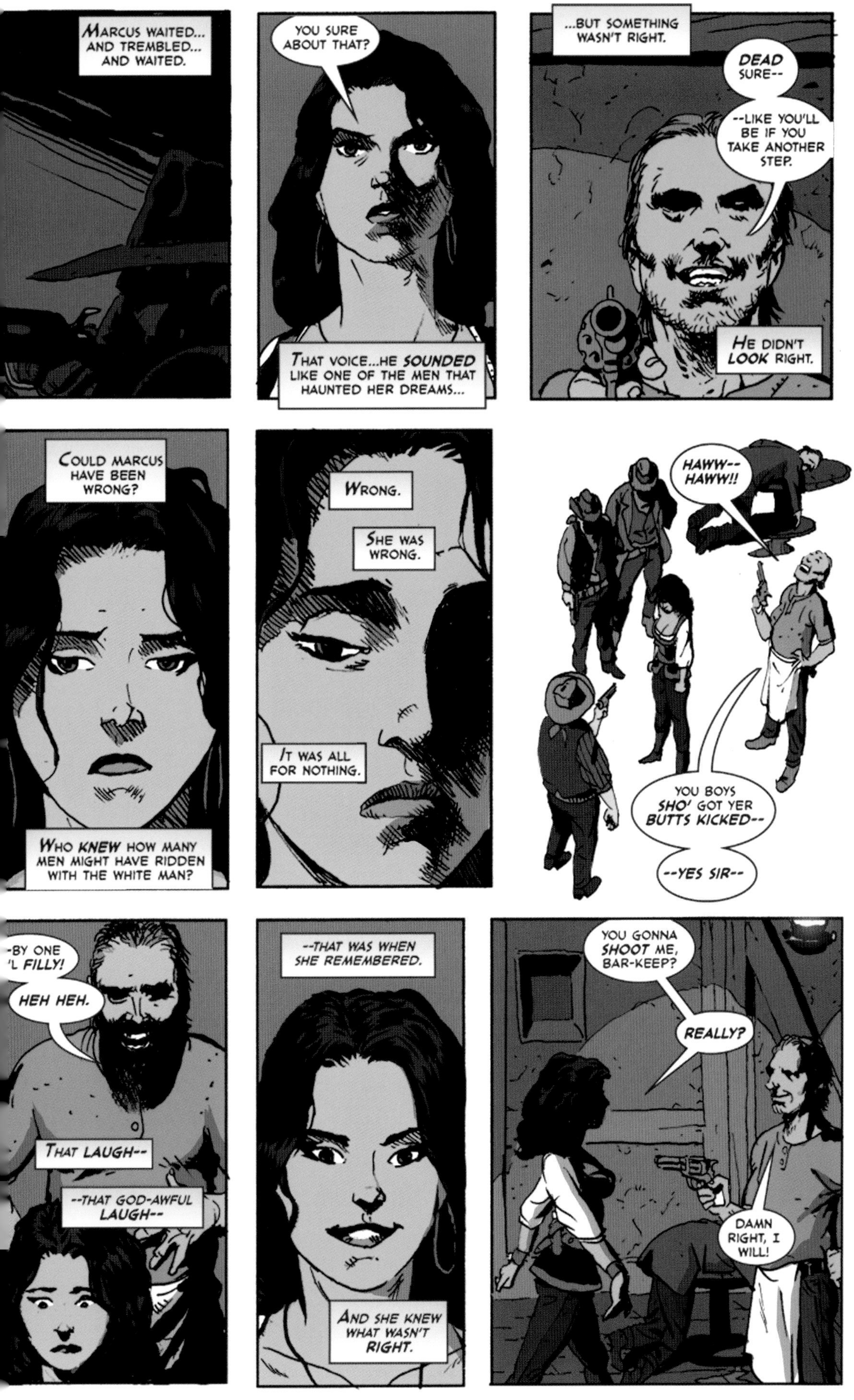
MARCUS WAITED... AND TREMBLED... AND WAITED.
YOU SURE ABOUT THAT?
THAT VOICE...HE SOUNDED LIKE ONE OF THE MEN THAT HAUNTED HER DREAMS...
...BUT SOMETHING WASN'T RIGHT.
DEAD SURE--
--LIKE YOU'LL BE IF YOU TAKE ANOTHER STEP.
HE DIDN'T LOOK RIGHT.
COULD MARCUS HAVE BEEN WRONG?
WHO KNEW HOW MANY MEN MIGHT HAVE RIDDEN WITH THE WHITE MAN?
WRONG.
SHE WAS WRONG.
IT WAS ALL FOR NOTHING.
HAWW-- HAWW!!
YOU BOYS SHO' GOT YER BUTTS KICKED--
--YES SIR--
-BY ONE
'L FILLY!
HEH HEH.
THAT LAUGH--
--THAT GOD-AWFUL LAUGH--
--THAT WAS WHEN SHE REMEMBERED.
AND SHE KNEW WHAT WASN'T RIGHT.
YOU GONNA SHOOT ME, BAR-KEEP?
REALLY?
DAMN RIGHT, I WILL!

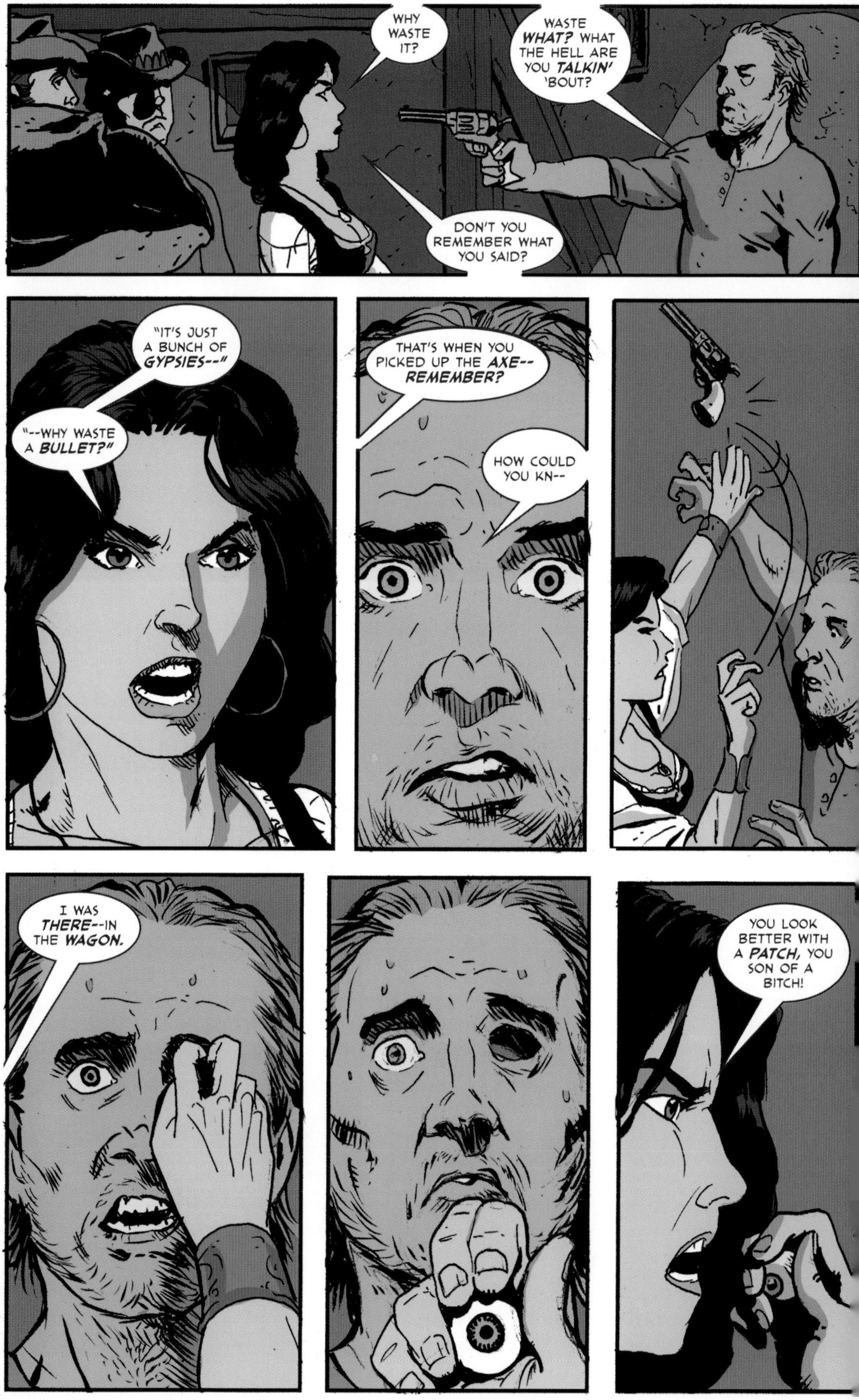
WHY WASTE IT?
WASTE *WHAT?* WHAT THE HELL ARE YOU *TALKIN'* 'BOUT?
DON'T YOU REMEMBER WHAT YOU SAID?
"IT'S JUST A BUNCH OF *GYPSIES--"*
"--WHY WASTE A *BULLET?"*
THAT'S WHEN YOU PICKED UP THE *AXE-- REMEMBER?*
HOW COULD YOU KN--
I WAS *THERE*--IN THE *WAGON.*
YOU LOOK BETTER WITH A *PATCH,* YOU SON OF A BITCH!

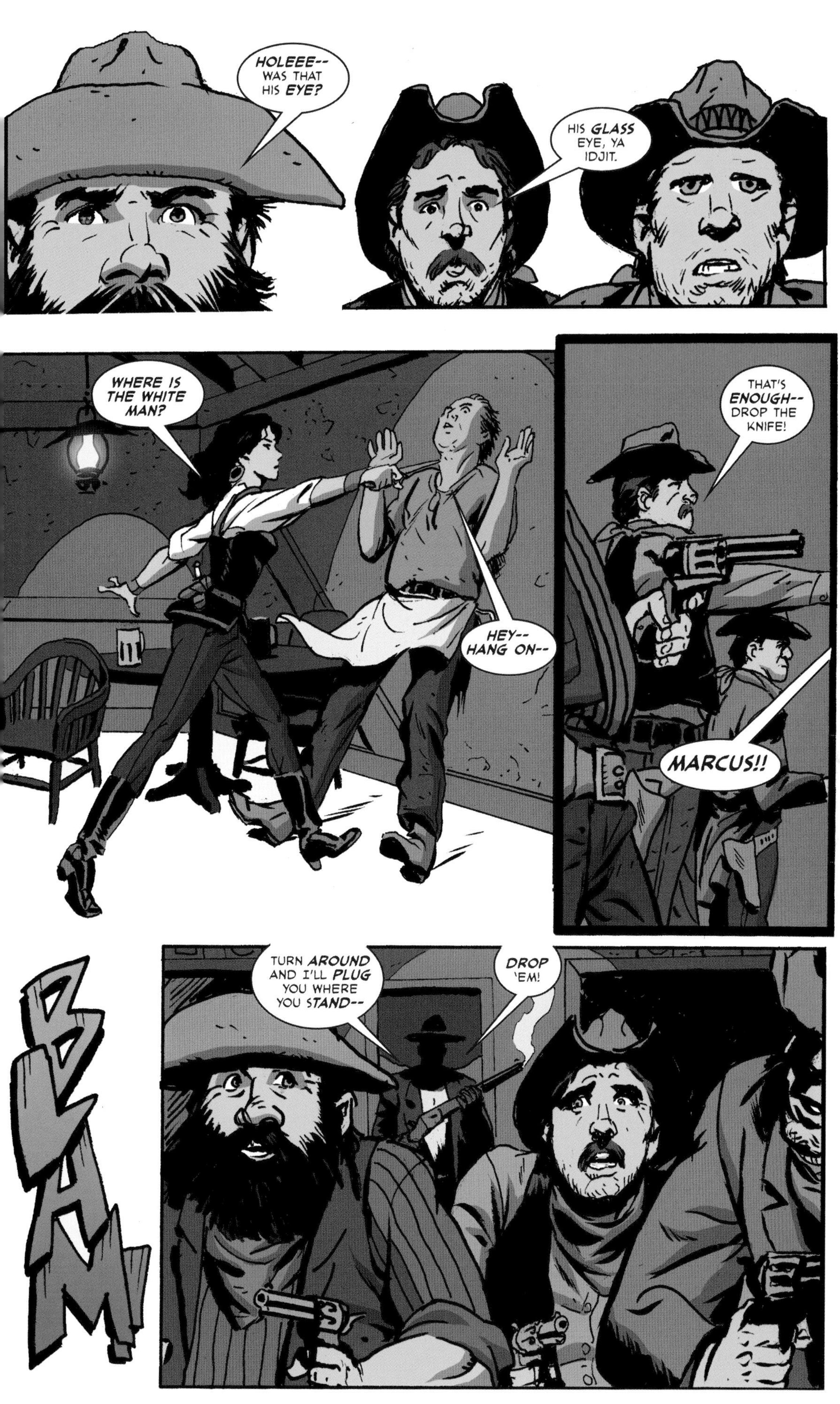
HOLEEE-- WAS THAT HIS EYE?
HIS GLASS EYE, YA IDJIT.
WHERE IS THE WHITE MAN?
HEY-- HANG ON--
THAT'S ENOUGH-- DROP THE KNIFE!
MARCUS!!
BLAM
TURN AROUND AND I'LL PLUG YOU WHERE YOU STAND--
DROP 'EM!

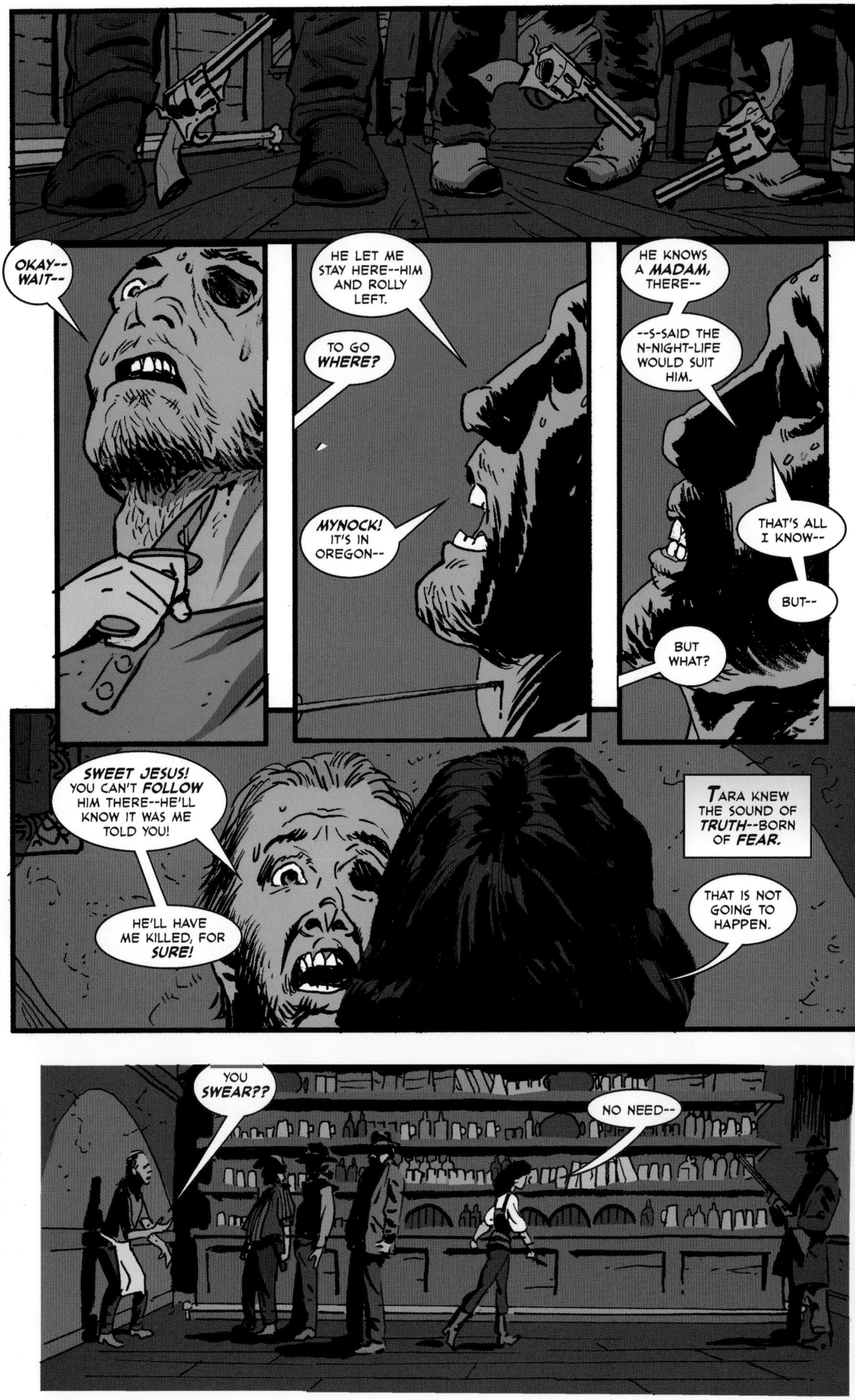
OKAY--
WAIT--
HE LET ME STAY HERE--HIM AND ROLLY LEFT.
TO GO WHERE?
MYNOCK! IT'S IN OREGON--
HE KNOWS A MADAM, THERE--
--S-SAID THE N-NIGHT-LIFE WOULD SUIT HIM.
THAT'S ALL I KNOW--
BUT--
BUT WHAT?
SWEET JESUS! YOU CAN'T FOLLOW HIM THERE--HE'LL KNOW IT WAS ME TOLD YOU!
HE'LL HAVE ME KILLED, FOR SURE!
TARA KNEW THE SOUND OF TRUTH--BORN OF FEAR.
THAT IS NOT GOING TO HAPPEN.
YOU SWEAR??
NO NEED--

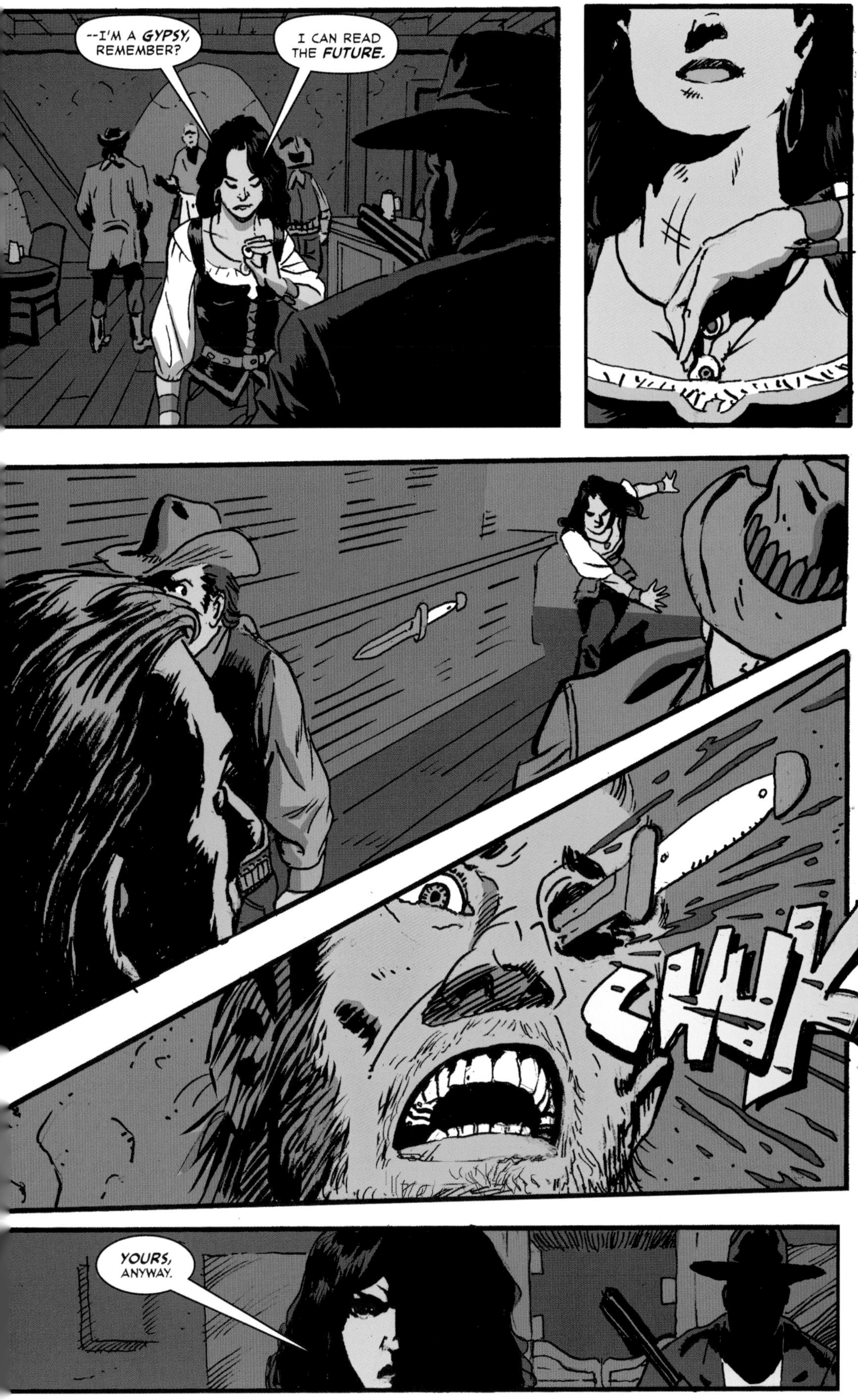
--I'M A GYPSY, REMEMBER?
I CAN READ THE FUTURE.
CHUK
YOURS, ANYWAY.

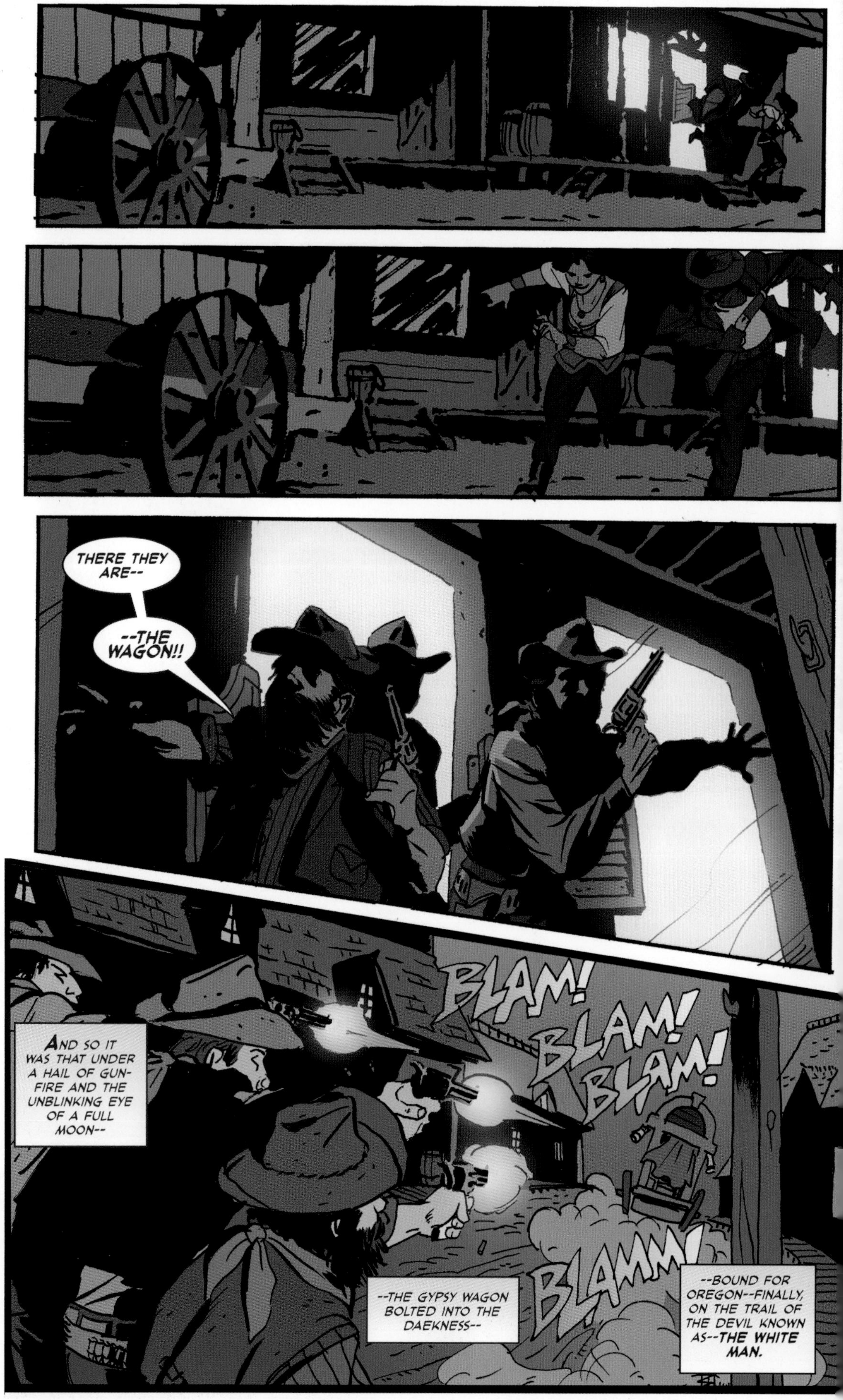
THERE THEY ARE--
--THE WAGON!!
AND SO IT WAS THAT UNDER A HAIL OF GUN-FIRE AND THE UNBLINKING EYE OF A FULL MOON--
BLAM!
BLAM!
BLAM!
BLAMM!
--THE GYPSY WAGON BOLTED INTO THE DAEKNESS--
--BOUND FOR OREGON--FINALLY, ON THE TRAIL OF THE DEVIL KNOWN AS--THE WHITE MAN.

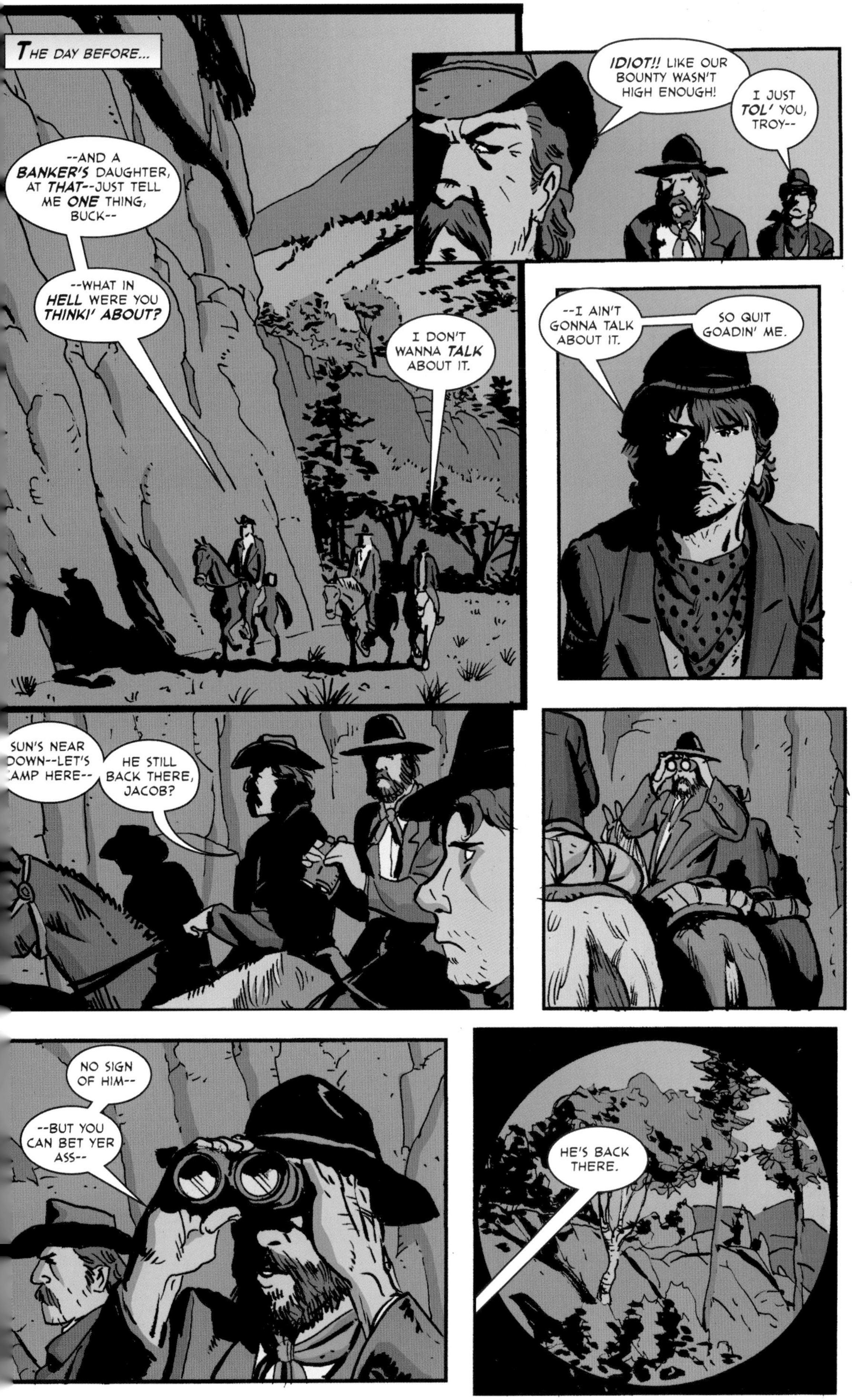
THE DAY BEFORE...
--AND A BANKER'S DAUGHTER, AT THAT--JUST TELL ME ONE THING, BUCK--
--WHAT IN HELL WERE YOU THINKI' ABOUT?
I DON'T WANNA TALK ABOUT IT.
IDIOT!! LIKE OUR BOUNTY WASN'T HIGH ENOUGH!
I JUST TOL' YOU, TROY--
--I AIN'T GONNA TALK ABOUT IT.
SO QUIT GOADIN' ME.
SUN'S NEAR DOWN--LET'S CAMP HERE--
HE STILL BACK THERE, JACOB?
NO SIGN OF HIM--
--BUT YOU CAN BET YER ASS--
HE'S BACK THERE.

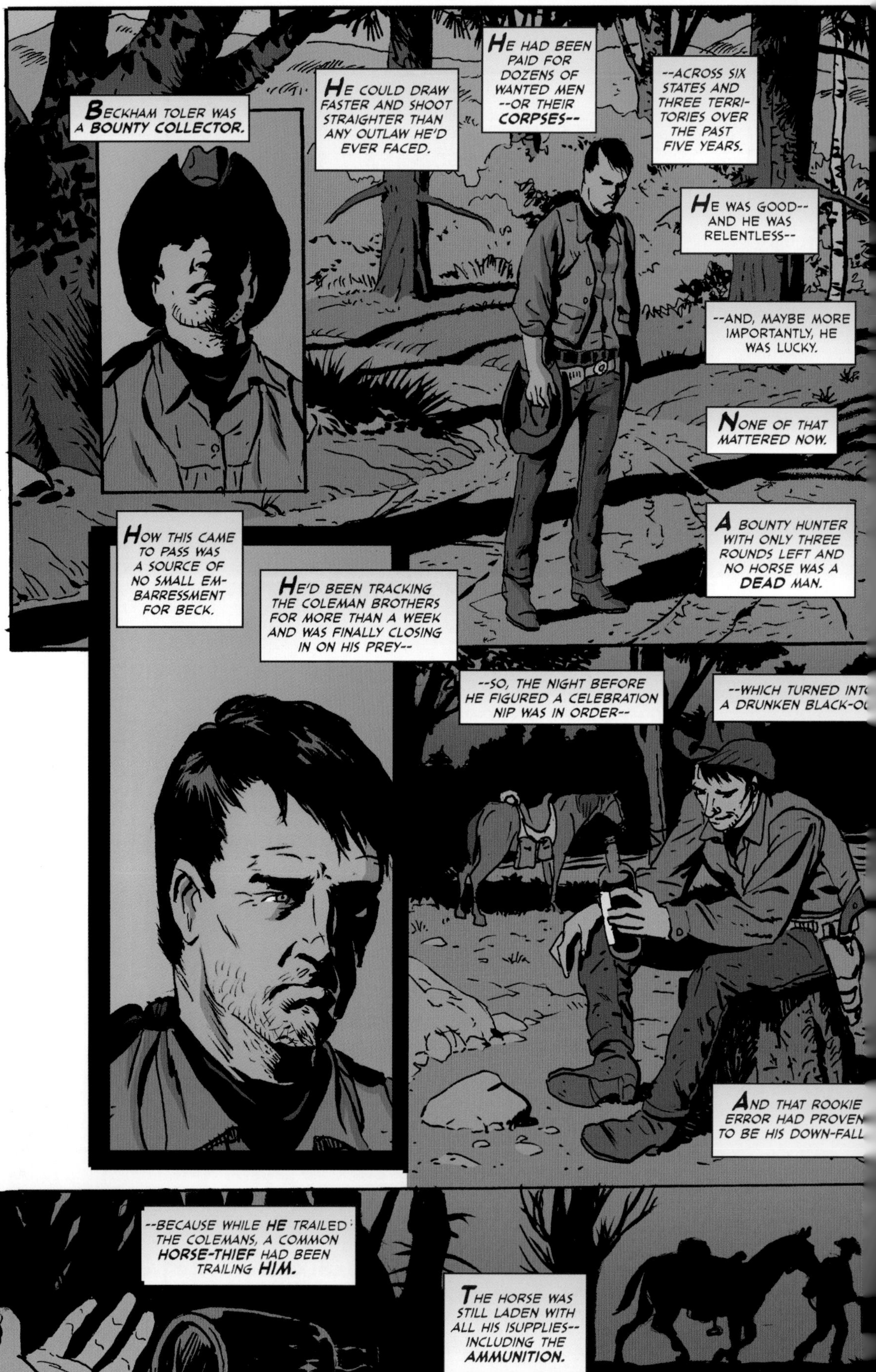
BECKHAM TOLER WAS A BOUNTY COLLECTOR.
HE COULD DRAW FASTER AND SHOOT STRAIGHTER THAN ANY OUTLAW HE'D EVER FACED.
HE HAD BEEN PAID FOR DOZENS OF WANTED MEN --OR THEIR CORPSES--
--ACROSS SIX STATES AND THREE TERRITORIES OVER THE PAST FIVE YEARS.
HE WAS GOOD-- AND HE WAS RELENTLESS--
--AND, MAYBE MORE IMPORTANTLY, HE WAS LUCKY.
NONE OF THAT MATTERED NOW.
A BOUNTY HUNTER WITH ONLY THREE ROUNDS LEFT AND NO HORSE WAS A DEAD MAN.
HOW THIS CAME TO PASS WAS A SOURCE OF NO SMALL EMBARRESSMENT FOR BECK.
HE'D BEEN TRACKING THE COLEMAN BROTHERS FOR MORE THAN A WEEK AND WAS FINALLY CLOSING IN ON HIS PREY--
--SO, THE NIGHT BEFORE HE FIGURED A CELEBRATION NIP WAS IN ORDER--
--WHICH TURNED INT
A DRUNKEN BLACK-O
AND THAT ROOKIE ERROR HAD PROVEN TO BE HIS DOWN-FALL
--BECAUSE WHILE HE TRAILED THE COLEMANS, A COMMON HORSE-THIEF HAD BEEN TRAILING HIM.
THE HORSE WAS STILL LADEN WITH ALL HIS ISUPPLIES-- INCLUDING THE AMMUNITION.

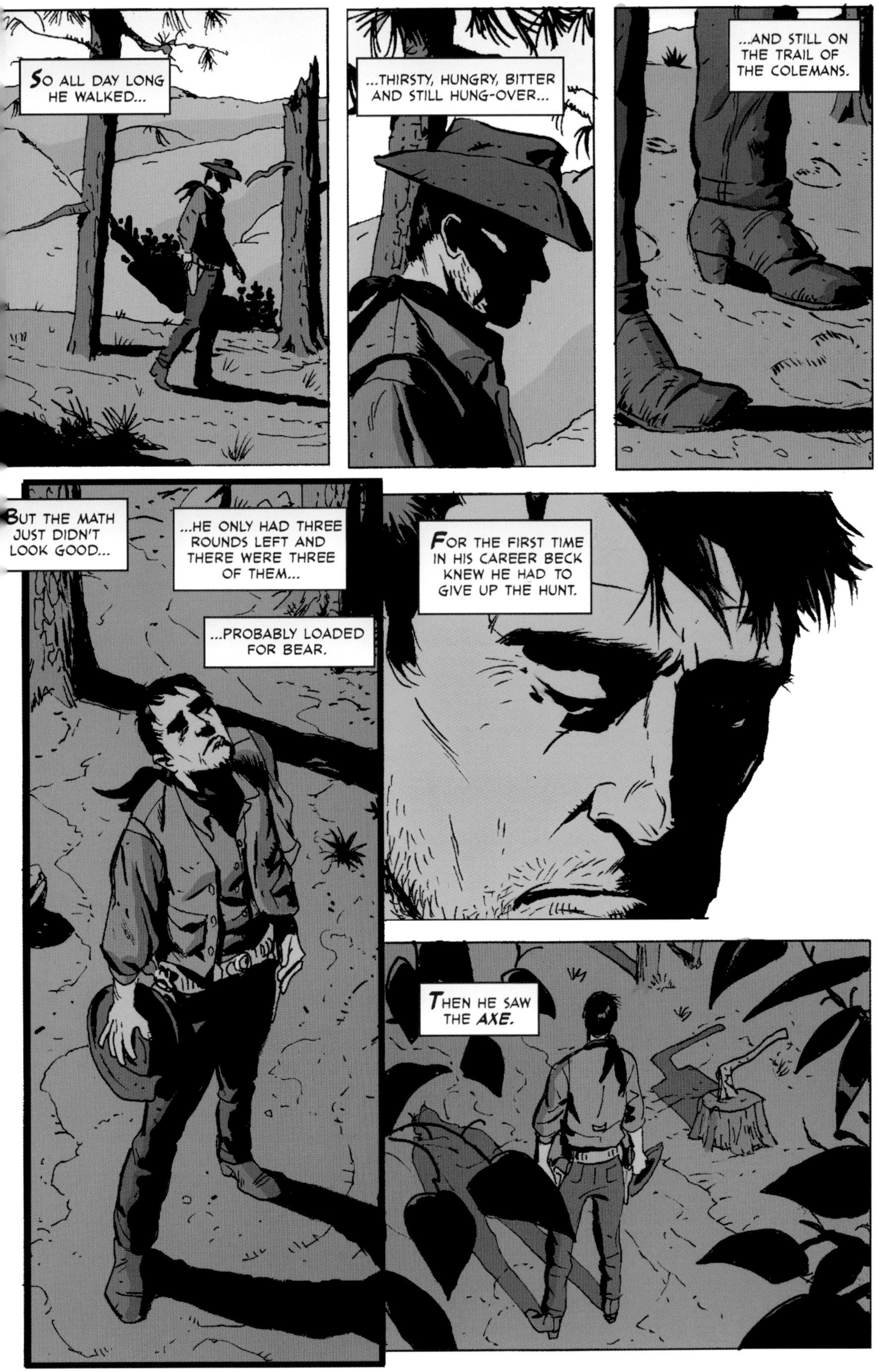
SO ALL DAY LONG HE WALKED...
...THIRSTY, HUNGRY, BITTER AND STILL HUNG-OVER...
...AND STILL ON THE TRAIL OF THE COLEMANS.
BUT THE MATH JUST DIDN'T LOOK GOOD...
...HE ONLY HAD THREE ROUNDS LEFT AND THERE WERE THREE OF THEM...
...PROBABLY LOADED FOR BEAR.
FOR THE FIRST TIME IN HIS CAREER BECK KNEW HE HAD TO GIVE UP THE HUNT.
THEN HE SAW THE AXE.

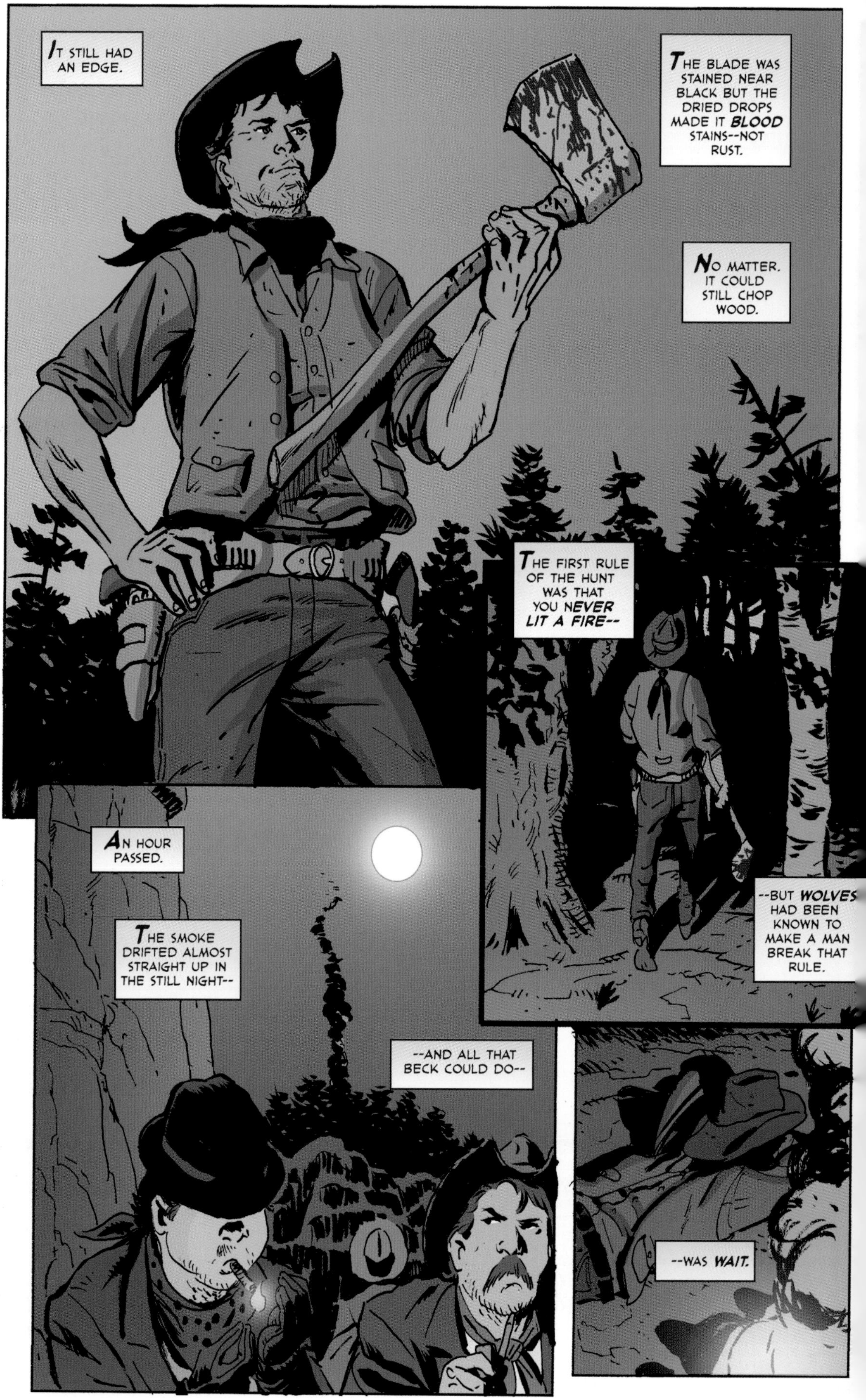
IT STILL HAD AN EDGE.
THE BLADE WAS STAINED NEAR BLACK BUT THE DRIED DROPS MADE IT BLOOD STAINS--NOT RUST.
NO MATTER. IT COULD STILL CHOP WOOD.
THE FIRST RULE OF THE HUNT WAS THAT YOU NEVER LIT A FIRE--
--BUT WOLVES HAD BEEN KNOWN TO MAKE A MAN BREAK THAT RULE.
AN HOUR PASSED.
THE SMOKE DRIFTED ALMOST STRAIGHT UP IN THE STILL NIGHT--
--AND ALL THAT BECK COULD DO--
--WAS WAIT.

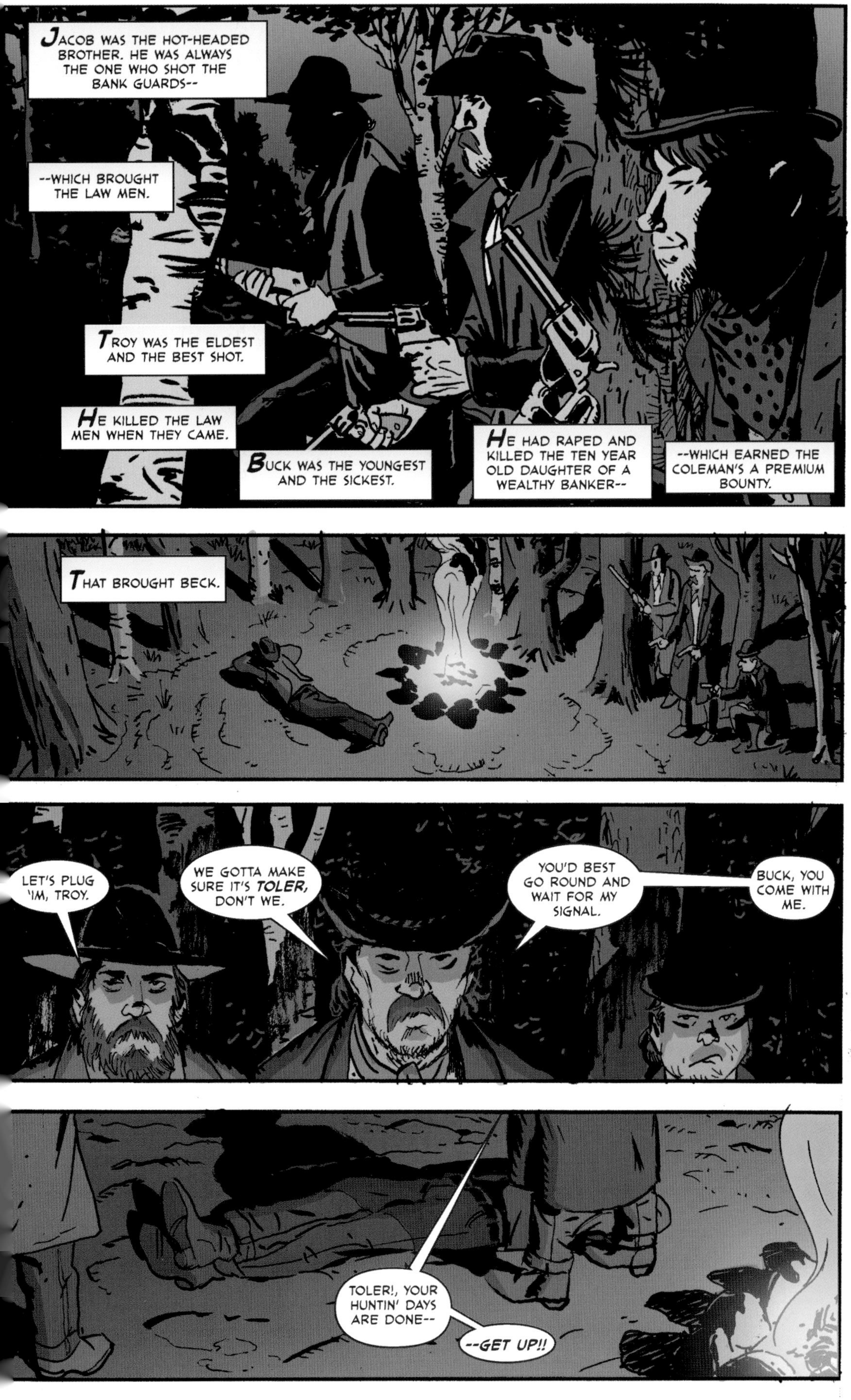
JACOB WAS THE HOT-HEADED BROTHER. HE WAS ALWAYS THE ONE WHO SHOT THE BANK GUARDS--
--WHICH BROUGHT THE LAW MEN.
TROY WAS THE ELDEST AND THE BEST SHOT.
HE KILLED THE LAW MEN WHEN THEY CAME.
BUCK WAS THE YOUNGEST AND THE SICKEST.
HE HAD RAPED AND KILLED THE TEN YEAR OLD DAUGHTER OF A WEALTHY BANKER--
--WHICH EARNED THE COLEMAN'S A PREMIUM BOUNTY.
THAT BROUGHT BECK.
LET'S PLUG 'IM, TROY.
WE GOTTA MAKE SURE IT'S TOLER, DON'T WE.
YOU'D BEST GO ROUND AND WAIT FOR MY SIGNAL.
BUCK, YOU COME WITH ME.
TOLER!, YOUR HUNTIN' DAYS ARE DONE--
--GET UP!!

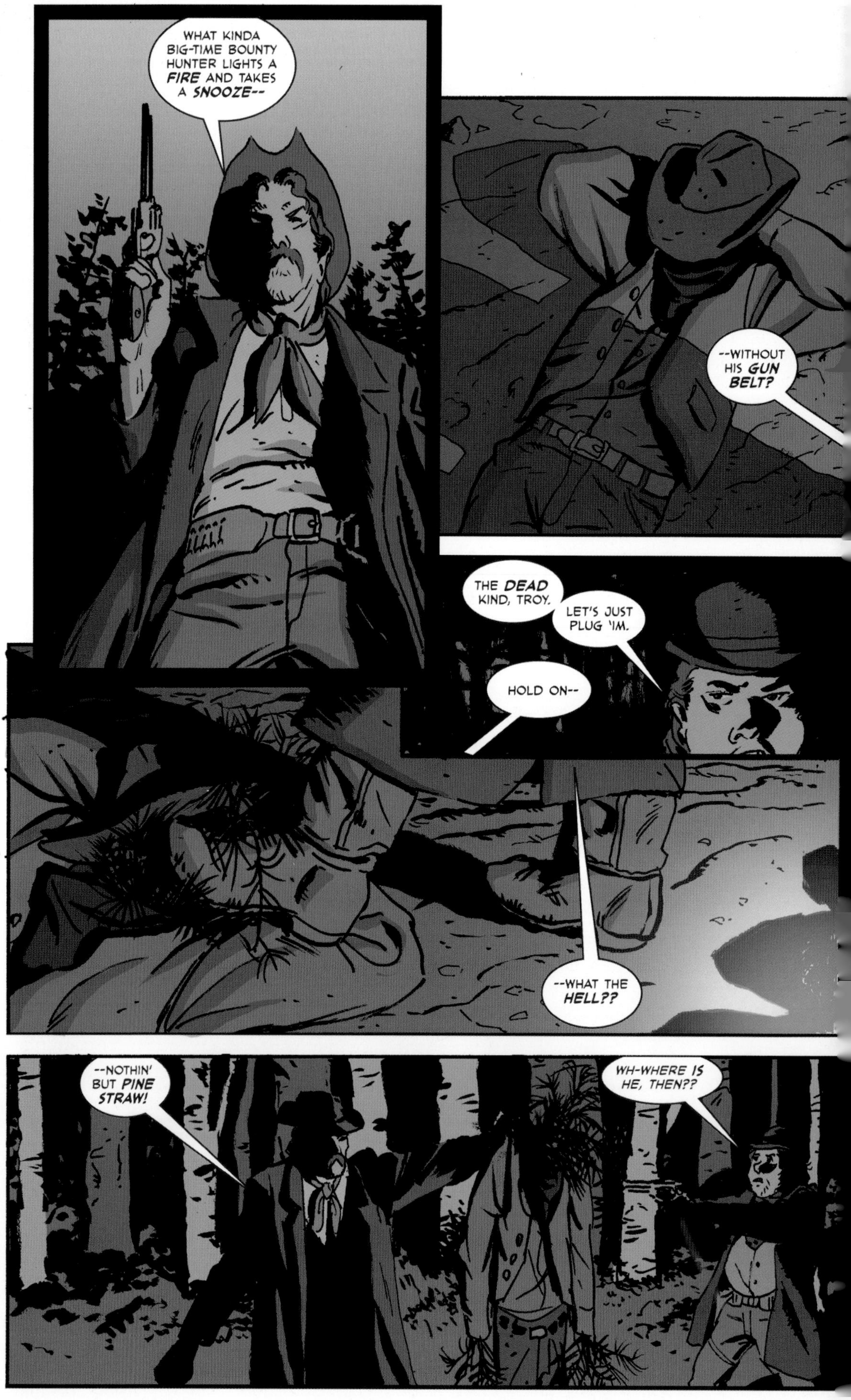
WHAT KINDA BIG-TIME BOUNTY HUNTER LIGHTS A FIRE AND TAKES A SNOOZE--
--WITHOUT HIS GUN BELT?
THE DEAD KIND, TROY.
LET'S JUST PLUG 'IM.
HOLD ON--
--WHAT THE HELL??
--NOTHIN' BUT PINE STRAW!
WH-WHERE IS HE, THEN??

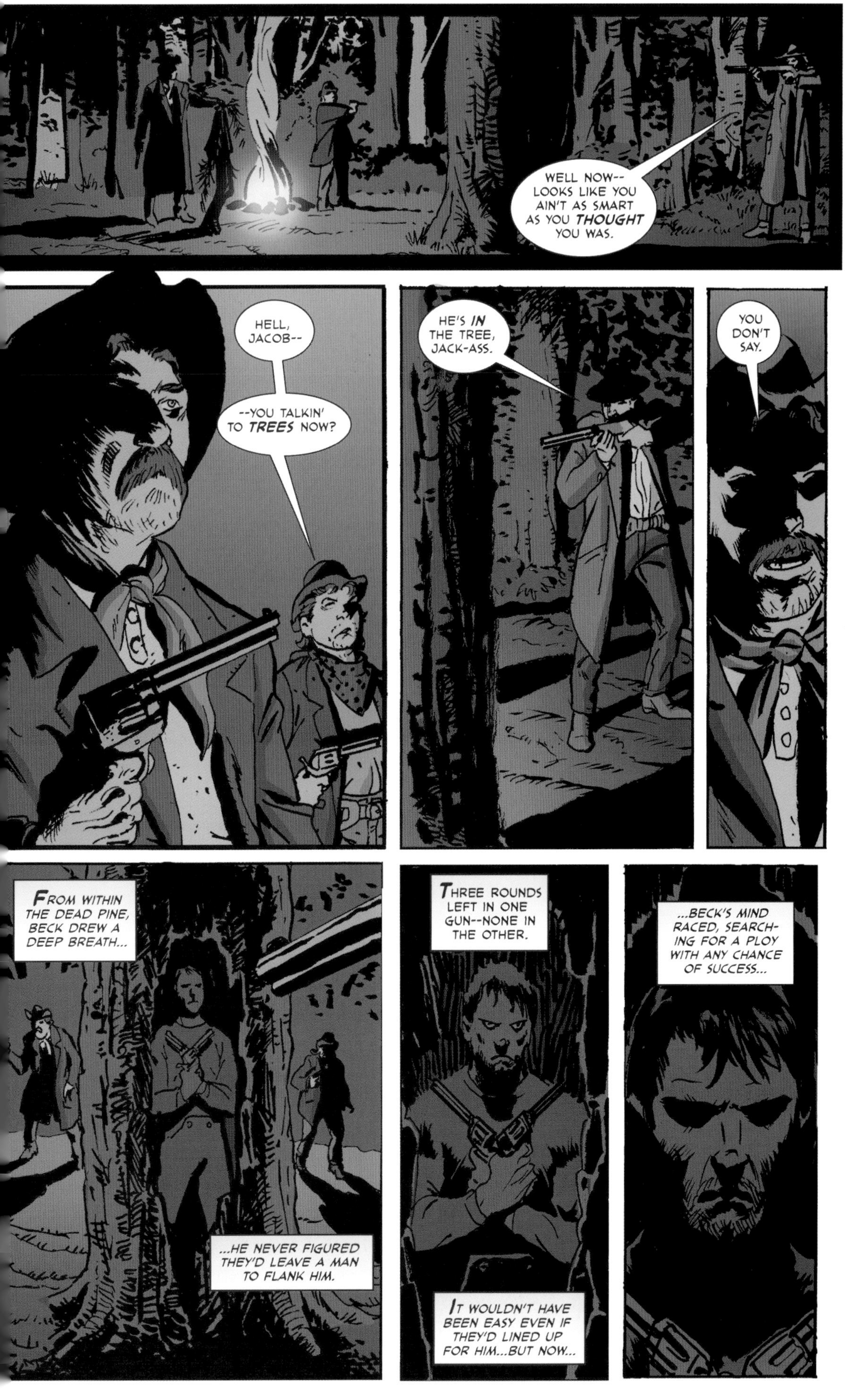
WELL NOW--
LOOKS LIKE YOU AIN'T AS SMART AS YOU THOUGHT YOU WAS.
HELL, JACOB--
--YOU TALKIN' TO TREES NOW?
HE'S IN THE TREE, JACK-ASS.
YOU DON'T SAY.
FROM WITHIN THE DEAD PINE, BECK DREW A DEEP BREATH...
...HE NEVER FIGURED THEY'D LEAVE A MAN TO FLANK HIM.
THREE ROUNDS LEFT IN ONE GUN--NONE IN THE OTHER.
IT WOULDN'T HAVE BEEN EASY EVEN IF THEY'D LINED UP FOR HIM...BUT NOW...
...BECK'S MIND RACED, SEARCHING FOR A PLOY WITH ANY CHANCE OF SUCCESS...

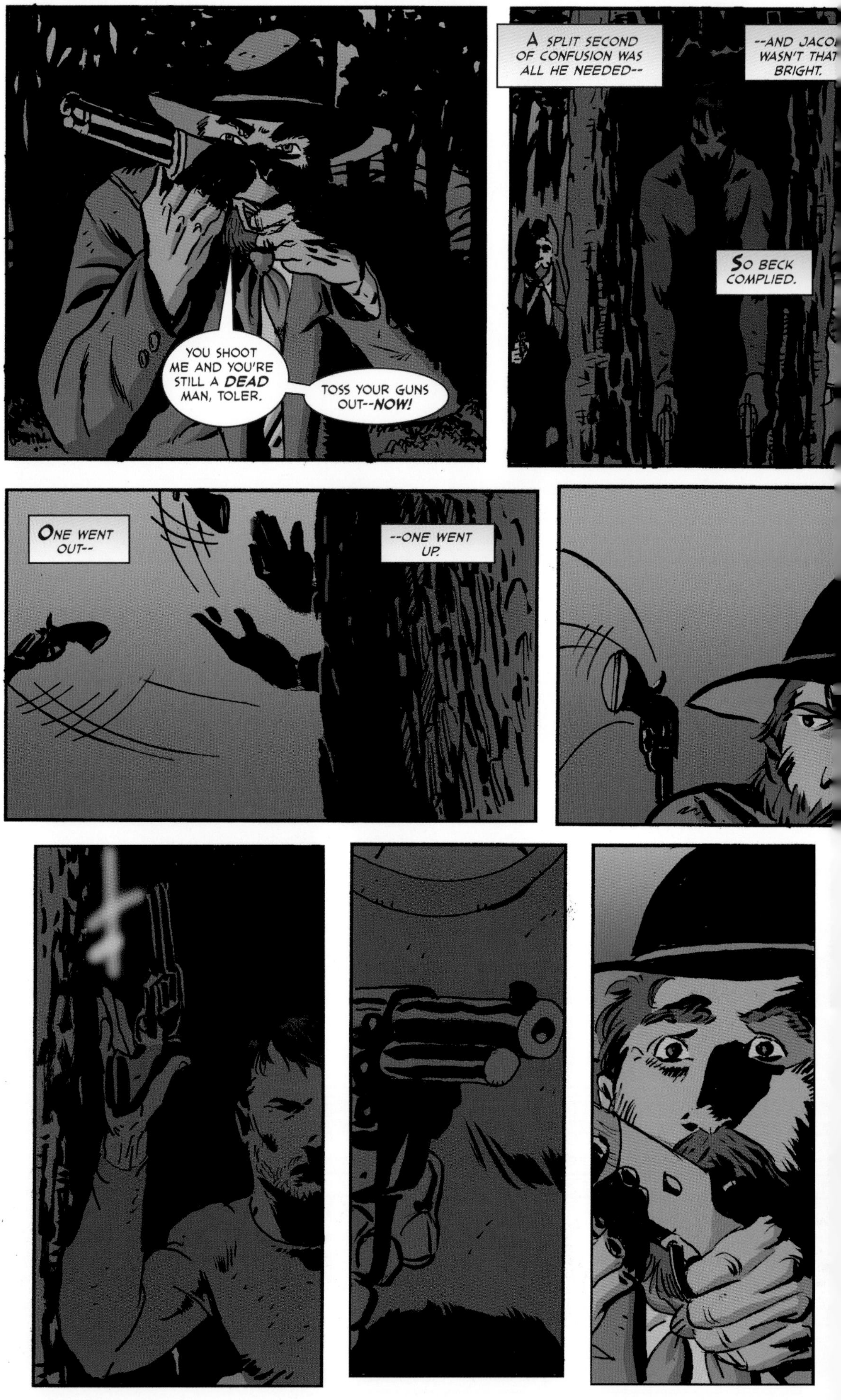
YOU SHOOT ME AND YOU'RE STILL A DEAD MAN, TOLER.
TOSS YOUR GUNS OUT--NOW!
A SPLIT SECOND OF CONFUSION WAS ALL HE NEEDED--
--AND JACO WASN'T THAT BRIGHT.
SO BECK COMPLIED.
ONE WENT OUT--
--ONE WENT UP.

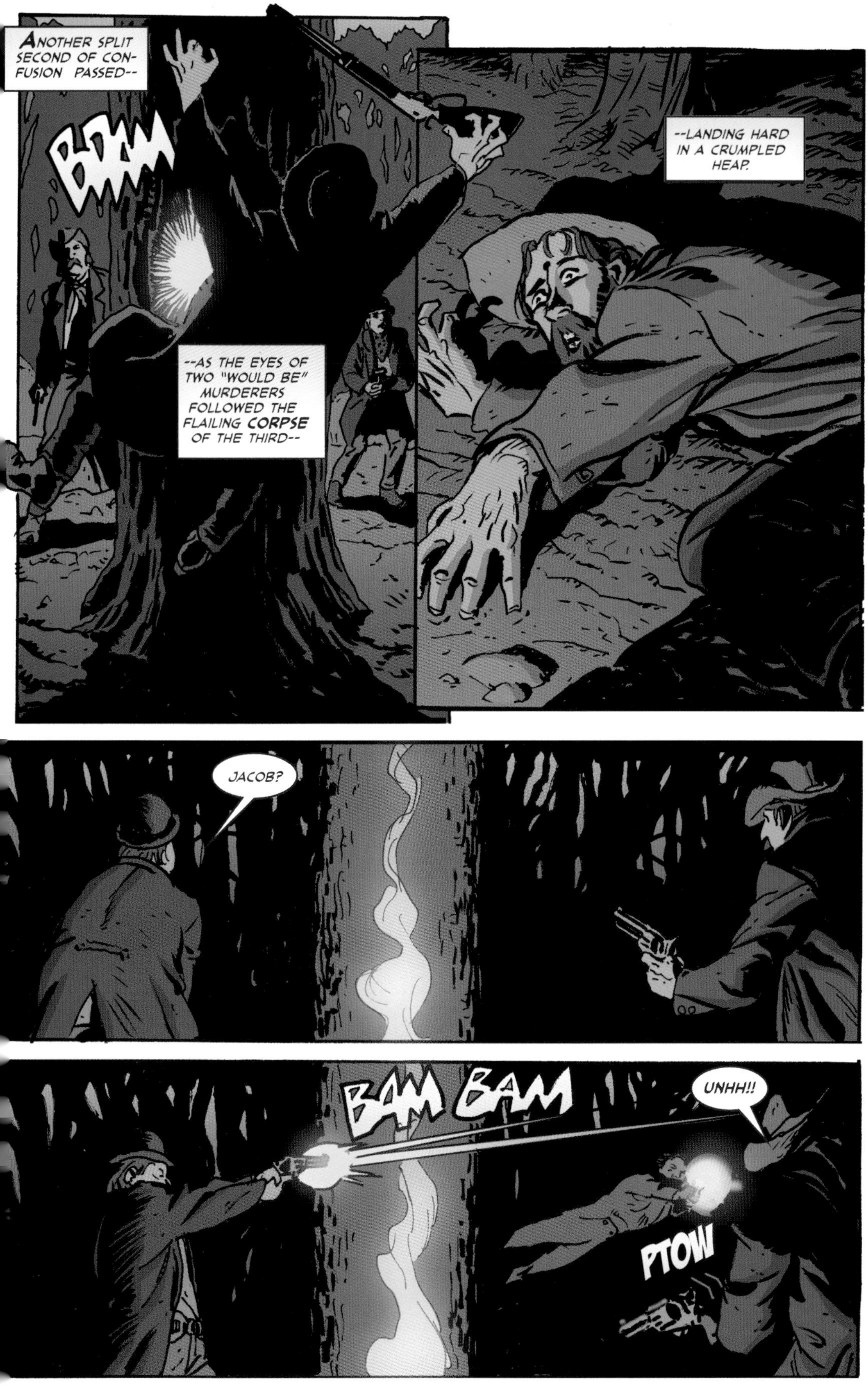
ANOTHER SPLIT SECOND OF CON-FUSION PASSED--
BLAM
--AS THE EYES OF TWO "WOULD BE" MURDERERS FOLLOWED THE FLAILING CORPSE OF THE THIRD--
--LANDING HARD IN A CRUMPLED HEAP.
JACOB?
BAM BAM
UNHH!!
PTOW

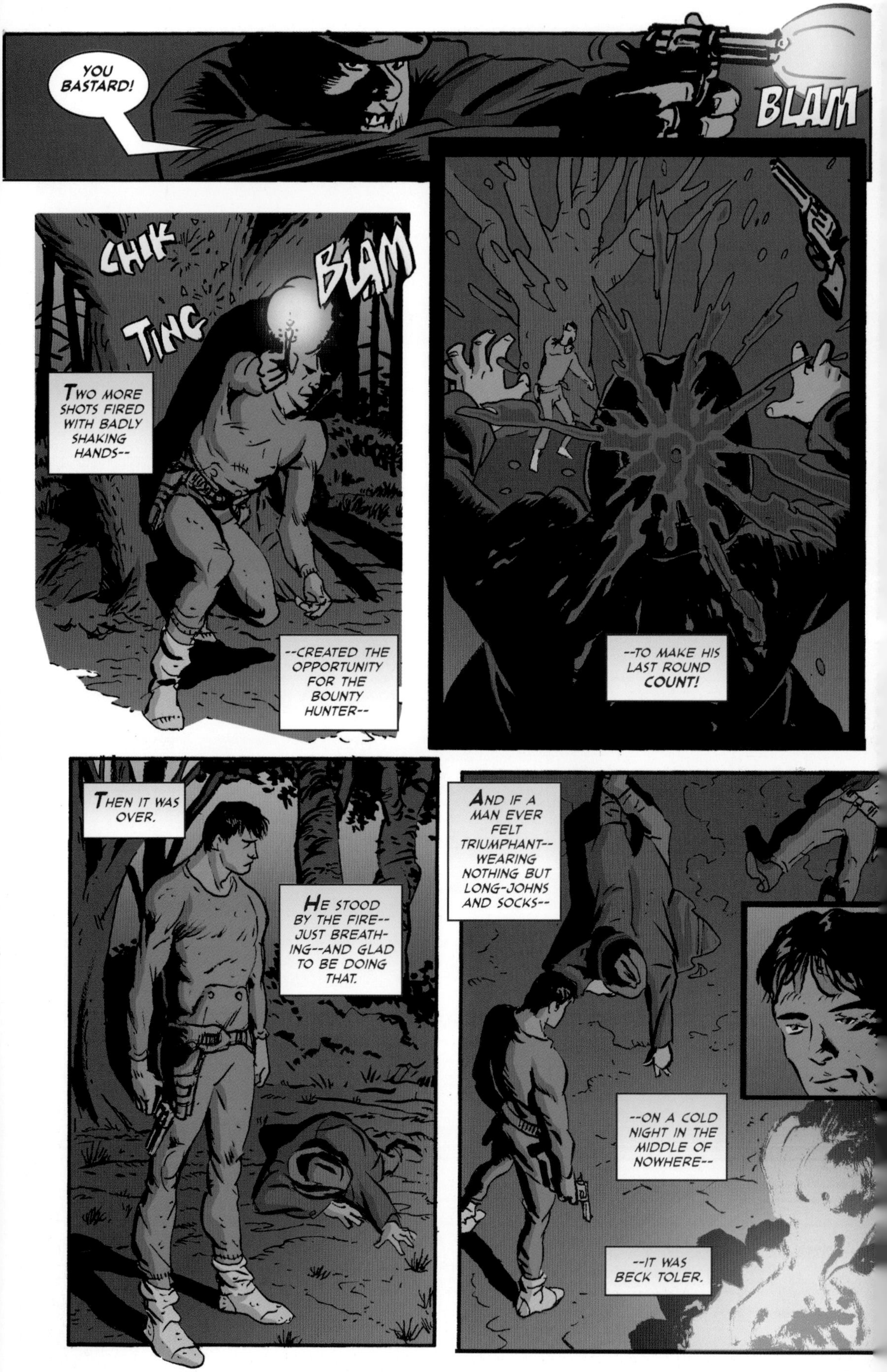
YOU BASTARD!
BLAM
CHIK
TING
BLAM
TWO MORE SHOTS FIRED WITH BADLY SHAKING HANDS--
--CREATED THE OPPORTUNITY FOR THE BOUNTY HUNTER--
--TO MAKE HIS LAST ROUND COUNT!
THEN IT WAS OVER.
HE STOOD BY THE FIRE--JUST BREATHING--AND GLAD TO BE DOING THAT.
AND IF A MAN EVER FELT TRIUMPHANT--WEARING NOTHING BUT LONG-JOHNS AND SOCKS--
--ON A COLD NIGHT IN THE MIDDLE OF NOWHERE--
--IT WAS BECK TOLER.

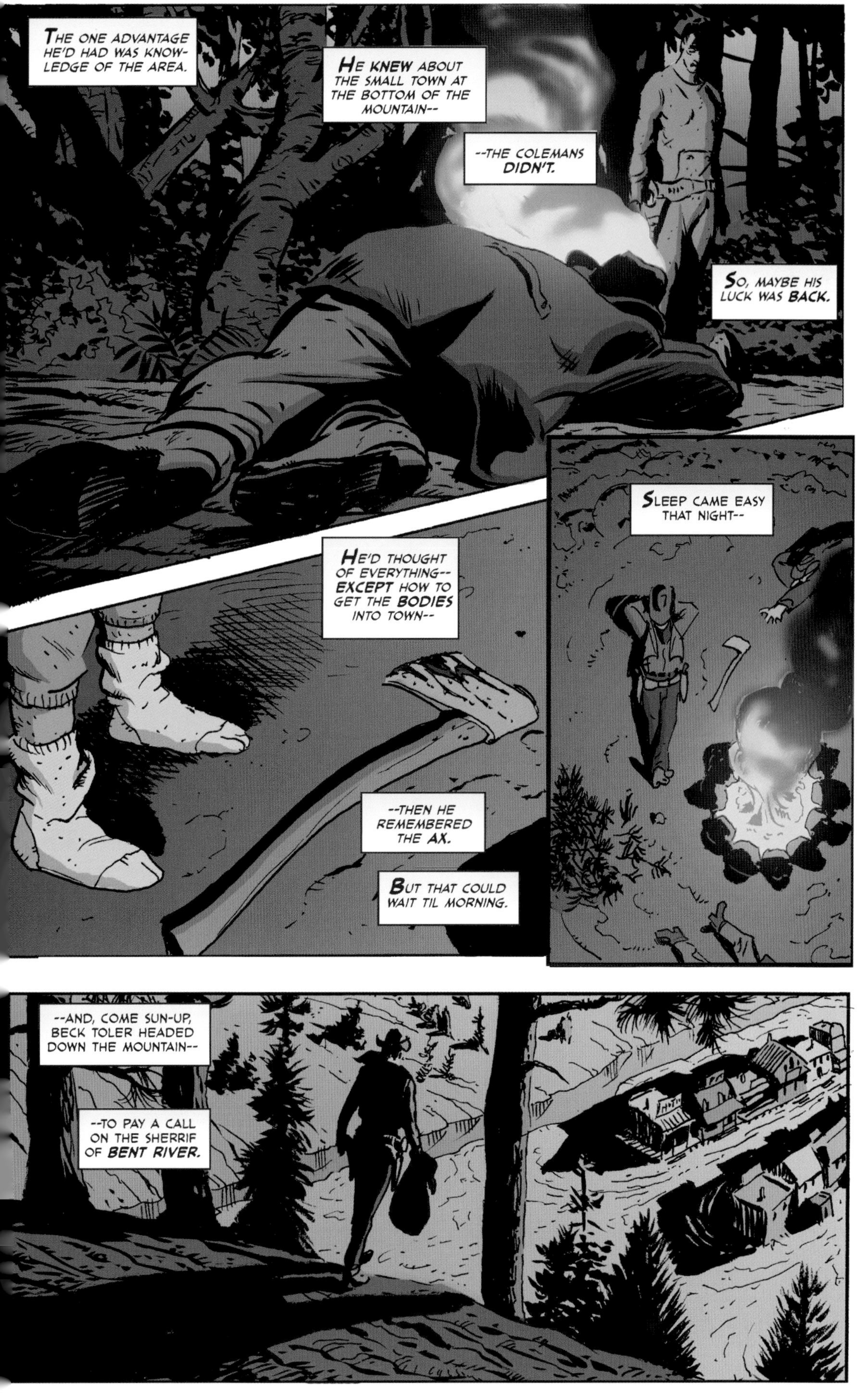
THE ONE ADVANTAGE HE'D HAD WAS KNOW-LEDGE OF THE AREA.
HE KNEW ABOUT THE SMALL TOWN AT THE BOTTOM OF THE MOUNTAIN--
--THE COLEMANS DIDN'T.
SO, MAYBE HIS LUCK WAS BACK.
HE'D THOUGHT OF EVERYTHING-- EXCEPT HOW TO GET THE BODIES INTO TOWN--
--THEN HE REMEMBERED THE AX.
BUT THAT COULD WAIT TIL MORNING.
SLEEP CAME EASY THAT NIGHT--
--AND, COME SUN-UP, BECK TOLER HEADED DOWN THE MOUNTAIN--
--TO PAY A CALL ON THE SHERRIF OF BENT RIVER.

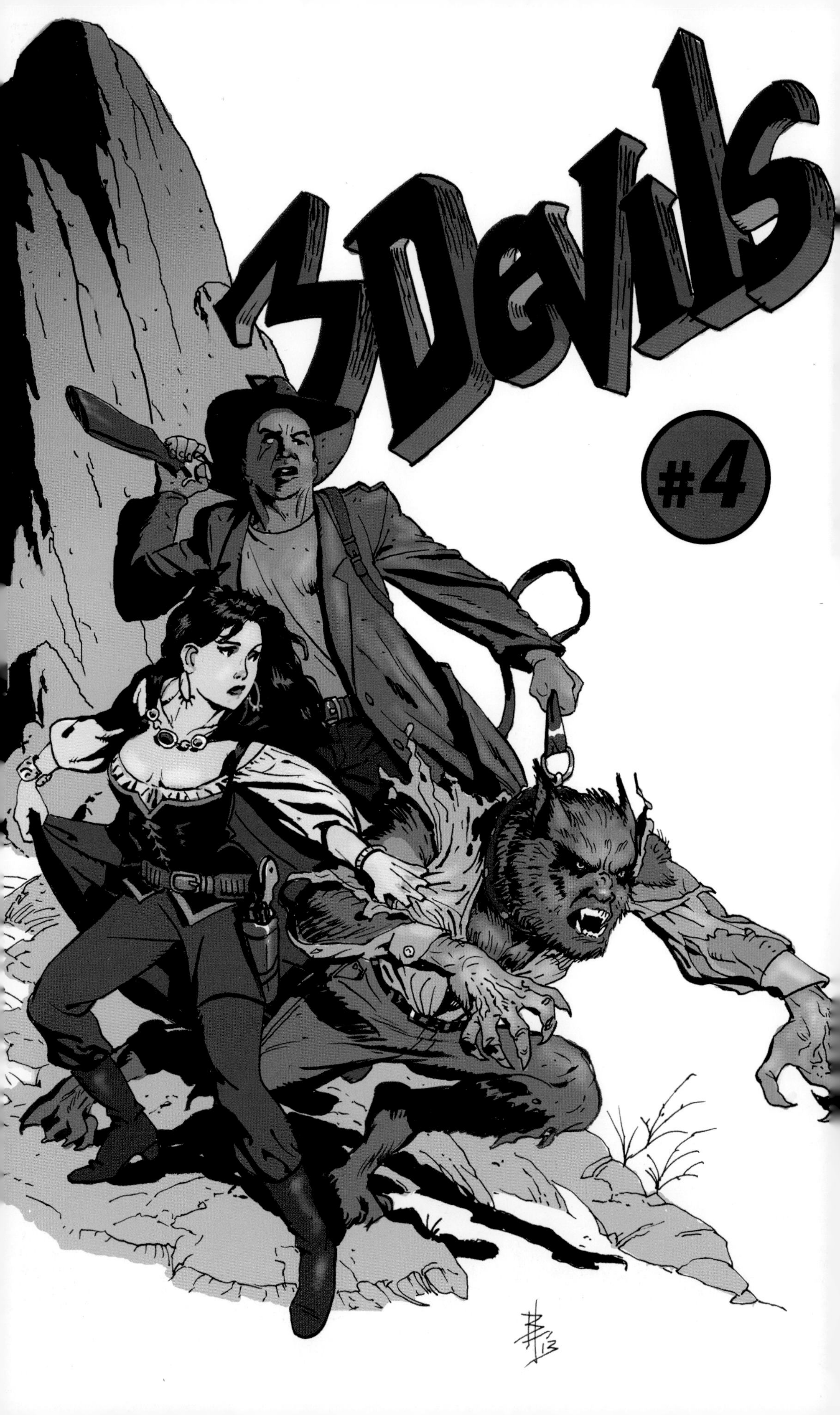
3 Devils
#4

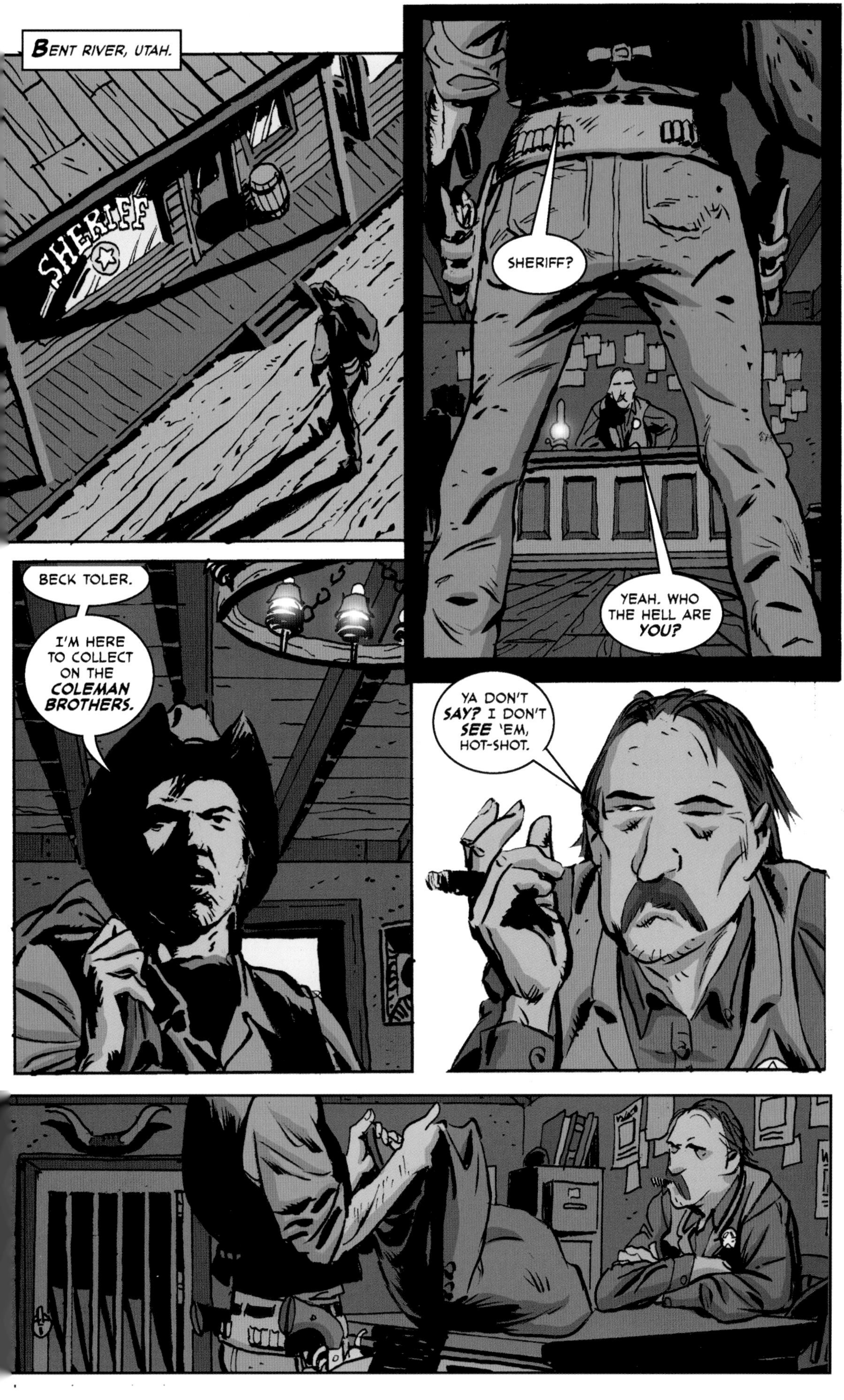
BENT RIVER, UTAH.
SHERIFF
SHERIFF?
YEAH. WHO THE HELL ARE *YOU?*
BECK TOLER.
I'M HERE TO COLLECT ON THE *COLEMAN BROTHERS.*
YA DON'T *SAY?* I DON'T *SEE* 'EM, HOT-SHOT.

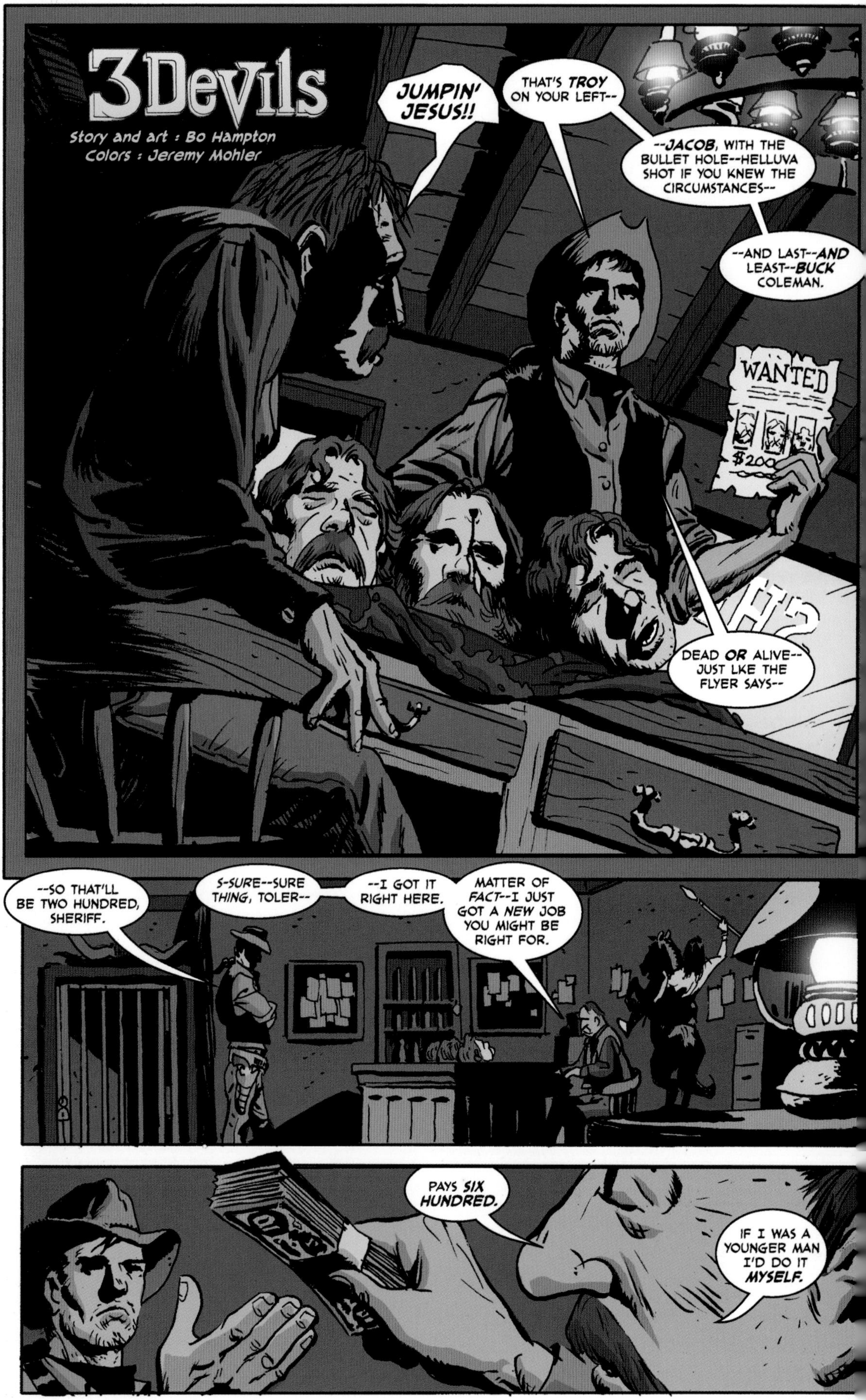
3Devils
Story and art : Bo Hampton
Colors : Jeremy Mohler
JUMPIN' JESUS!!
THAT'S TROY ON YOUR LEFT--
--JACOB, WITH THE BULLET HOLE--HELLUVA SHOT IF YOU KNEW THE CIRCUMSTANCES--
--AND LAST--AND LEAST--BUCK COLEMAN.
WANTED
DEAD OR ALIVE--JUST LKE THE FLYER SAYS--
--SO THAT'LL BE TWO HUNDRED, SHERIFF.
S-SURE--SURE THING, TOLER--
--I GOT IT RIGHT HERE.
MATTER OF FACT--I JUST GOT A NEW JOB YOU MIGHT BE RIGHT FOR.
PAYS SIX HUNDRED.
IF I WAS A YOUNGER MAN I'D DO IT MYSELF.

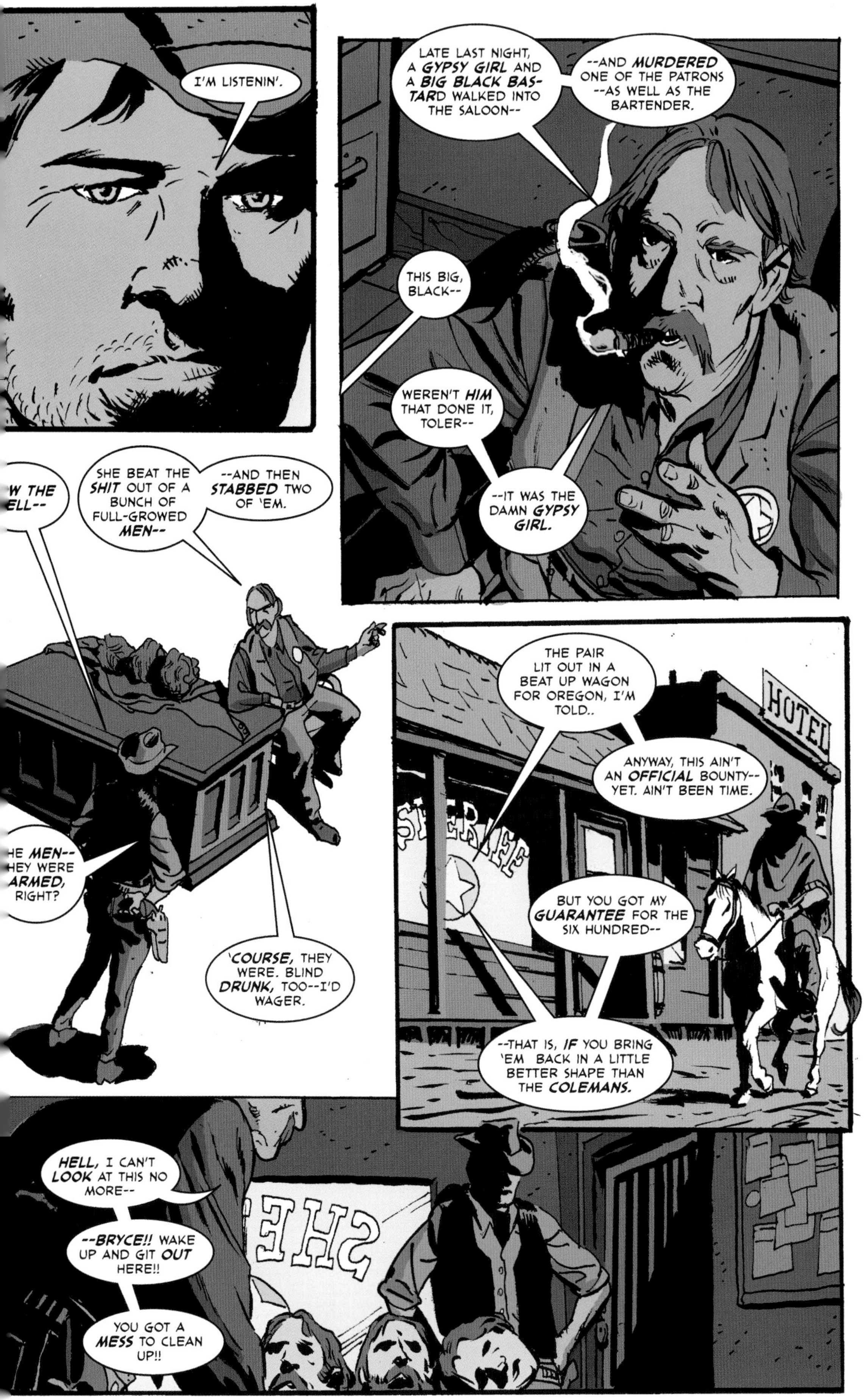
I'M LISTENIN'.
LATE LAST NIGHT, A GYPSY GIRL AND A BIG BLACK BASTARD WALKED INTO THE SALOON--
--AND MURDERED ONE OF THE PATRONS --AS WELL AS THE BARTENDER.
THIS BIG, BLACK--
WEREN'T HIM THAT DONE IT, TOLER--
--IT WAS THE DAMN GYPSY GIRL.
SHE BEAT THE SHIT OUT OF A BUNCH OF FULL-GROWED MEN--
--AND THEN STABBED TWO OF 'EM.
HE MEN-- HEY WERE ARMED, RIGHT?
'COURSE, THEY WERE. BLIND DRUNK, TOO--I'D WAGER.
THE PAIR LIT OUT IN A BEAT UP WAGON FOR OREGON, I'M TOLD..
HOTEL
ANYWAY, THIS AIN'T AN OFFICIAL BOUNTY-- YET. AIN'T BEEN TIME.
BUT YOU GOT MY GUARANTEE FOR THE SIX HUNDRED--
--THAT IS, IF YOU BRING 'EM BACK IN A LITTLE BETTER SHAPE THAN THE COLEMANS.
HELL, I CAN'T LOOK AT THIS NO MORE--
--BRYCE!! WAKE UP AND GIT OUT HERE!!
YOU GOT A MESS TO CLEAN UP!!

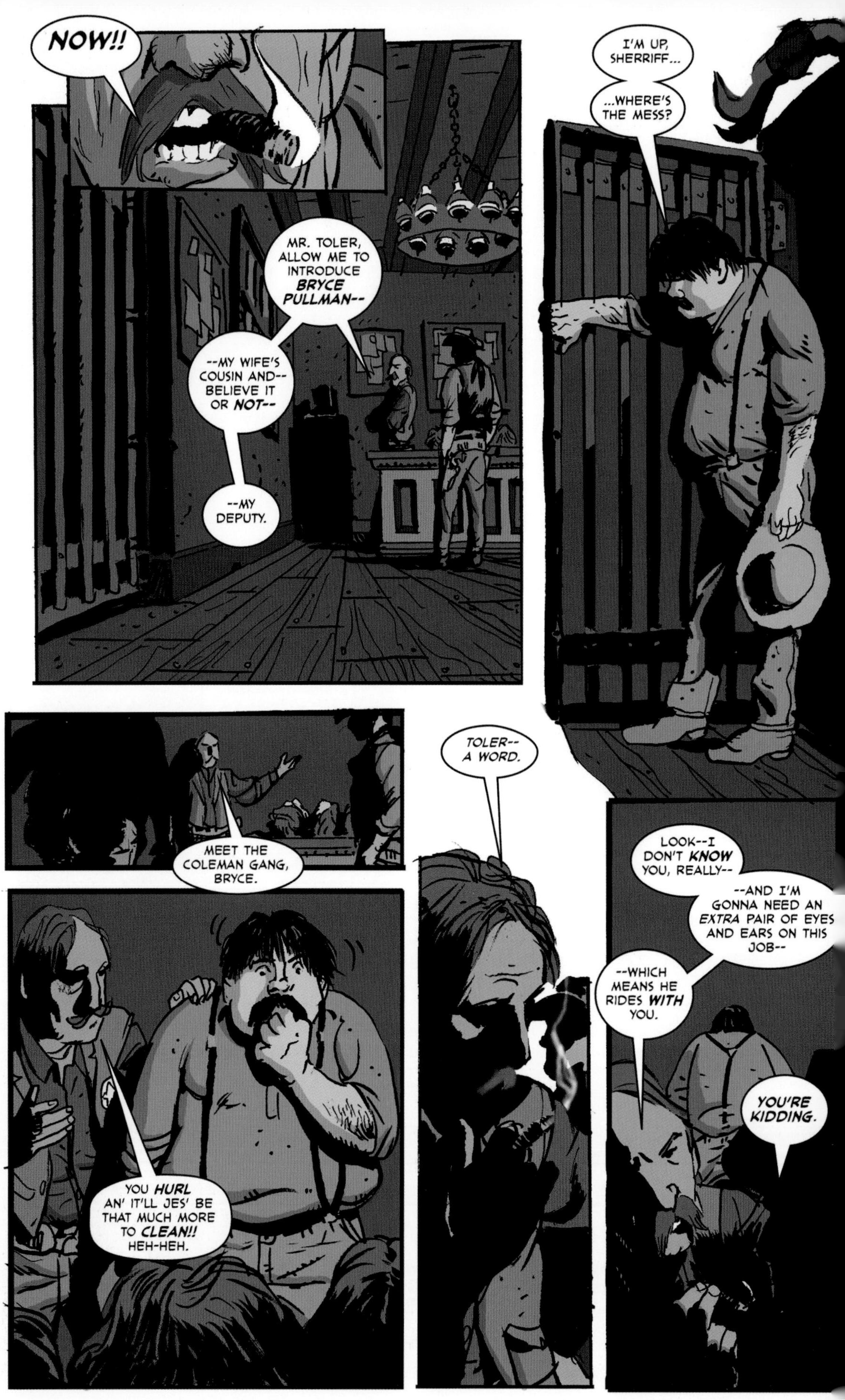
NOW!!
MR. TOLER, ALLOW ME TO INTRODUCE BRYCE PULLMAN--
--MY WIFE'S COUSIN AND-- BELIEVE IT OR NOT--
--MY DEPUTY.
I'M UP, SHERRIFF...
...WHERE'S THE MESS?
MEET THE COLEMAN GANG, BRYCE.
YOU HURL AN' IT'LL JES' BE THAT MUCH MORE TO CLEAN!! HEH-HEH.
TOLER-- A WORD.
LOOK--I DON'T KNOW YOU, REALLY--
--AND I'M GONNA NEED AN EXTRA PAIR OF EYES AND EARS ON THIS JOB--
--WHICH MEANS HE RIDES WITH YOU.
YOU'RE KIDDING.

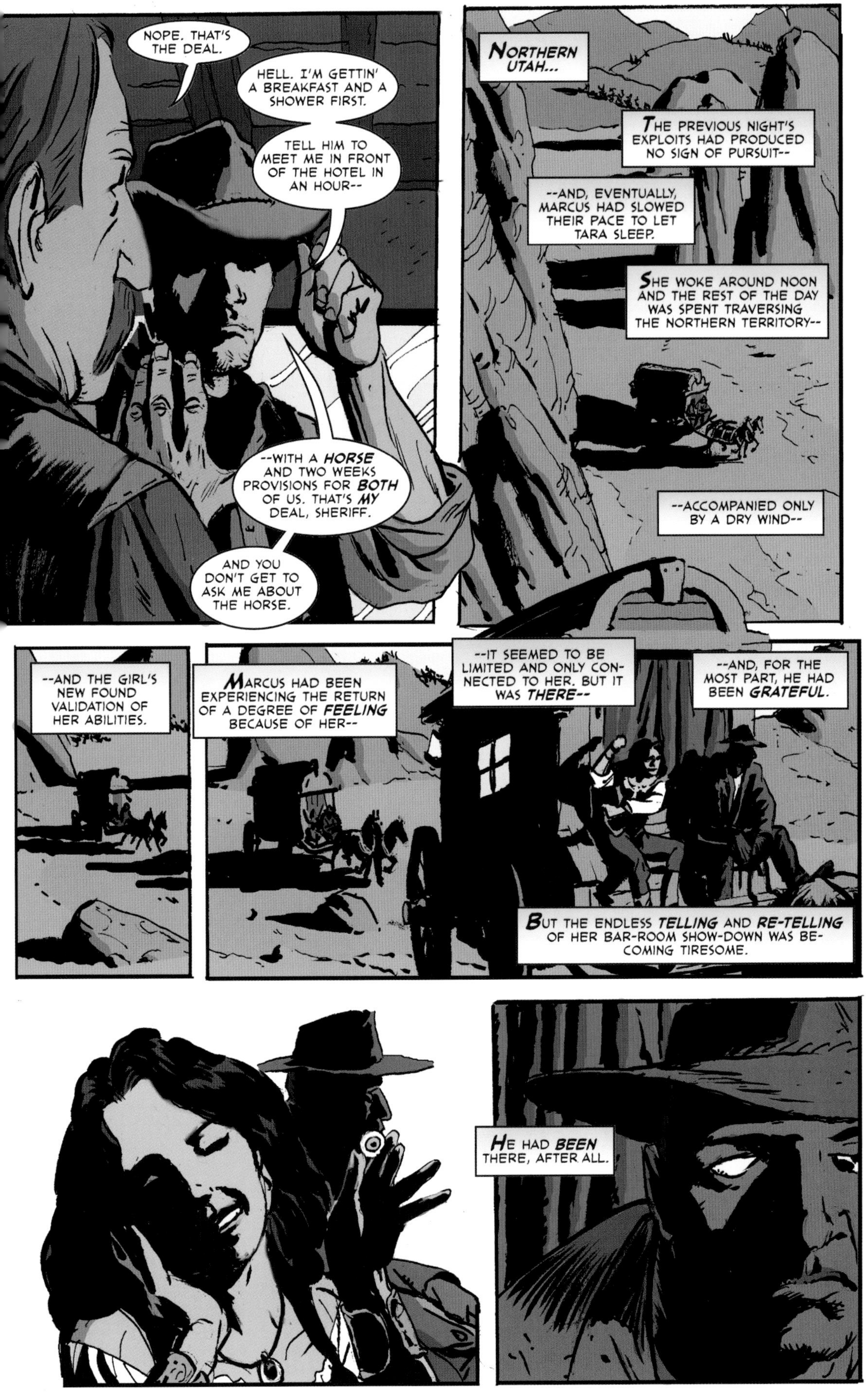
NOPE. THAT'S THE DEAL.
HELL. I'M GETTIN' A BREAKFAST AND A SHOWER FIRST.
TELL HIM TO MEET ME IN FRONT OF THE HOTEL IN AN HOUR--
--WITH A HORSE AND TWO WEEKS PROVISIONS FOR BOTH OF US. THAT'S MY DEAL, SHERIFF.
AND YOU DON'T GET TO ASK ME ABOUT THE HORSE.
NORTHERN UTAH...
THE PREVIOUS NIGHT'S EXPLOITS HAD PRODUCED NO SIGN OF PURSUIT--
--AND, EVENTUALLY, MARCUS HAD SLOWED THEIR PACE TO LET TARA SLEEP.
SHE WOKE AROUND NOON AND THE REST OF THE DAY WAS SPENT TRAVERSING THE NORTHERN TERRITORY--
--ACCOMPANIED ONLY BY A DRY WIND--
--AND THE GIRL'S NEW FOUND VALIDATION OF HER ABILITIES.
MARCUS HAD BEEN EXPERIENCING THE RETURN OF A DEGREE OF FEELING BECAUSE OF HER--
--IT SEEMED TO BE LIMITED AND ONLY CONNECTED TO HER. BUT IT WAS THERE--
--AND, FOR THE MOST PART, HE HAD BEEN GRATEFUL.
BUT THE ENDLESS TELLING AND RE-TELLING OF HER BAR-ROOM SHOW-DOWN WAS BECOMING TIRESOME.
HE HAD BEEN THERE, AFTER ALL.

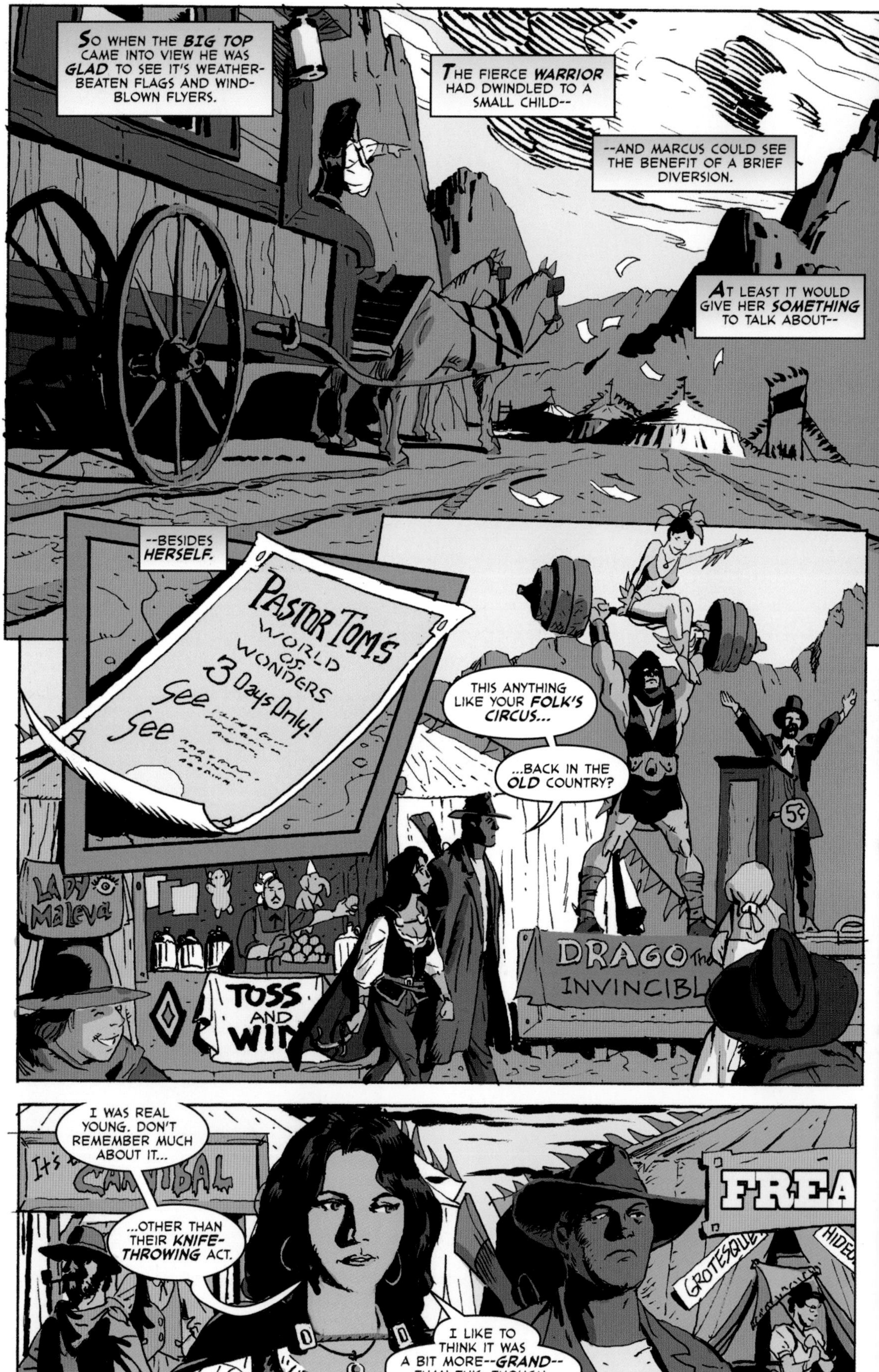
SO WHEN THE BIG TOP CAME INTO VIEW HE WAS GLAD TO SEE IT'S WEATHER-BEATEN FLAGS AND WIND-BLOWN FLYERS.
THE FIERCE WARRIOR HAD DWINDLED TO A SMALL CHILD--
--AND MARCUS COULD SEE THE BENEFIT OF A BRIEF DIVERSION.
AT LEAST IT WOULD GIVE HER SOMETHING TO TALK ABOUT--
--BESIDES HERSELF.
PASTOR TOM'S WORLD OF WONDERS 3 Days Only! See See
THIS ANYTHING LIKE YOUR FOLK'S CIRCUS...
...BACK IN THE OLD COUNTRY?
5¢
LADY MALEVA
TOSS AND WIN
DRAGO The INVINCIBL
I WAS REAL YOUNG. DON'T REMEMBER MUCH ABOUT IT...
...OTHER THAN THEIR KNIFE-THROWING ACT.
I LIKE TO THINK IT WAS A BIT MORE--GRAND--THAN THIS, THOUGH.
It's CANNIBAL
FREA
GROTESQUE
HIDEO

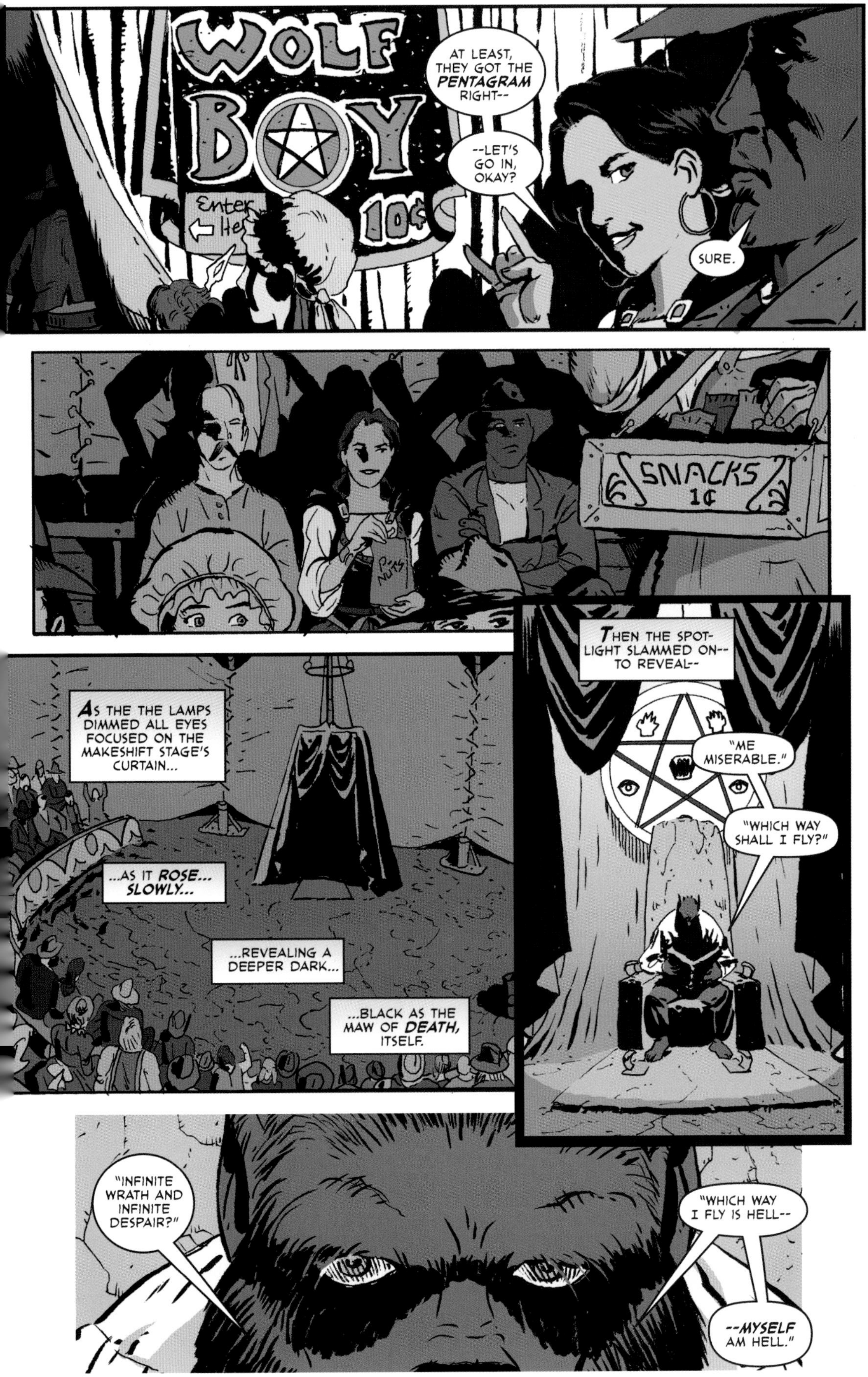
WOLF BOY
Enter Here
10¢
AT LEAST, THEY GOT THE PENTAGRAM RIGHT--
--LET'S GO IN, OKAY?
SURE.
SNACKS 1¢
THEN THE SPOT-LIGHT SLAMMED ON-- TO REVEAL--
AS THE THE LAMPS DIMMED ALL EYES FOCUSED ON THE MAKESHIFT STAGE'S CURTAIN...
...AS IT ROSE... SLOWLY...
...REVEALING A DEEPER DARK...
...BLACK AS THE MAW OF DEATH, ITSELF.
"ME MISERABLE."
"WHICH WAY SHALL I FLY?"
"INFINITE WRATH AND INFINITE DESPAIR?"
"WHICH WAY I FLY IS HELL--
--MYSELF AM HELL."

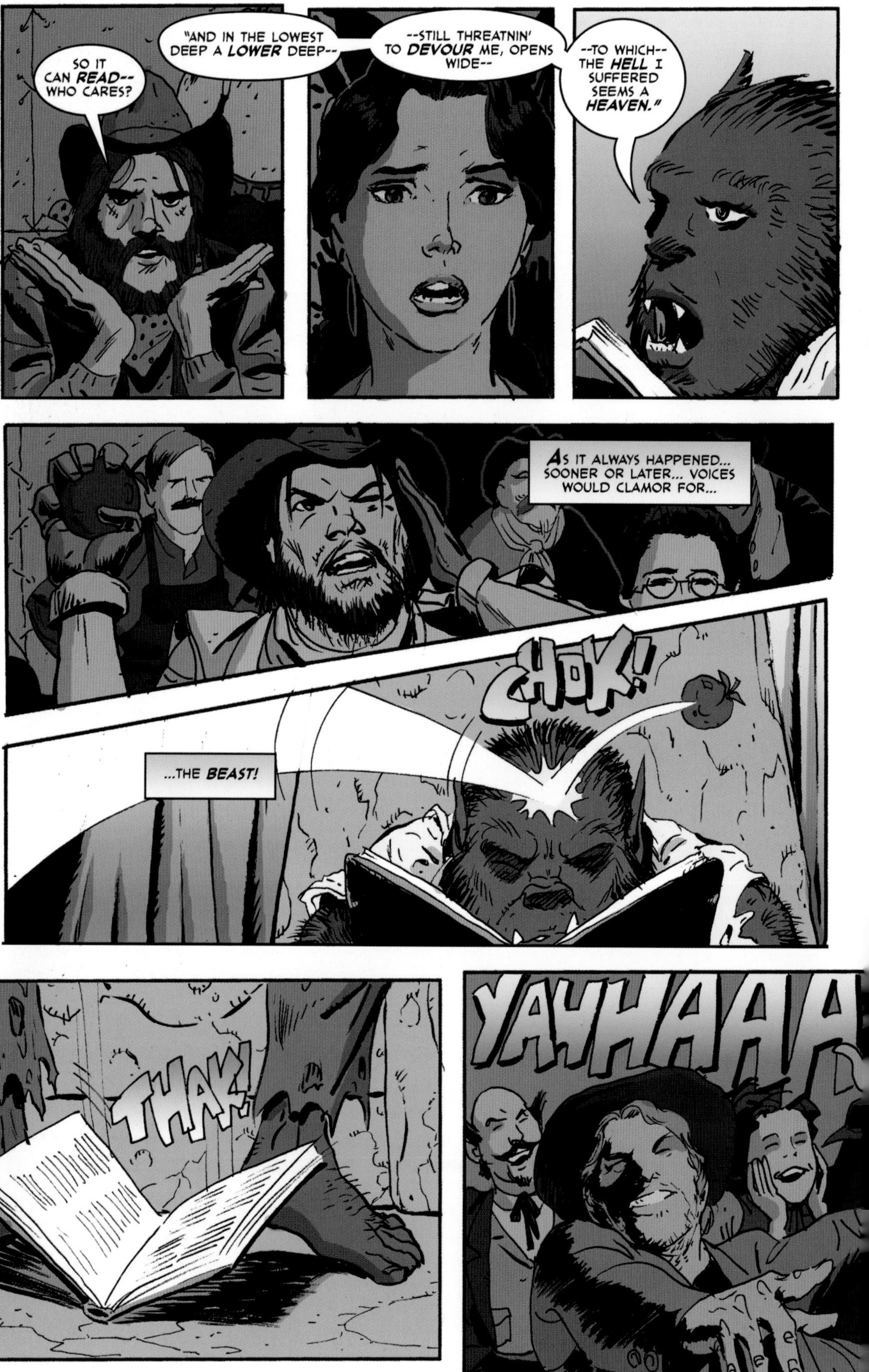
SO IT CAN READ-- WHO CARES?
"AND IN THE LOWEST DEEP A LOWER DEEP--
--STILL THREATNIN' TO DEVOUR ME, OPENS WIDE--
--TO WHICH-- THE HELL I SUFFERED SEEMS A HEAVEN."
AS IT ALWAYS HAPPENED... SOONER OR LATER... VOICES WOULD CLAMOR FOR...
CHOK!
...THE BEAST!
THAK!
YAYHAAA

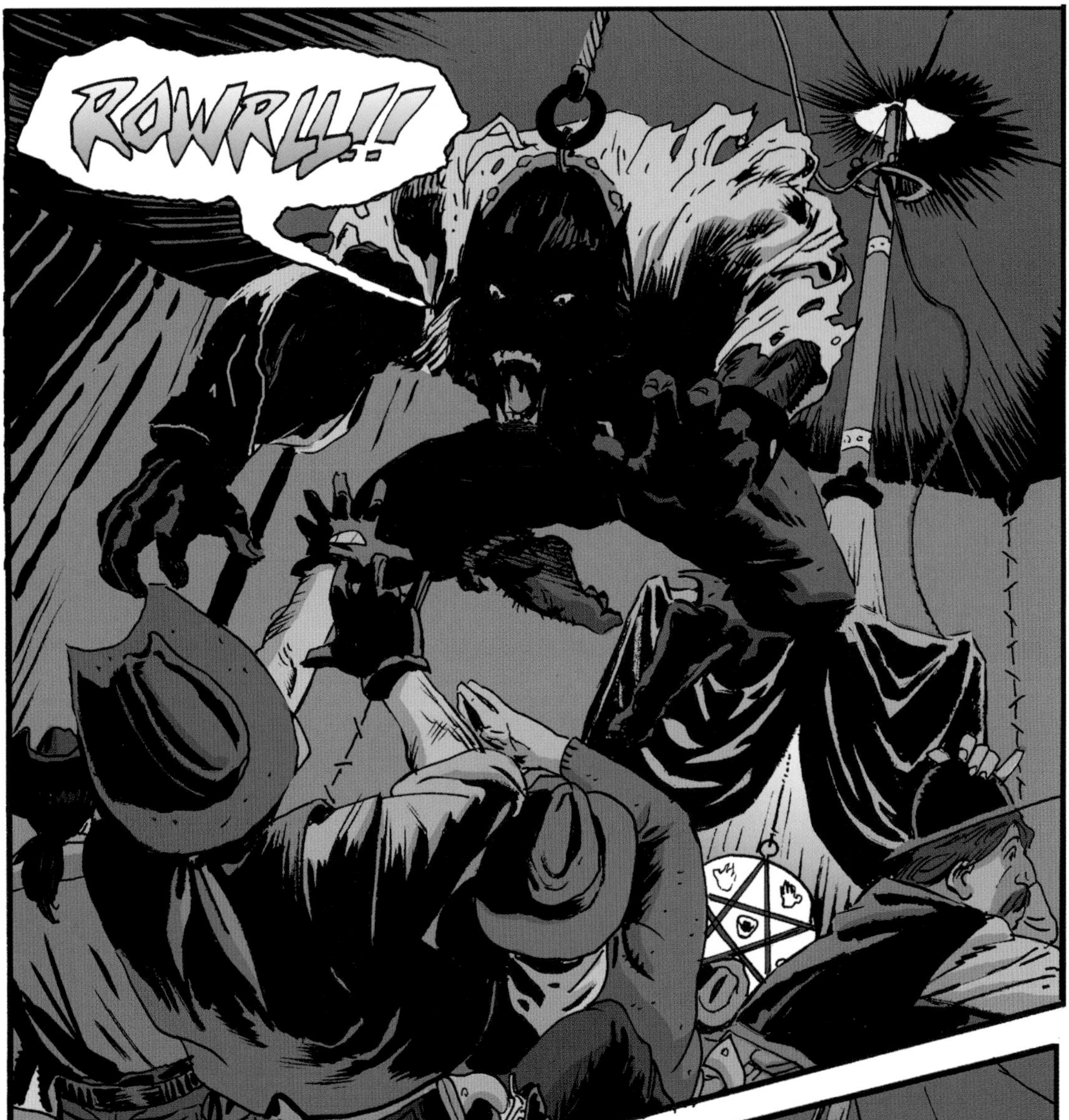
ROWRLL!!

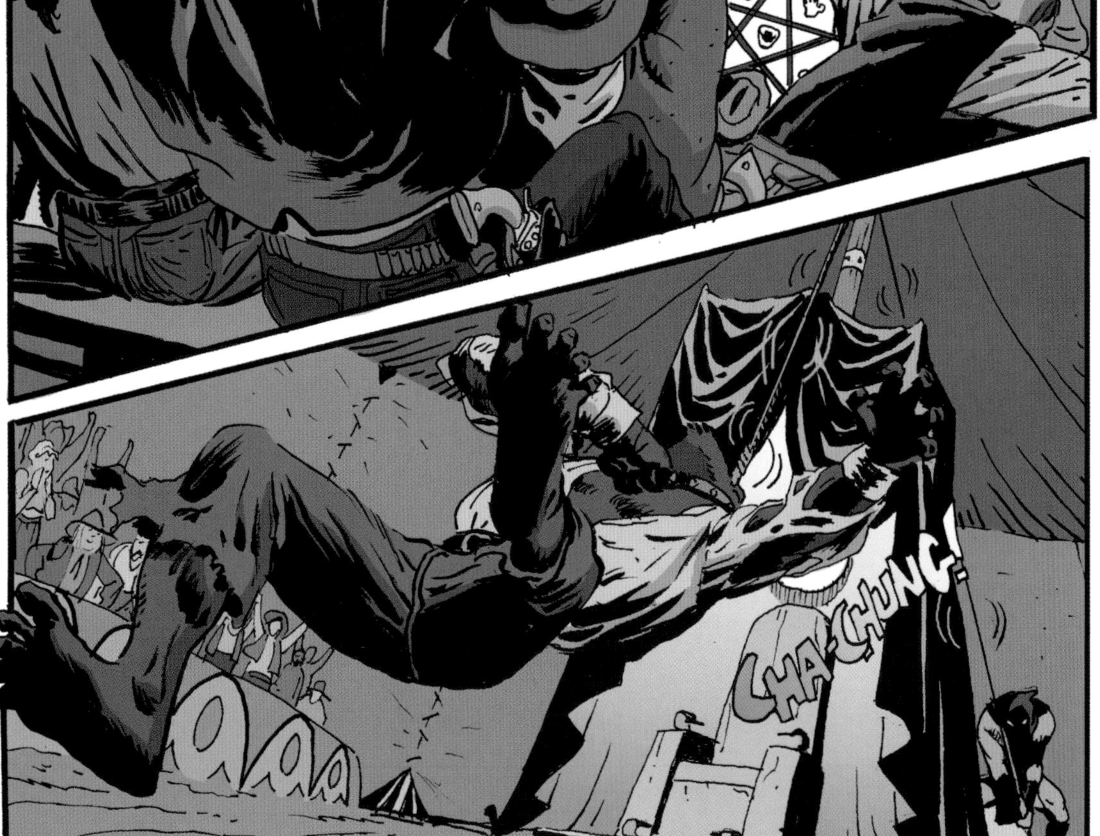
CHA-CHUNG!

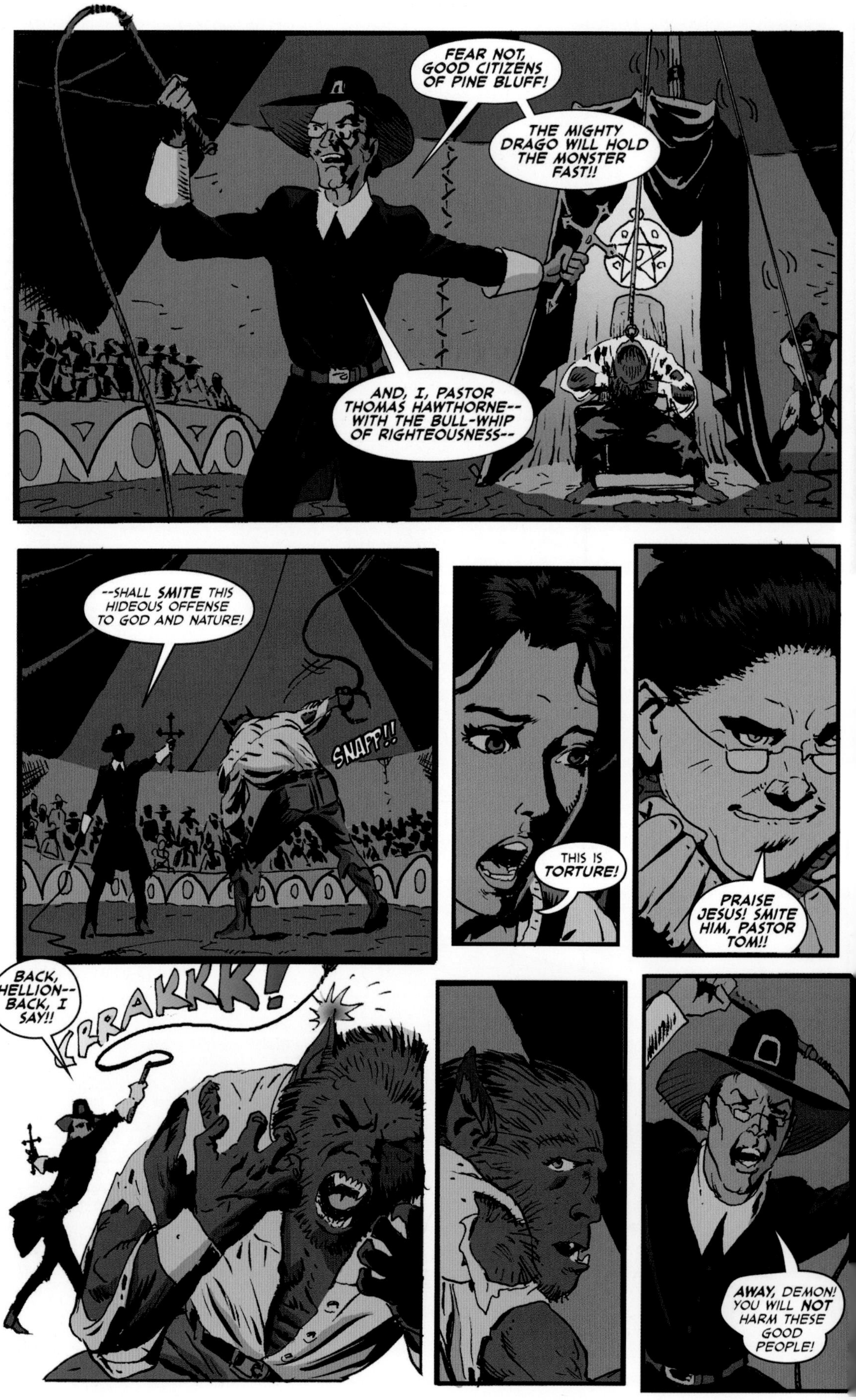
FEAR NOT, GOOD CITIZENS OF PINE BLUFF!
THE MIGHTY DRAGO WILL HOLD THE MONSTER FAST!!
AND, I, PASTOR THOMAS HAWTHORNE-- WITH THE BULL-WHIP OF RIGHTEOUSNESS--
--SHALL SMITE THIS HIDEOUS OFFENSE TO GOD AND NATURE!
SNAPP!!
THIS IS TORTURE!
PRAISE JESUS! SMITE HIM, PASTOR TOM!!
BACK, HELLION-- BACK, I SAY!!
CRRAKKK!
AWAY, DEMON! YOU WILL NOT HARM THESE GOOD PEOPLE!

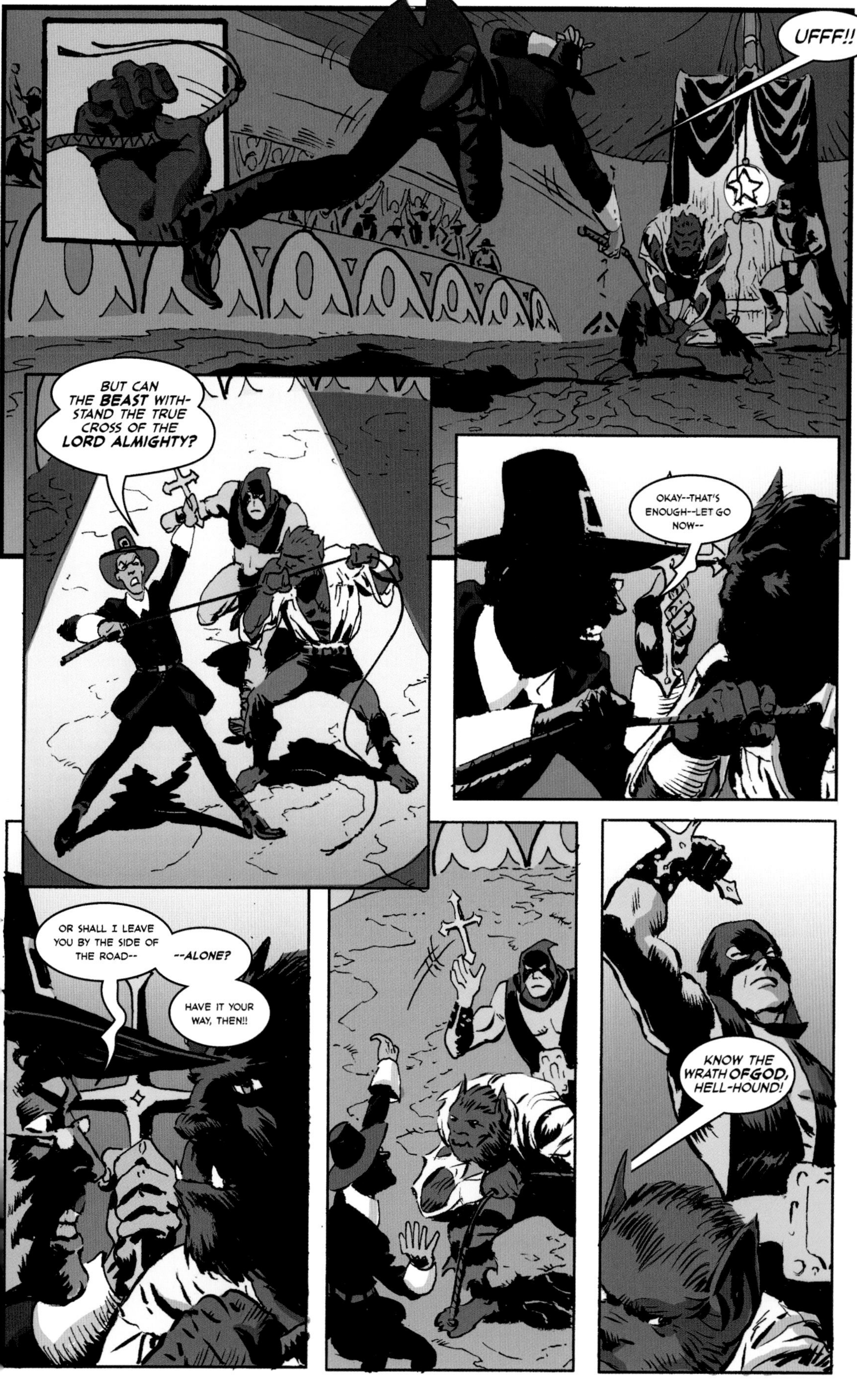
UFFF!!
BUT CAN THE BEAST WITH-STAND THE TRUE CROSS OF THE LORD ALMIGHTY?
OKAY--THAT'S ENOUGH--LET GO NOW--
OR SHALL I LEAVE YOU BY THE SIDE OF THE ROAD--
--ALONE?
HAVE IT YOUR WAY, THEN!!
KNOW THE WRATH OF GOD, HELL-HOUND!

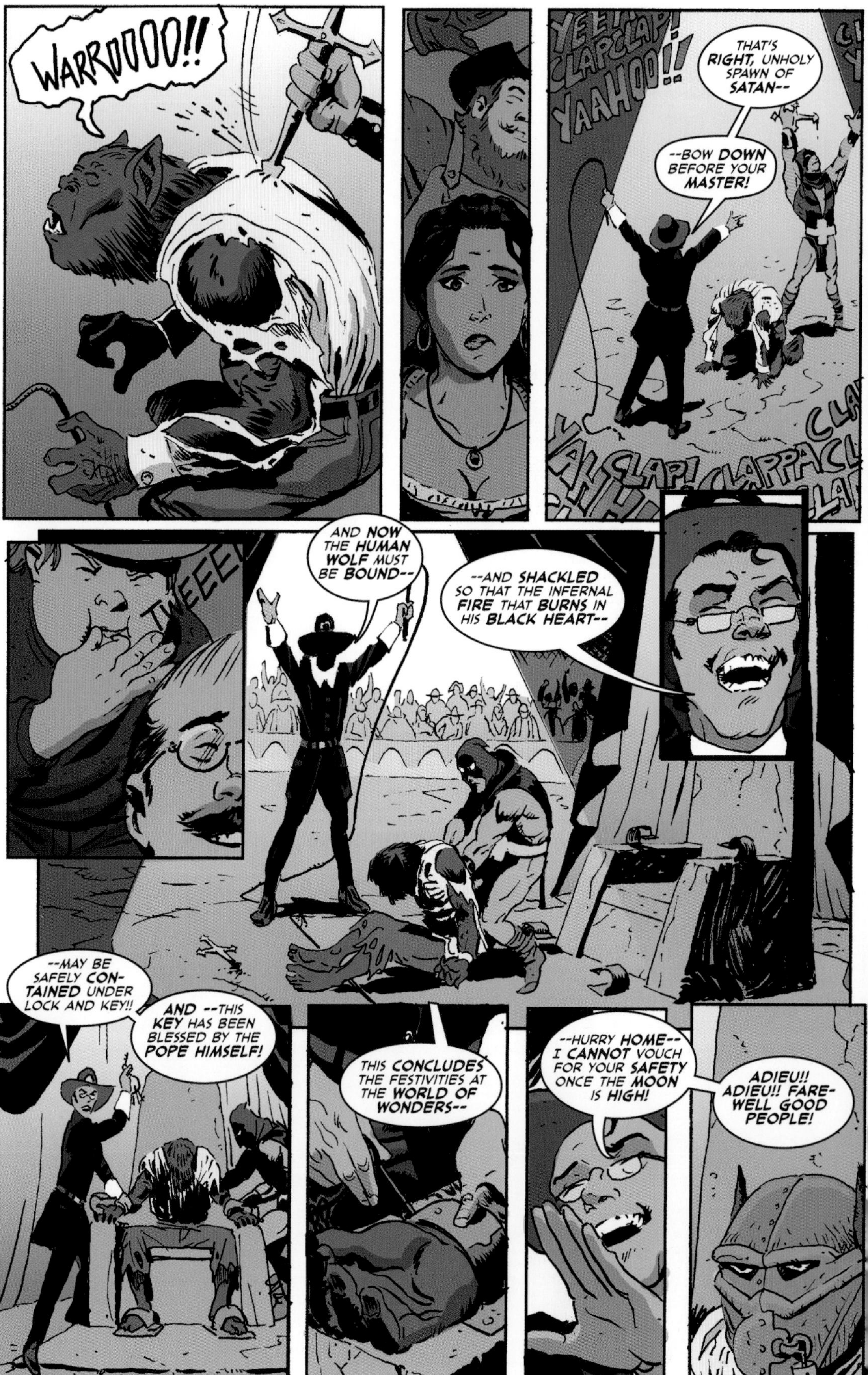
WARROOOO!!
YEEHA! CLAPCLAP! YAAHOO!!
THAT'S RIGHT, UNHOLY SPAWN OF SATAN--
--BOW DOWN BEFORE YOUR MASTER!
YAH! CLAP! CLAPPACLAP
AND NOW THE HUMAN WOLF MUST BE BOUND--
--AND SHACKLED SO THAT THE INFERNAL FIRE THAT BURNS IN HIS BLACK HEART--
--MAY BE SAFELY CONTAINED UNDER LOCK AND KEY!!
AND --THIS KEY HAS BEEN BLESSED BY THE POPE HIMSELF!
THIS CONCLUDES THE FESTIVITIES AT THE WORLD OF WONDERS--
--HURRY HOME-- I CANNOT VOUCH FOR YOUR SAFETY ONCE THE MOON IS HIGH!
ADIEU!! ADIEU!! FARE-WELL GOOD PEOPLE!

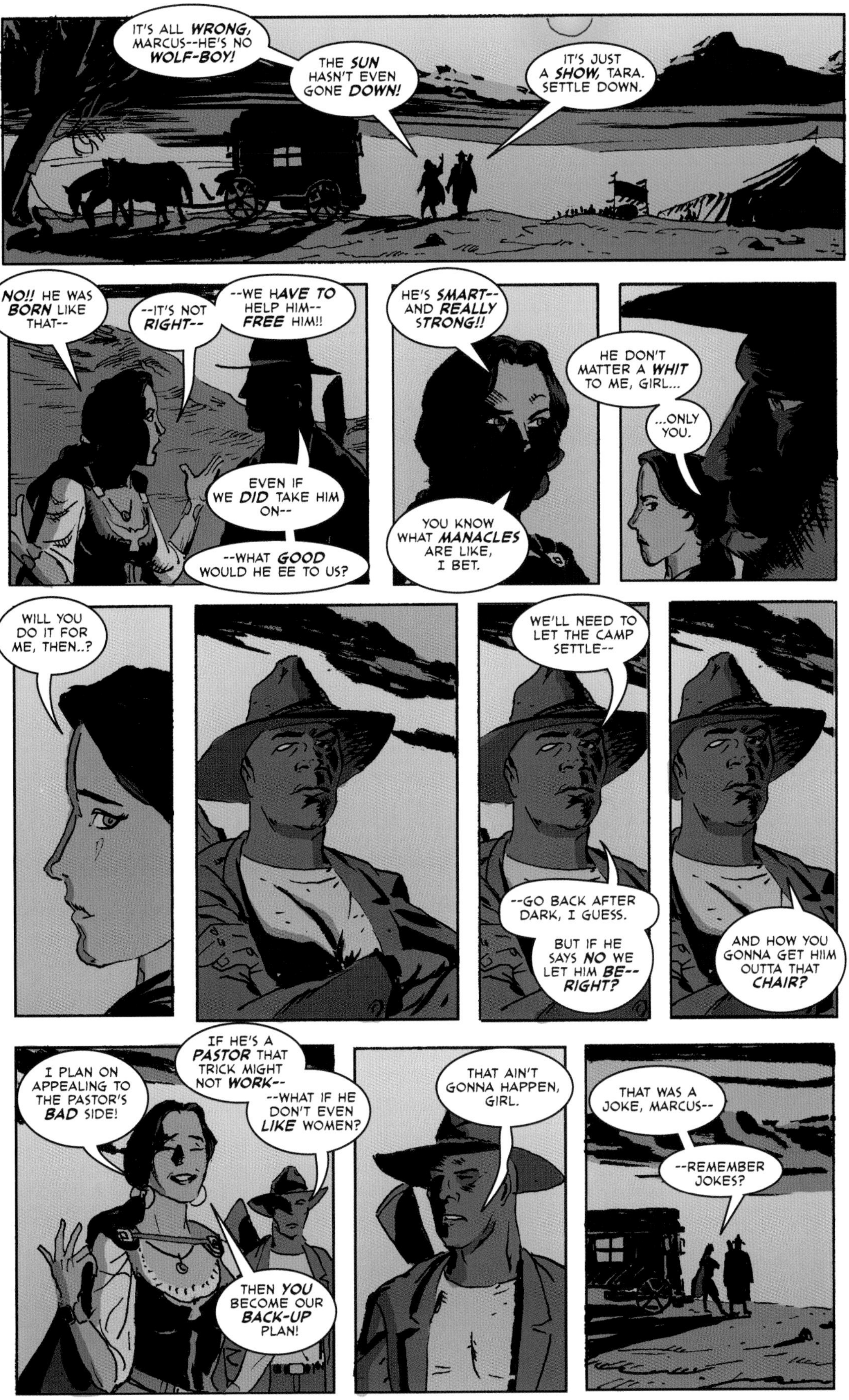
IT'S ALL WRONG, MARCUS--HE'S NO WOLF-BOY!
THE SUN HASN'T EVEN GONE DOWN!
IT'S JUST A SHOW, TARA. SETTLE DOWN.
NO!! HE WAS BORN LIKE THAT--
--IT'S NOT RIGHT--
--WE HAVE TO HELP HIM--FREE HIM!!
EVEN IF WE DID TAKE HIM ON--
--WHAT GOOD WOULD HE EE TO US?
HE'S SMART--AND REALLY STRONG!!
YOU KNOW WHAT MANACLES ARE LIKE, I BET.
HE DON'T MATTER A WHIT TO ME, GIRL...
...ONLY YOU.
WILL YOU DO IT FOR ME, THEN..?
WE'LL NEED TO LET THE CAMP SETTLE--
--GO BACK AFTER DARK, I GUESS.
BUT IF HE SAYS NO WE LET HIM BE--RIGHT?
AND HOW YOU GONNA GET HIIM OUTTA THAT CHAIR?
I PLAN ON APPEALING TO THE PASTOR'S BAD SIDE!
IF HE'S A PASTOR THAT TRICK MIGHT NOT WORK--
--WHAT IF HE DON'T EVEN LIKE WOMEN?
THEN YOU BECOME OUR BACK-UP PLAN!
THAT AIN'T GONNA HAPPEN, GIRL.
THAT WAS A JOKE, MARCUS--
--REMEMBER JOKES?

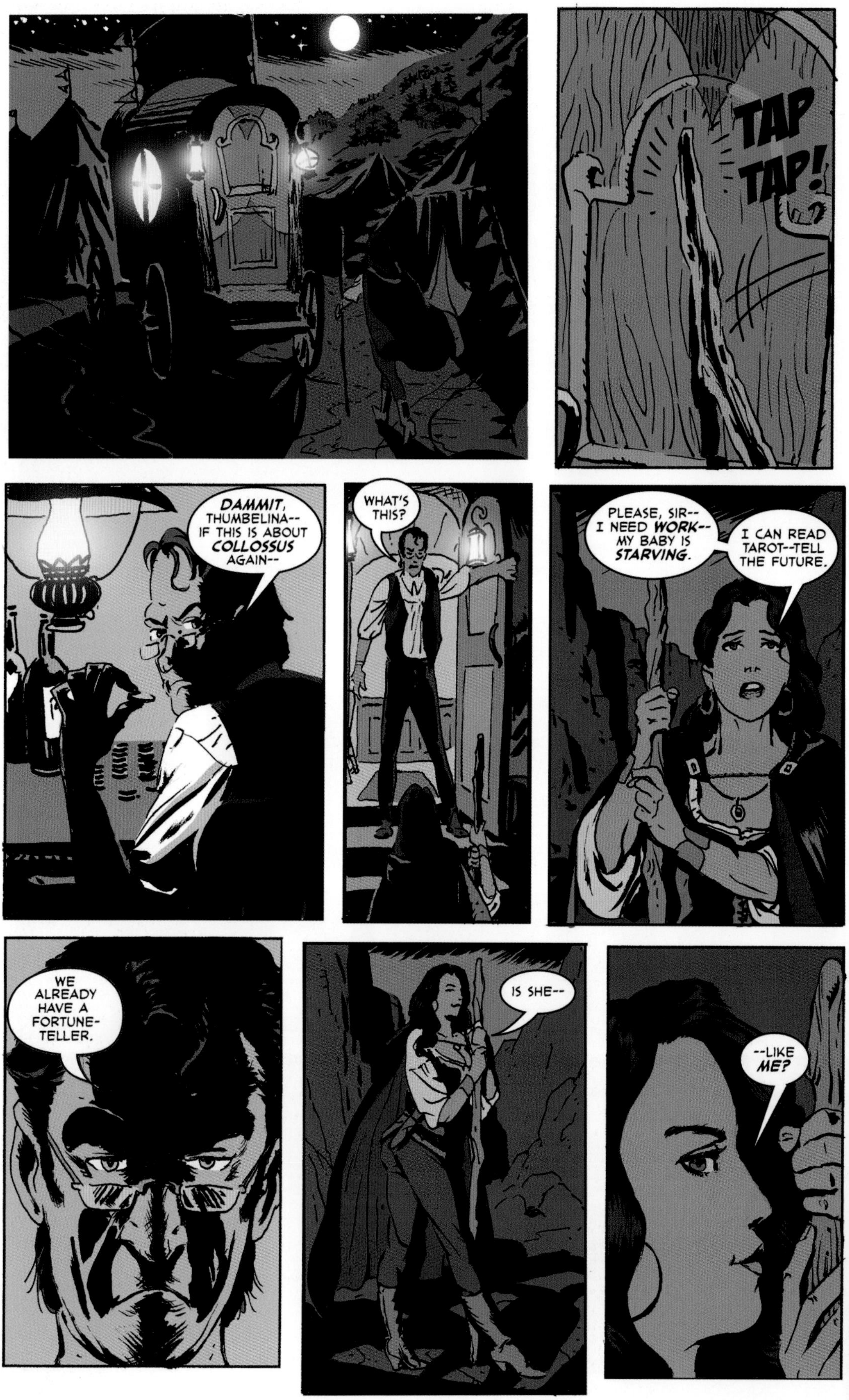
TAP TAP!
DAMMIT, THUMBELINA-- IF THIS IS ABOUT COLLOSSUS AGAIN--
WHAT'S THIS?
PLEASE, SIR-- I NEED WORK-- MY BABY IS STARVING.
I CAN READ TAROT--TELL THE FUTURE.
WE ALREADY HAVE A FORTUNE-TELLER.
IS SHE--
--LIKE ME?

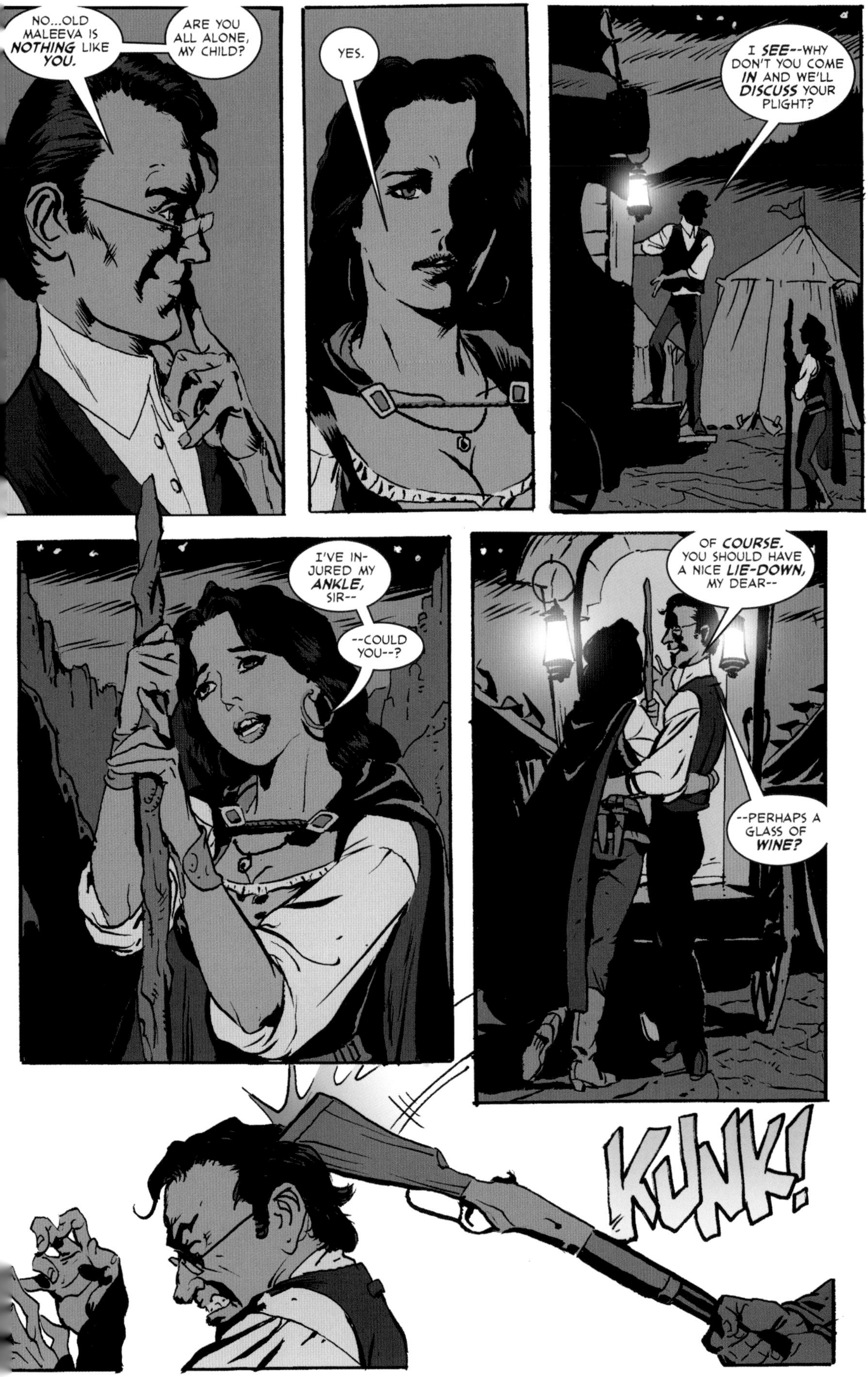
ARE YOU ALL ALONE, MY CHILD?
NO...OLD MALEEVA IS NOTHING LIKE YOU.
YES.
I SEE--WHY DON'T YOU COME IN AND WE'LL DISCUSS YOUR PLIGHT?
I'VE INJURED MY ANKLE, SIR--
--COULD YOU--?
OF COURSE. YOU SHOULD HAVE A NICE LIE-DOWN, MY DEAR--
--PERHAPS A GLASS OF WINE?
KUNK!

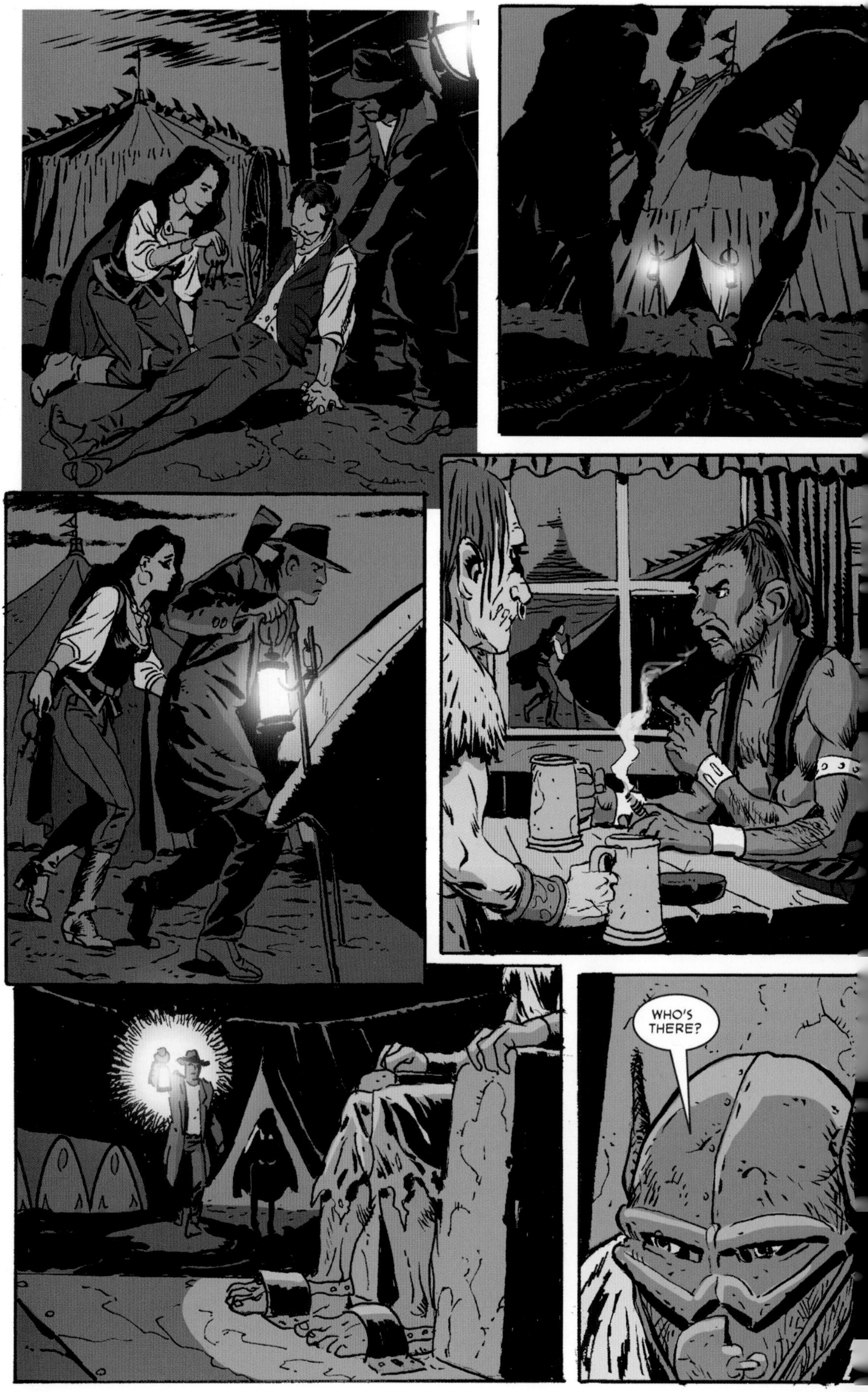
WHO'S THERE?

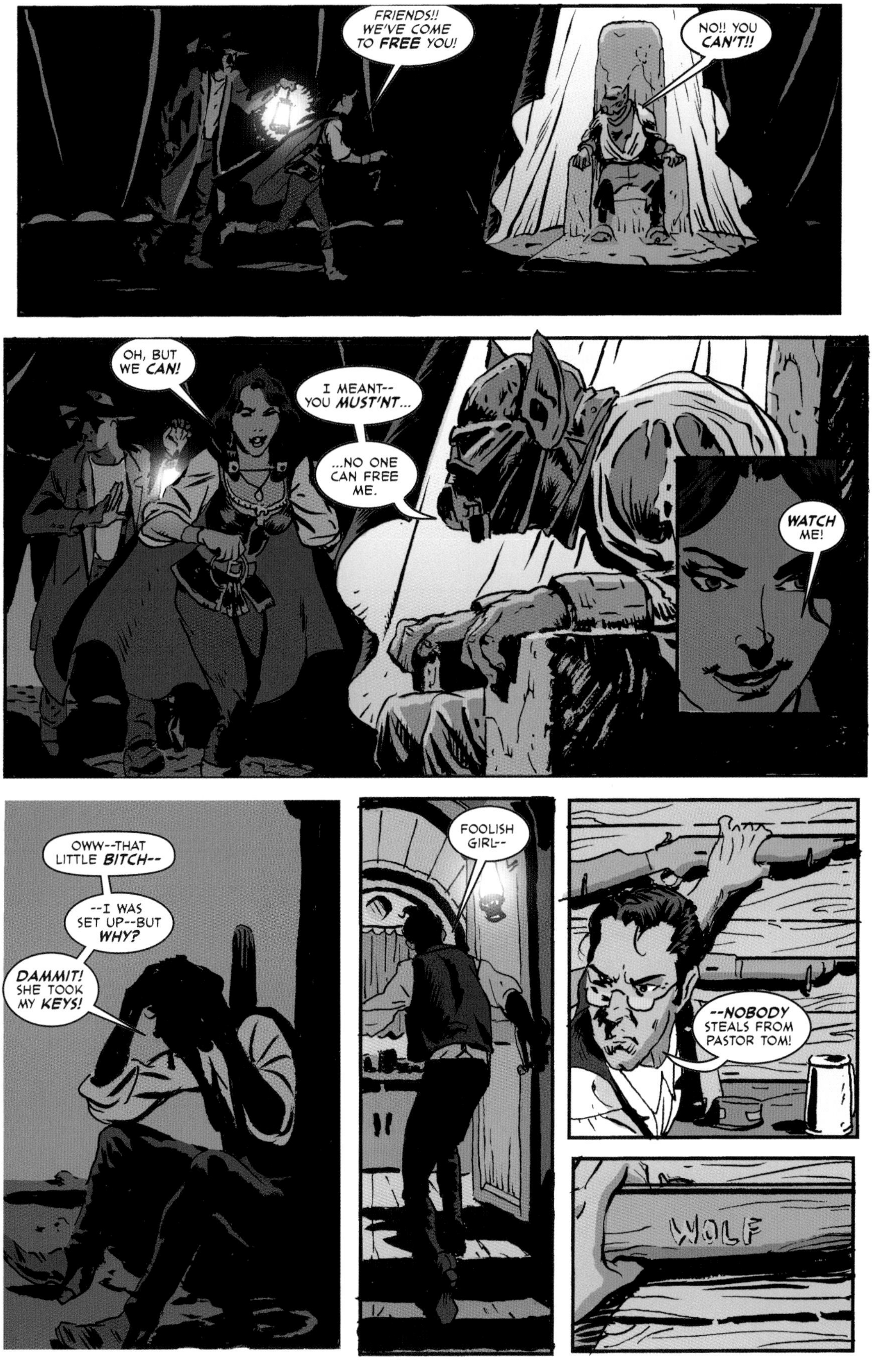
FRIENDS!! WE'VE COME TO FREE YOU!
NO!! YOU CAN'T!!
OH, BUT WE CAN!
I MEANT-- YOU MUST'NT...
...NO ONE CAN FREE ME.
WATCH ME!
OWW--THAT LITTLE BITCH--
--I WAS SET UP--BUT WHY?
DAMMIT! SHE TOOK MY KEYS!
FOOLISH GIRL--
--NOBODY STEALS FROM PASTOR TOM!
WOLF

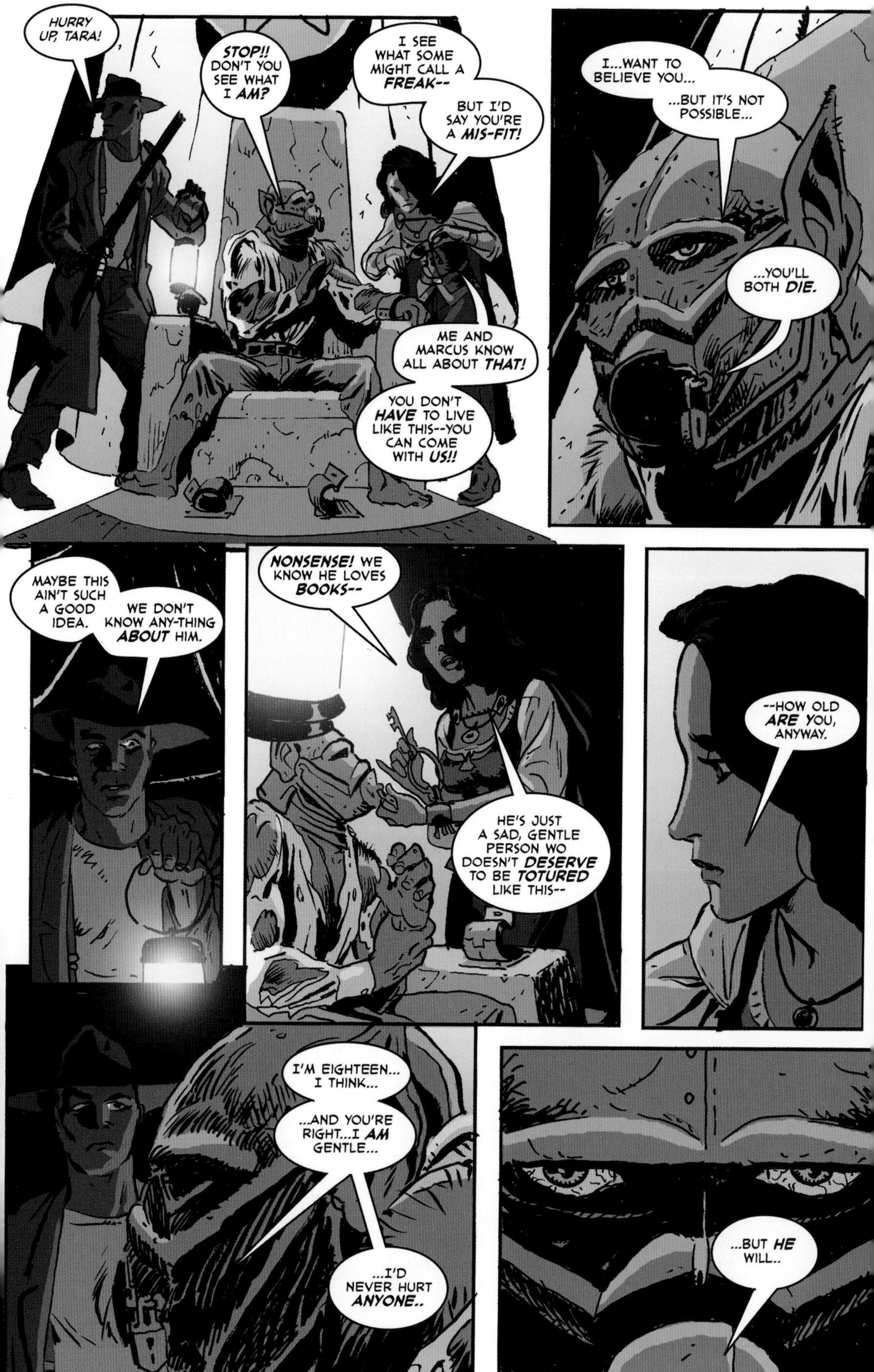
HURRY UP, TARA!
STOP!! DON'T YOU SEE WHAT I AM?
I SEE WHAT SOME MIGHT CALL A FREAK--
BUT I'D SAY YOU'RE A MIS-FIT!
ME AND MARCUS KNOW ALL ABOUT THAT!
YOU DON'T HAVE TO LIVE LIKE THIS--YOU CAN COME WITH US!!
I...WANT TO BELIEVE YOU...
...BUT IT'S NOT POSSIBLE...
...YOU'LL BOTH DIE.
MAYBE THIS AIN'T SUCH A GOOD IDEA.
WE DON'T KNOW ANY-THING ABOUT HIM.
NONSENSE! WE KNOW HE LOVES BOOKS--
HE'S JUST A SAD, GENTLE PERSON WO DOESN'T DESERVE TO BE TOTURED LIKE THIS--
--HOW OLD ARE YOU, ANYWAY.
I'M EIGHTEEN... I THINK...
...AND YOU'RE RIGHT...I AM GENTLE...
...I'D NEVER HURT ANYONE..
...BUT HE WILL..

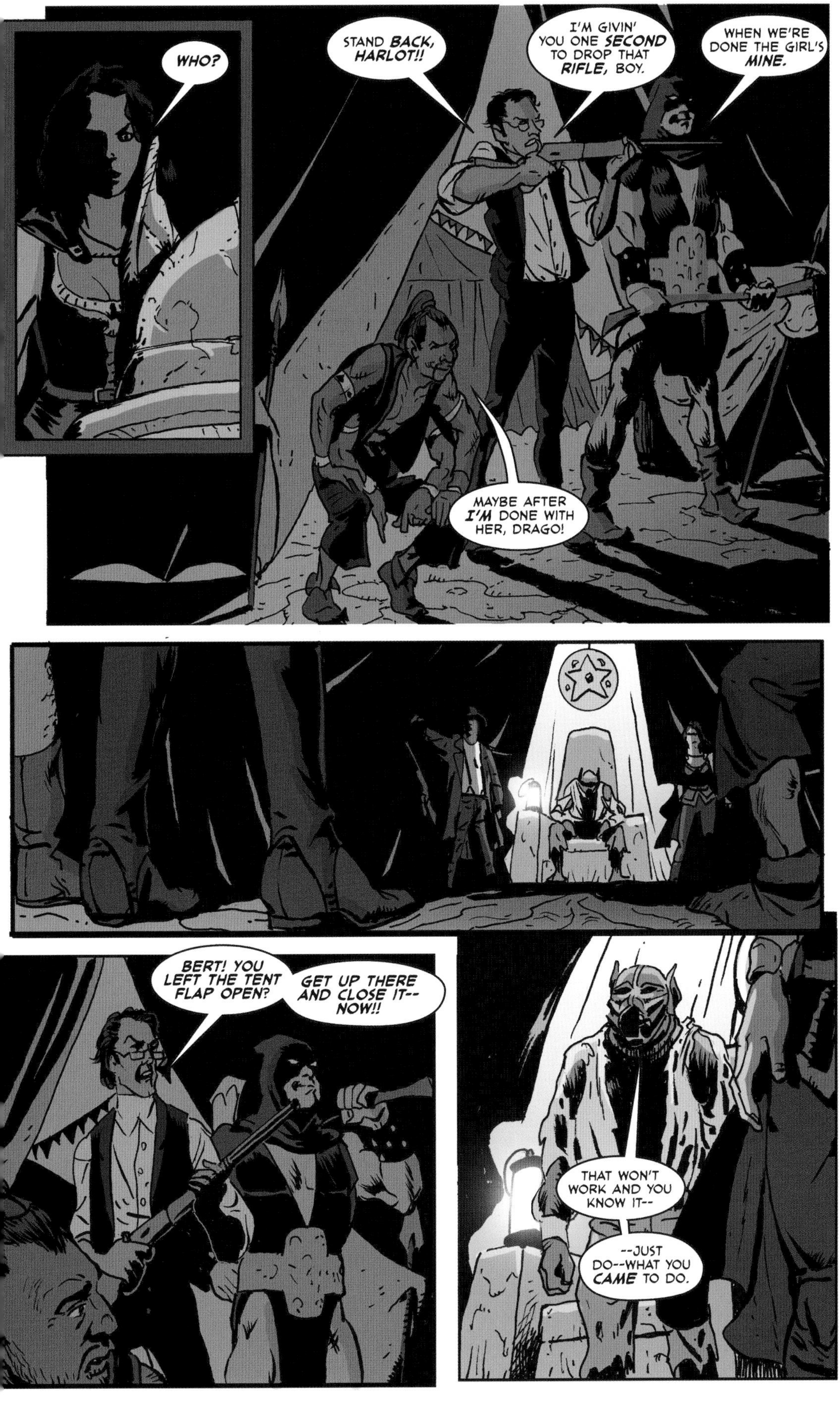
WHO?
STAND BACK, HARLOT!!
I'M GIVIN' YOU ONE SECOND TO DROP THAT RIFLE, BOY.
WHEN WE'RE DONE THE GIRL'S MINE.
MAYBE AFTER I'M DONE WITH HER, DRAGO!
BERT! YOU LEFT THE TENT FLAP OPEN?
GET UP THERE AND CLOSE IT-- NOW!!
THAT WON'T WORK AND YOU KNOW IT--
--JUST DO--WHAT YOU CAME TO DO.

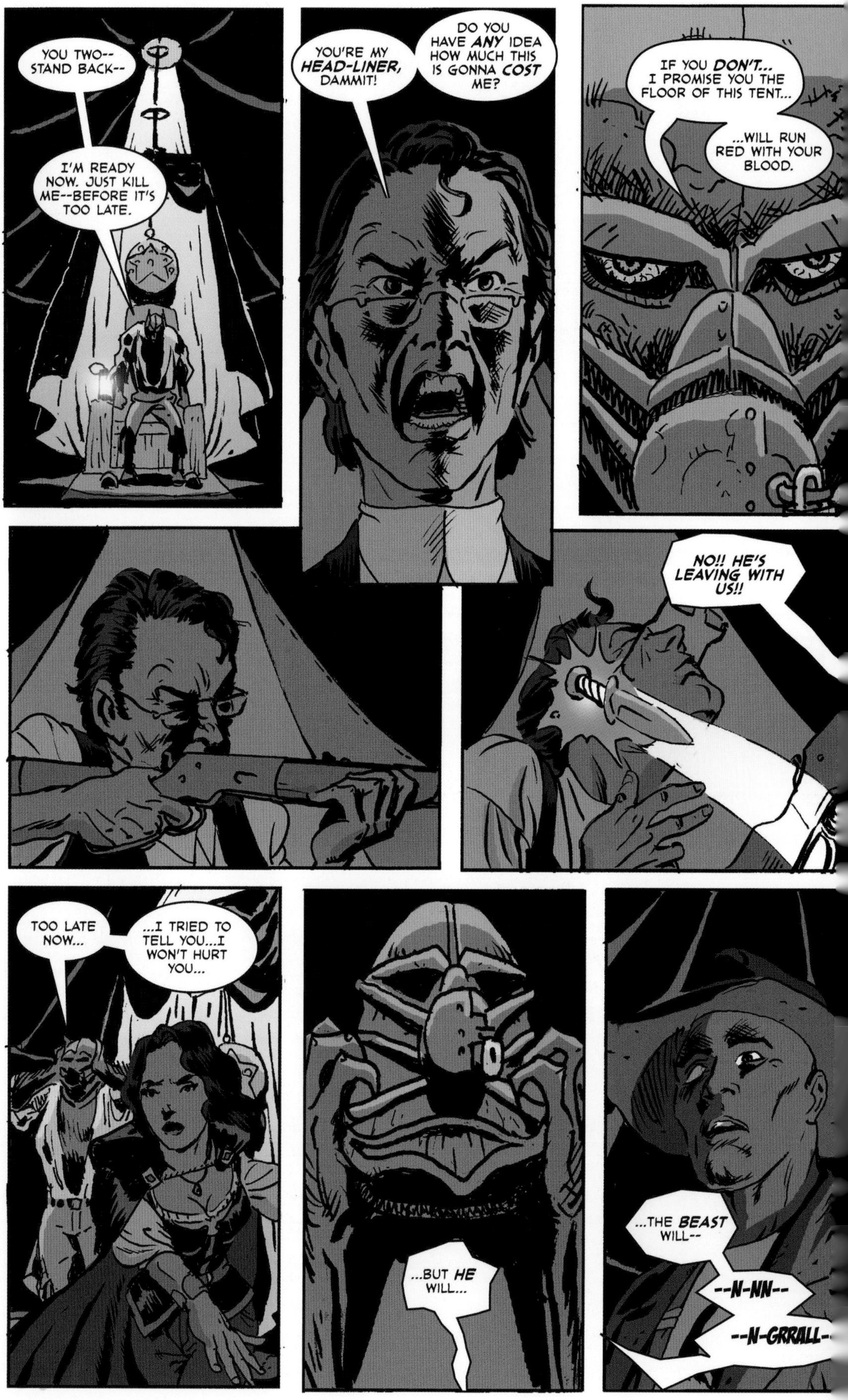
YOU TWO-- STAND BACK--
I'M READY NOW. JUST KILL ME--BEFORE IT'S TOO LATE.
YOU'RE MY HEAD-LINER, DAMMIT!
DO YOU HAVE ANY IDEA HOW MUCH THIS IS GONNA COST ME?
IF YOU DON'T... I PROMISE YOU THE FLOOR OF THIS TENT...
...WILL RUN RED WITH YOUR BLOOD.
NO!! HE'S LEAVING WITH US!!
TOO LATE NOW...
...I TRIED TO TELL YOU...I WON'T HURT YOU...
...BUT HE WILL...
...THE BEAST WILL--
--N-NN--
--N-GRRALL-

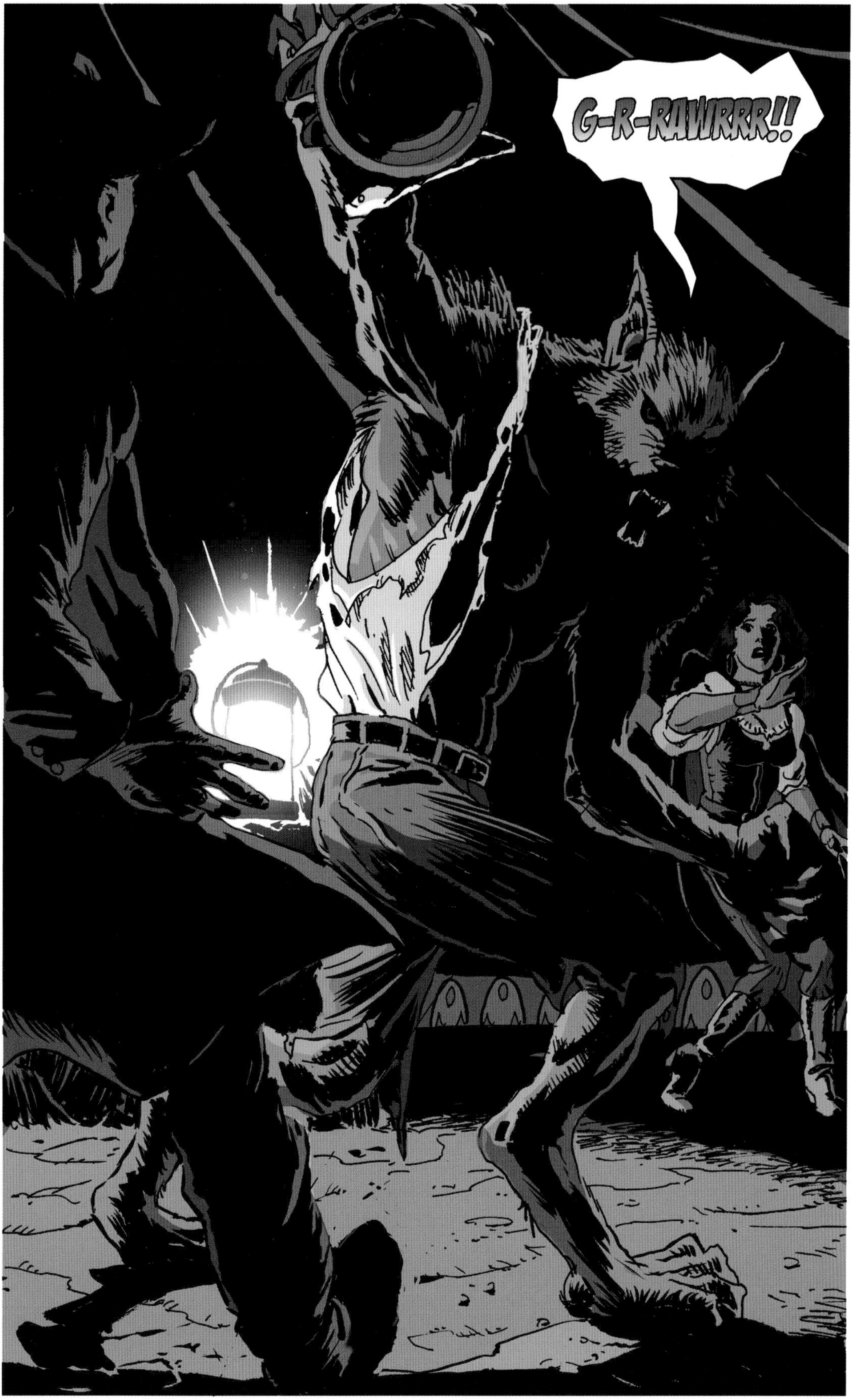
G-R-RAWRRR!!

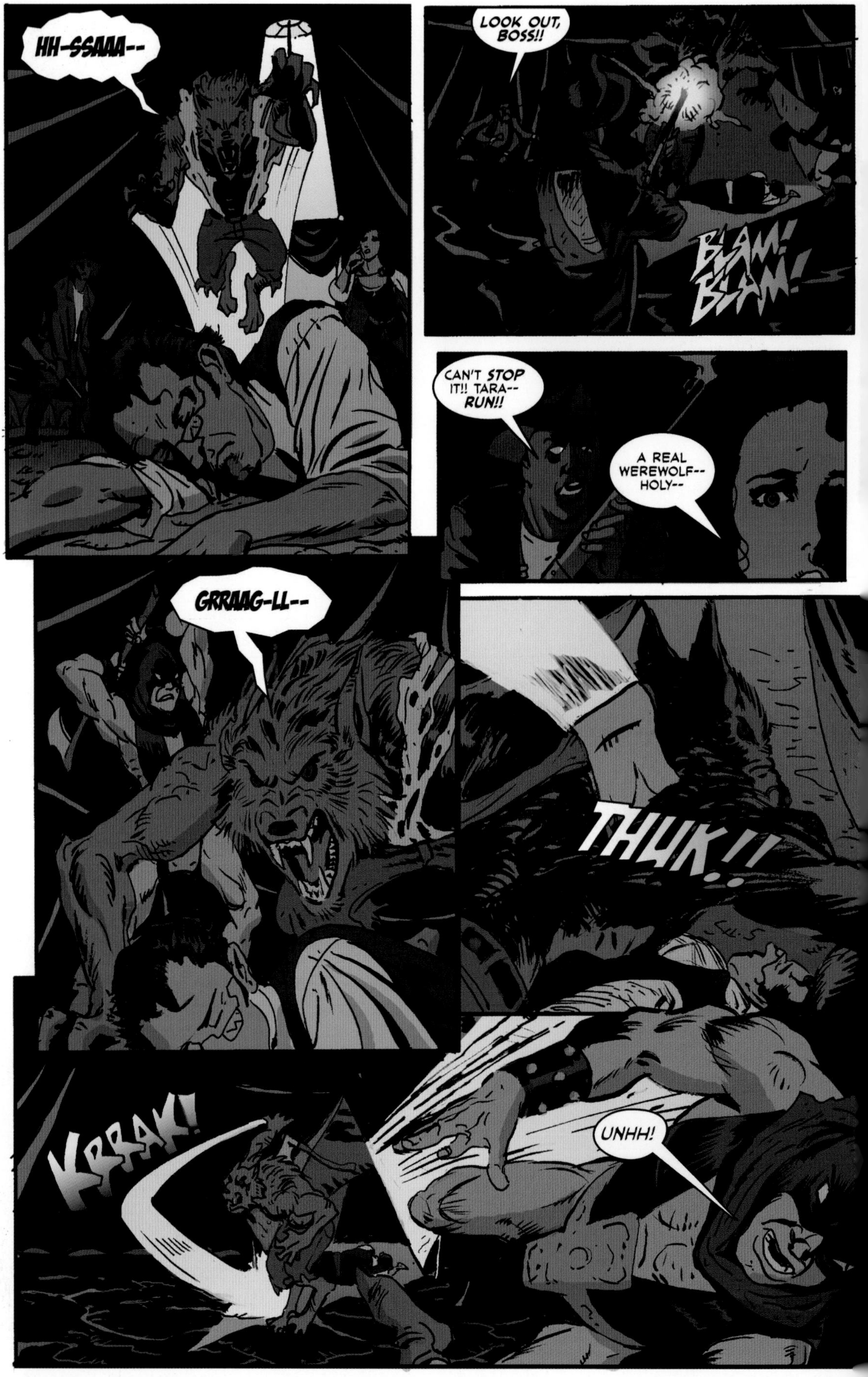
HH-SSAAA--
LOOK OUT, BOSS!!
BLAM! BLAM!
CAN'T STOP IT!! TARA-- RUN!!
A REAL WEREWOLF-- HOLY--
GRRAAG-LL--
THUK!!
KRRAK!
UNHH!

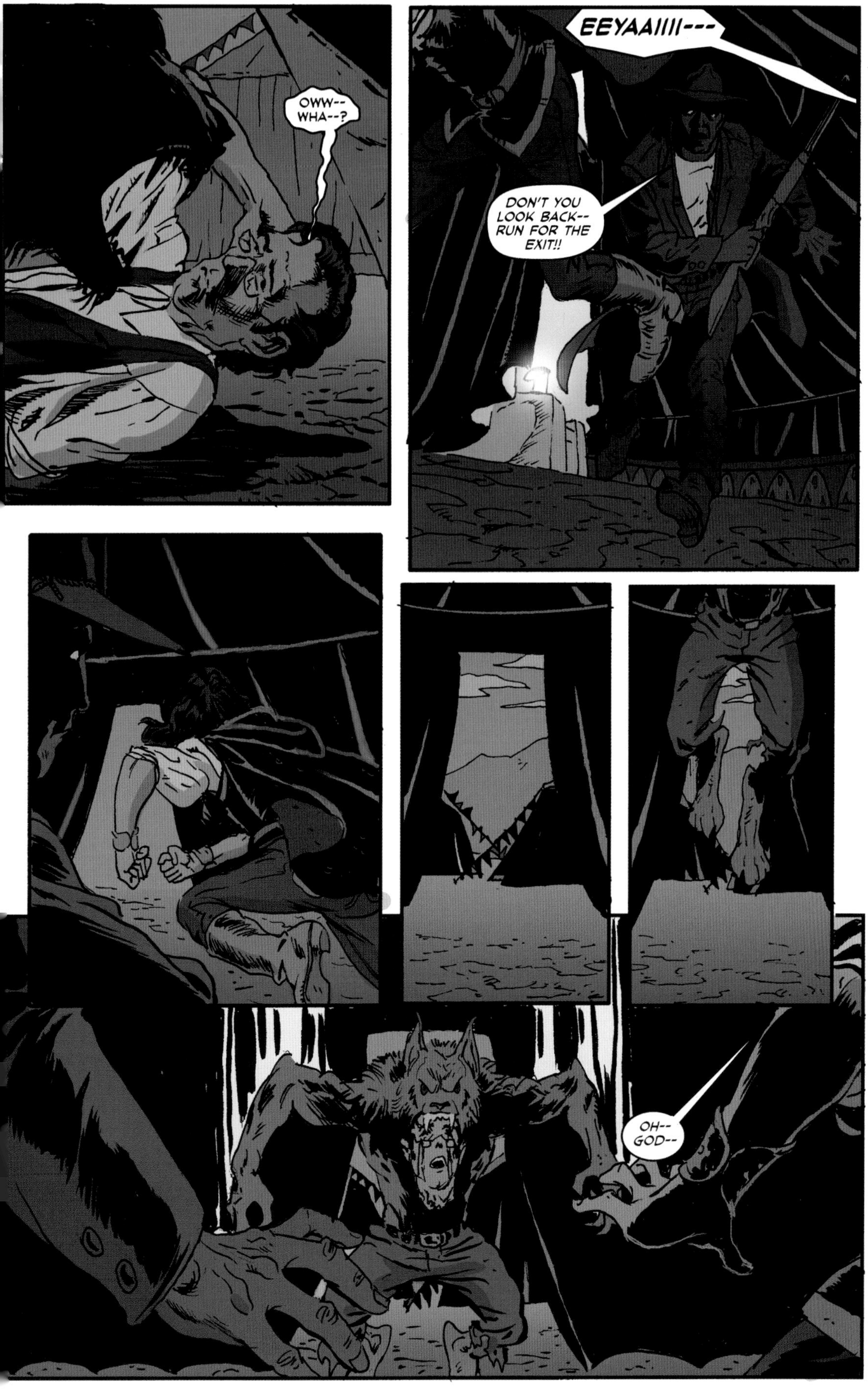
OWW--
WHA--?
EEYAAIIII---
DON'T YOU LOOK BACK-- RUN FOR THE EXIT!!
OH-- GOD--

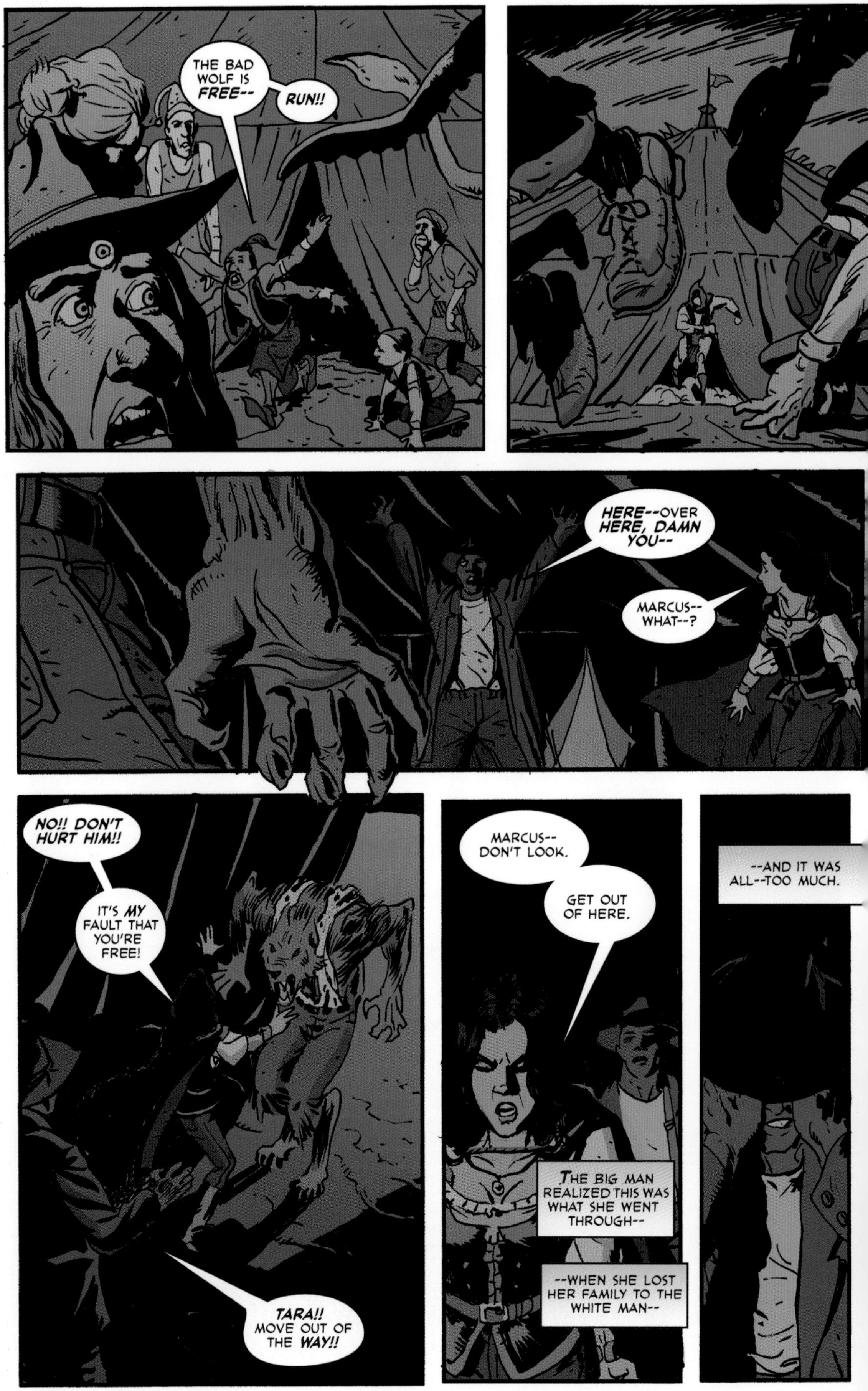
THE BAD WOLF IS FREE--
RUN!!
HERE--OVER HERE, DAMN YOU--
MARCUS-- WHAT--?
NO!! DON'T HURT HIM!!
IT'S MY FAULT THAT YOU'RE FREE!
TARA!! MOVE OUT OF THE WAY!!
MARCUS-- DON'T LOOK.
GET OUT OF HERE.
THE BIG MAN REALIZED THIS WAS WHAT SHE WENT THROUGH--
--WHEN SHE LOST HER FAMILY TO THE WHITE MAN--
--AND IT WAS ALL--TOO MUCH.

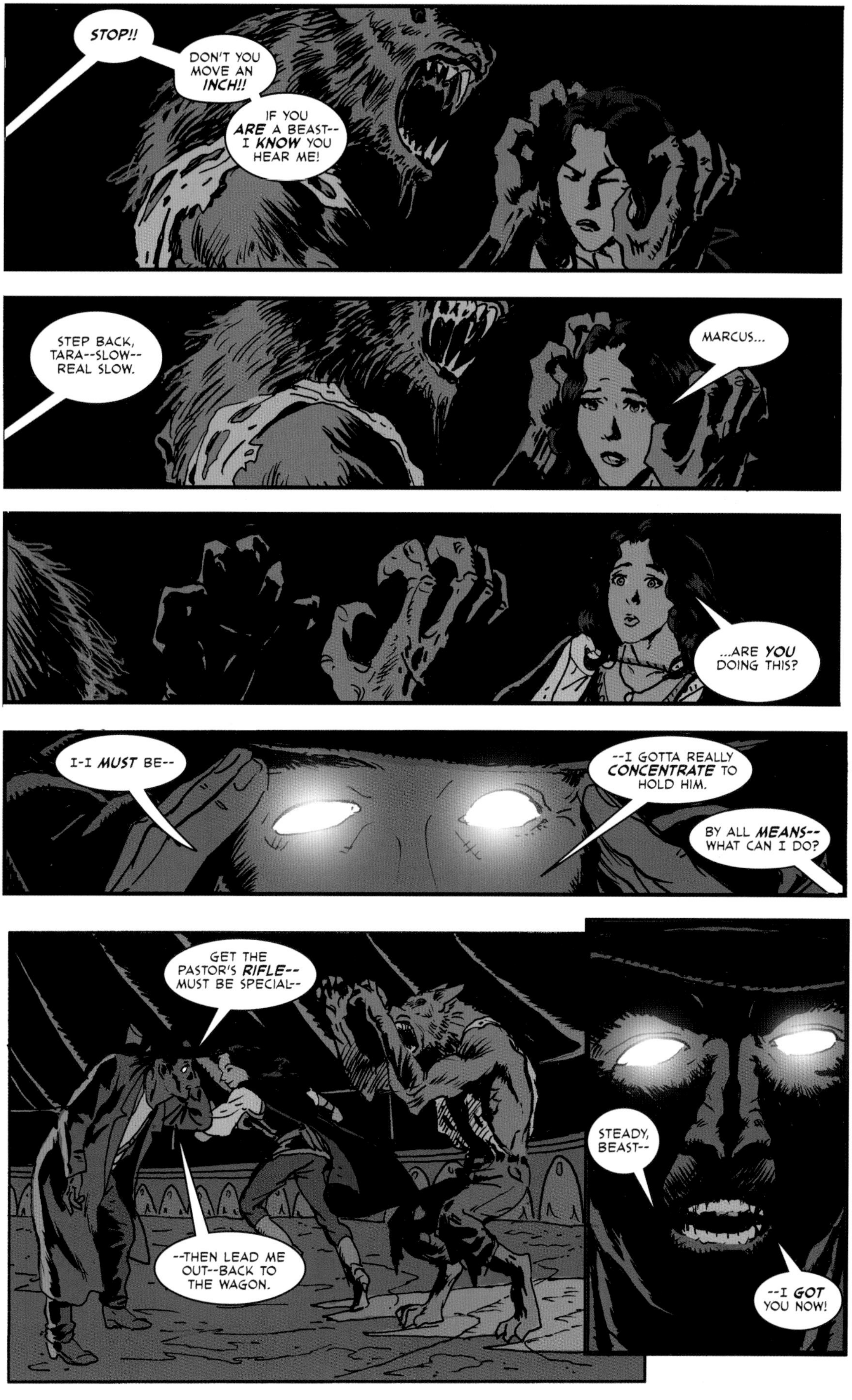
STOP!!
DON'T YOU MOVE AN INCH!!
IF YOU ARE A BEAST-- I KNOW YOU HEAR ME!
STEP BACK, TARA--SLOW-- REAL SLOW.
MARCUS...
...ARE YOU DOING THIS?
I-I MUST BE--
--I GOTTA REALLY CONCENTRATE TO HOLD HIM.
BY ALL MEANS-- WHAT CAN I DO?
GET THE PASTOR'S RIFLE-- MUST BE SPECIAL--
--THEN LEAD ME OUT--BACK TO THE WAGON.
STEADY, BEAST--
--I GOT YOU NOW!

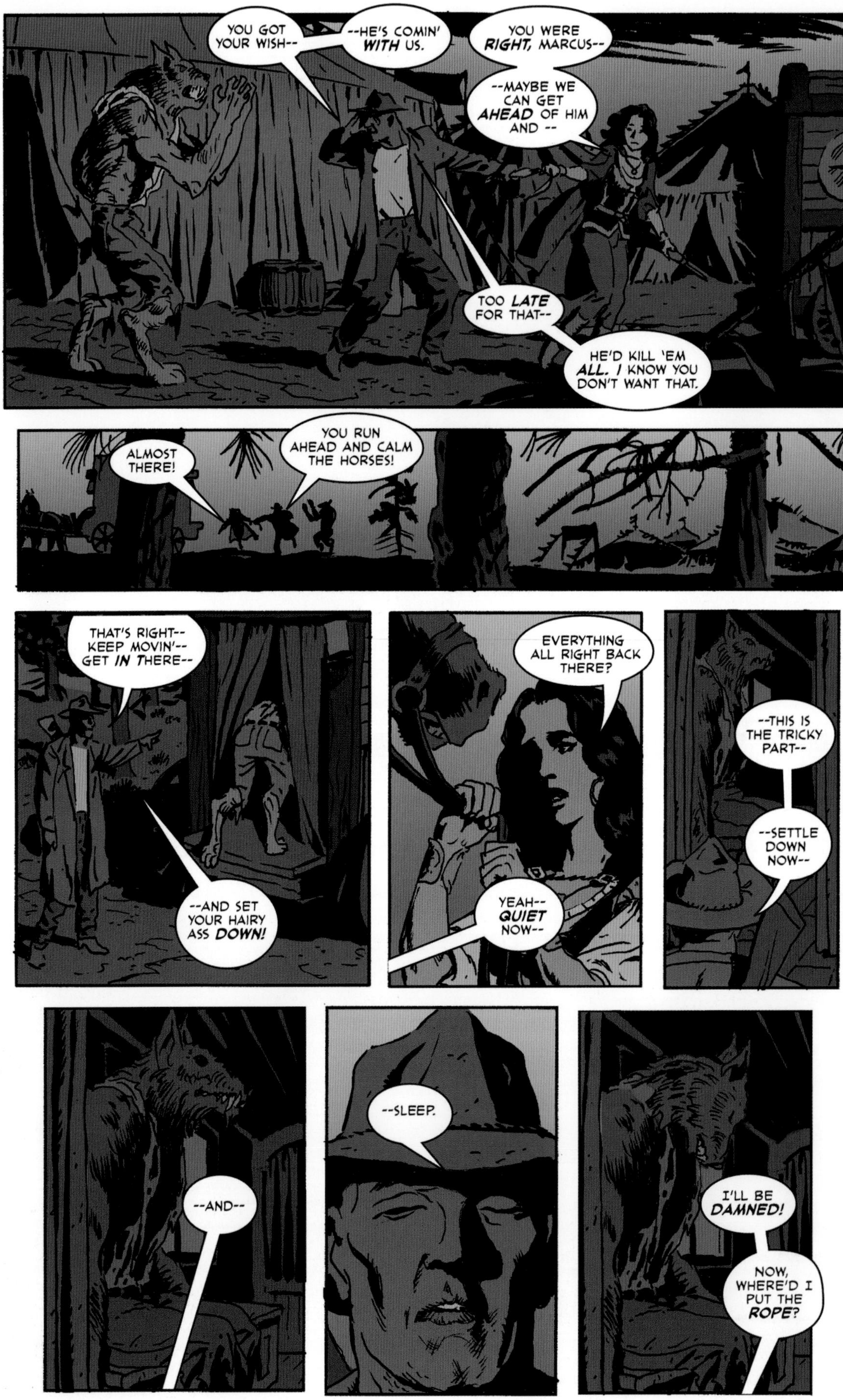
YOU GOT YOUR WISH--
--HE'S COMIN' WITH US.
YOU WERE RIGHT, MARCUS--
--MAYBE WE CAN GET AHEAD OF HIM AND --
TOO LATE FOR THAT--
HE'D KILL 'EM ALL. I KNOW YOU DON'T WANT THAT.
ALMOST THERE!
YOU RUN AHEAD AND CALM THE HORSES!
THAT'S RIGHT-- KEEP MOVIN'-- GET IN THERE--
--AND SET YOUR HAIRY ASS DOWN!
EVERYTHING ALL RIGHT BACK THERE?
YEAH-- QUIET NOW--
--THIS IS THE TRICKY PART--
--SETTLE DOWN NOW--
--AND--
--SLEEP.
I'LL BE DAMNED!
NOW, WHERE'D I PUT THE ROPE?

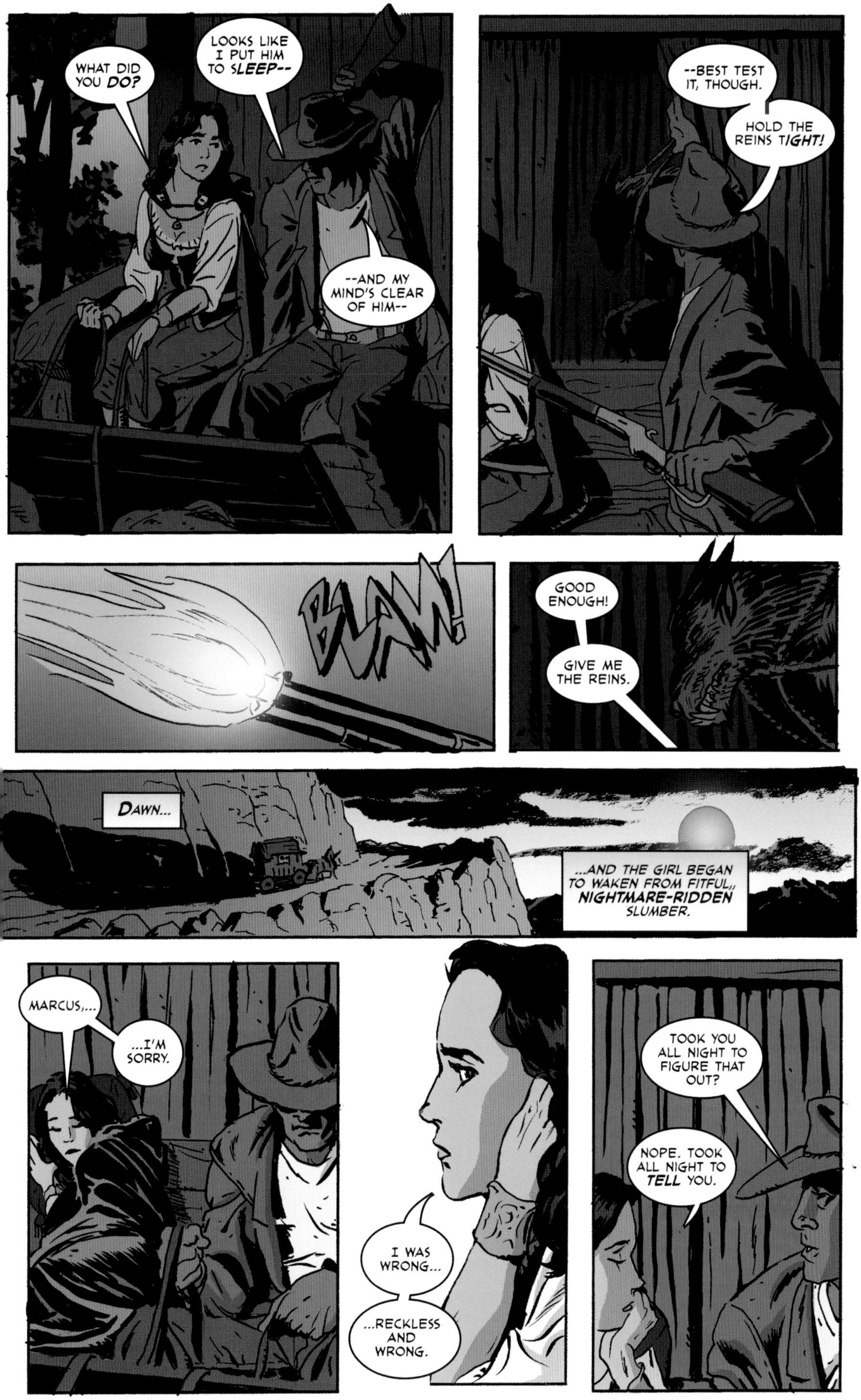
WHAT DID YOU DO?
LOOKS LIKE I PUT HIM TO SLEEP--
--AND MY MIND'S CLEAR OF HIM--
--BEST TEST IT, THOUGH.
HOLD THE REINS TIGHT!
BLAM!
GOOD ENOUGH!
GIVE ME THE REINS.
DAWN...
...AND THE GIRL BEGAN TO WAKEN FROM FITFUL,, NIGHTMARE-RIDDEN SLUMBER.
MARCUS,...
...I'M SORRY.
I WAS WRONG...
...RECKLESS AND WRONG.
TOOK YOU ALL NIGHT TO FIGURE THAT OUT?
NOPE. TOOK ALL NIGHT TO TELL YOU.

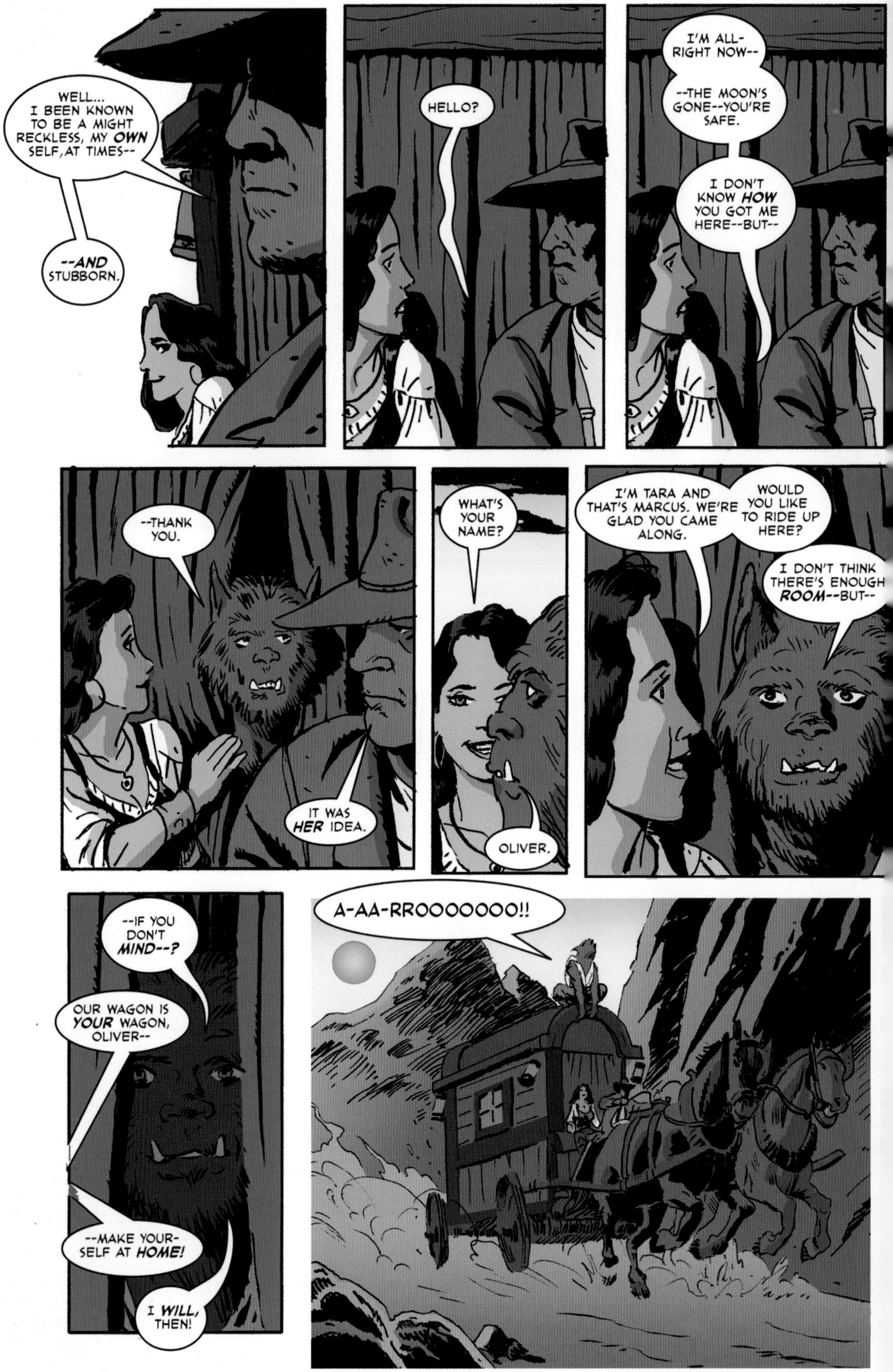
WELL... I BEEN KNOWN TO BE A MIGHT RECKLESS, MY OWN SELF, AT TIMES--
--AND STUBBORN.
HELLO?
I'M ALL-RIGHT NOW--
--THE MOON'S GONE--YOU'RE SAFE.
I DON'T KNOW HOW YOU GOT ME HERE--BUT--
--THANK YOU.
IT WAS HER IDEA.
WHAT'S YOUR NAME?
OLIVER.
I'M TARA AND THAT'S MARCUS. WE'RE GLAD YOU CAME ALONG.
WOULD YOU LIKE TO RIDE UP HERE?
I DON'T THINK THERE'S ENOUGH ROOM--BUT--
--IF YOU DON'T MIND--?
OUR WAGON IS YOUR WAGON, OLIVER--
--MAKE YOUR-SELF AT HOME!
I WILL, THEN!
A-AA-RROOOOOOO!!

These are the first two pages done to help sell the series. It's interesting to see how the bar scene changed and the action page with the Wolfman is actually from a future scene–if a second arc should ever materialize.

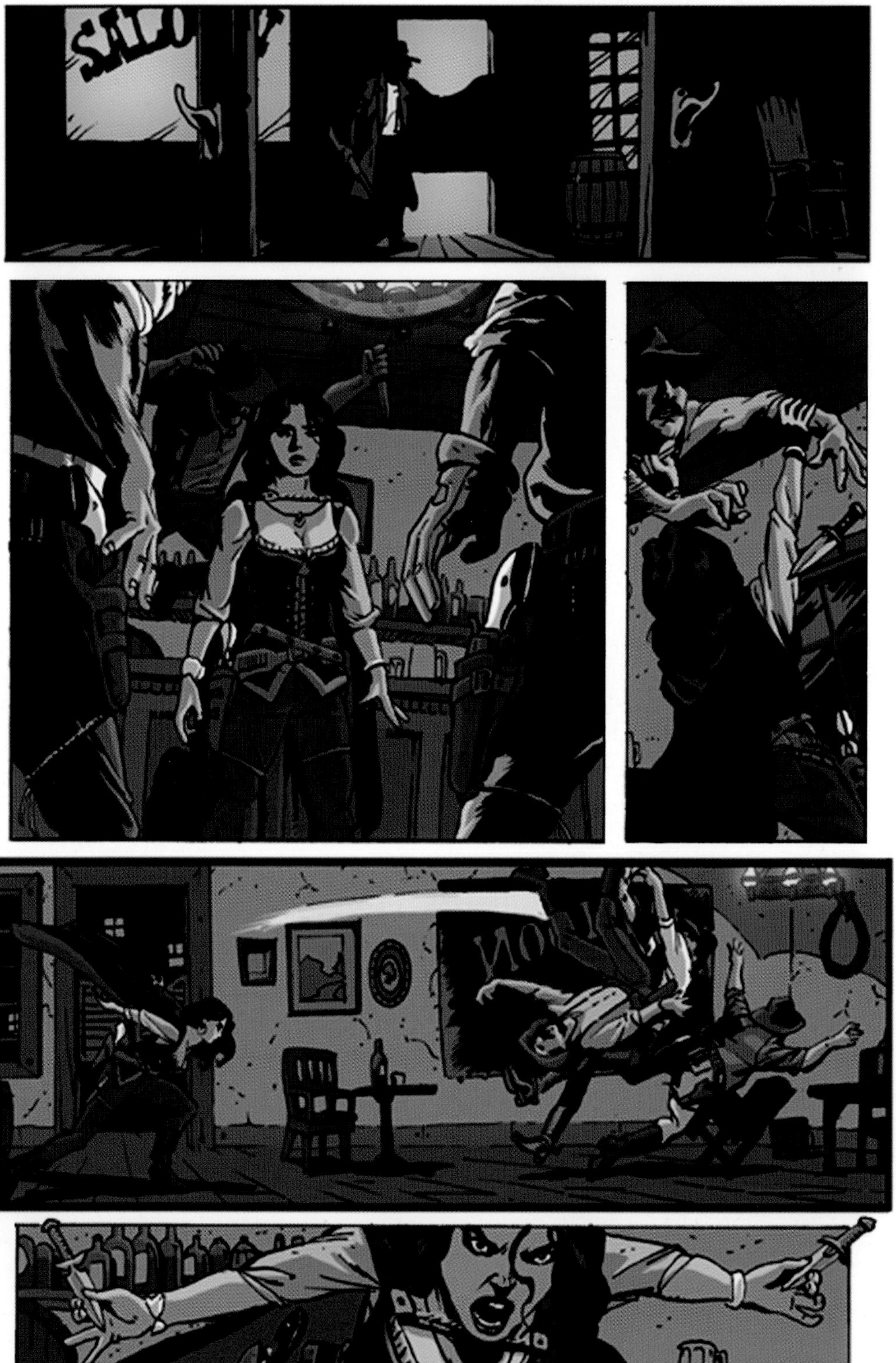
SALO

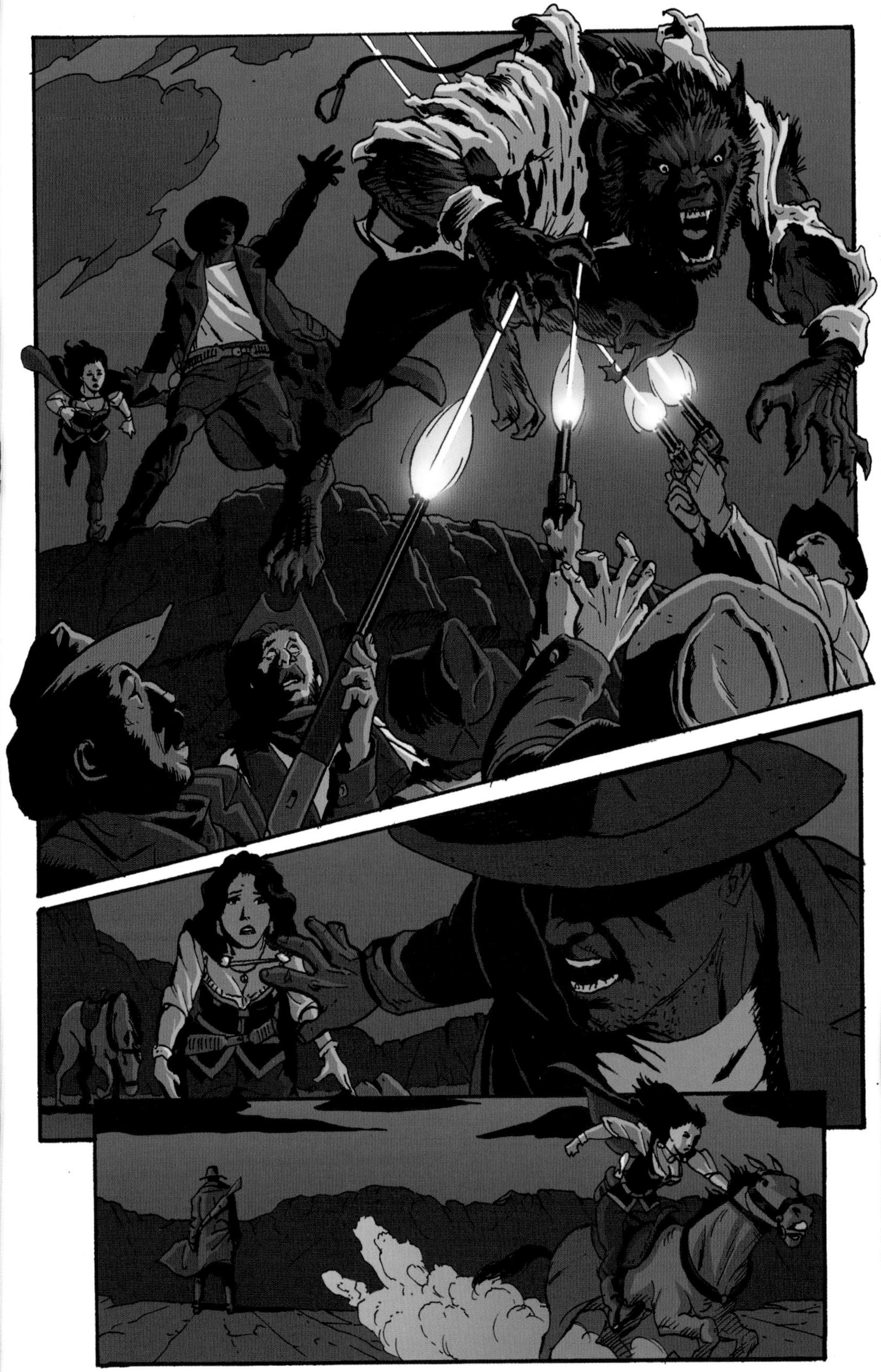

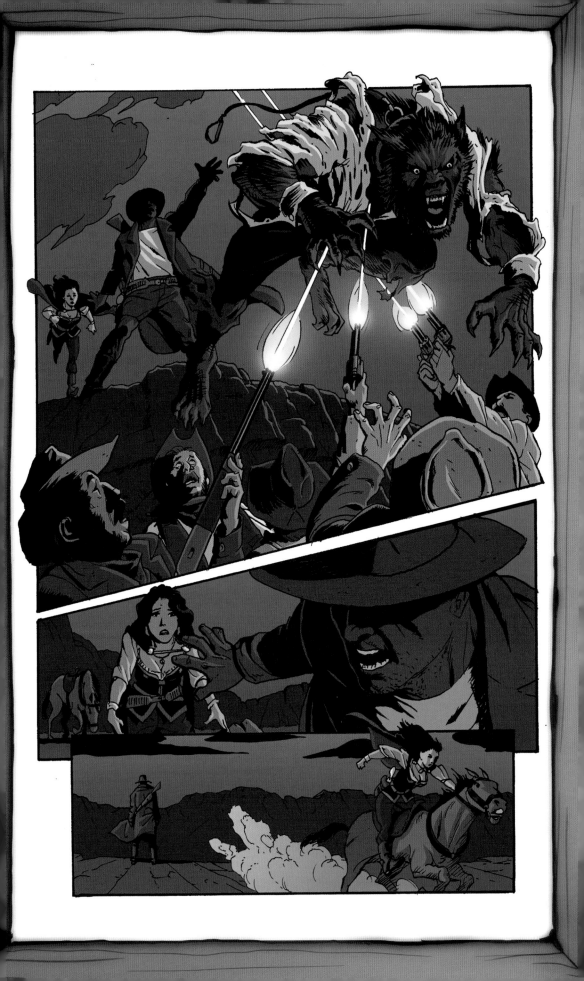

Tara Character Design

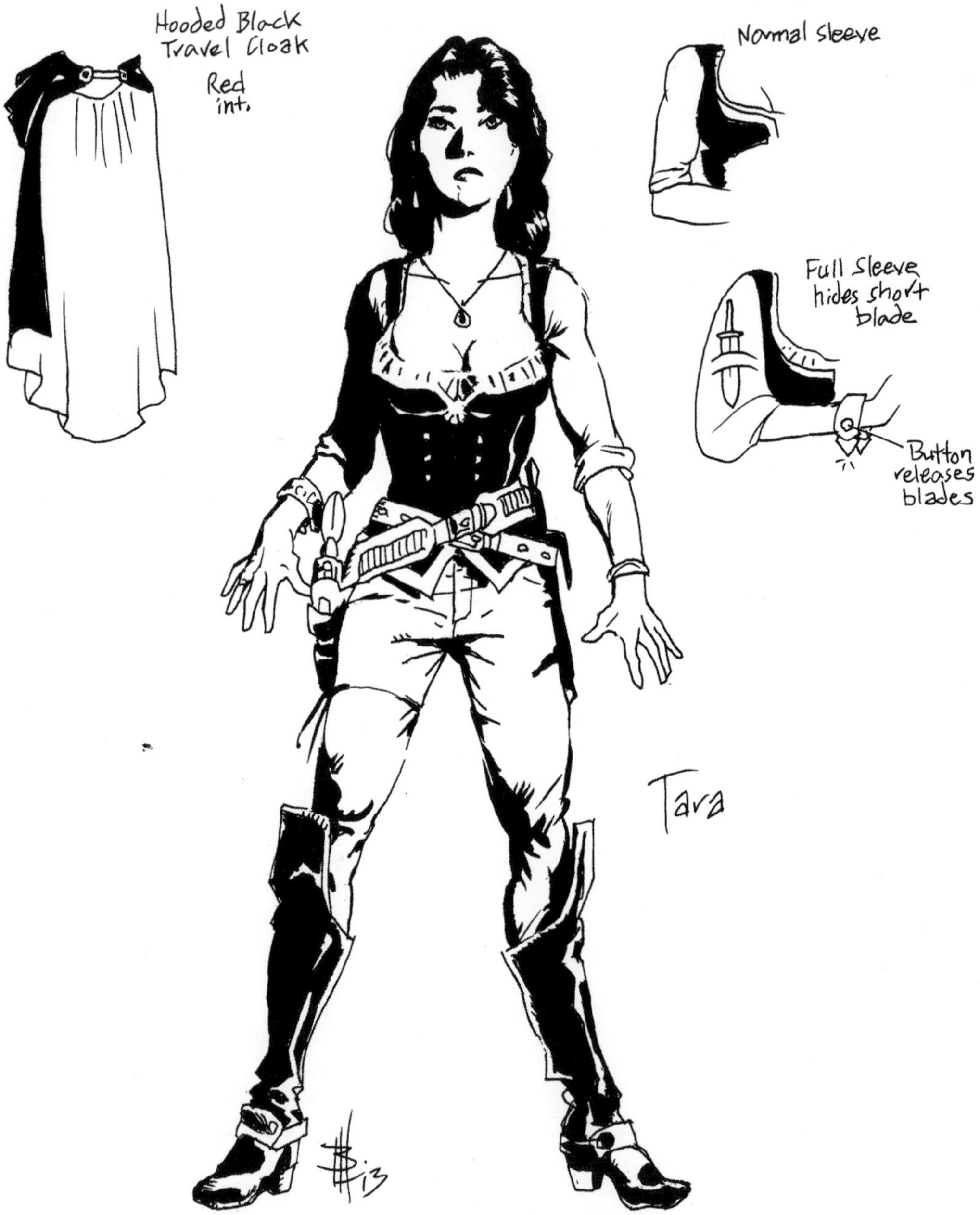
Hooded Black Travel Cloak
Red int.
Normal sleeve
Full Sleeve hides short blade
Button releases blades
Tara
'13

Tara Character Design

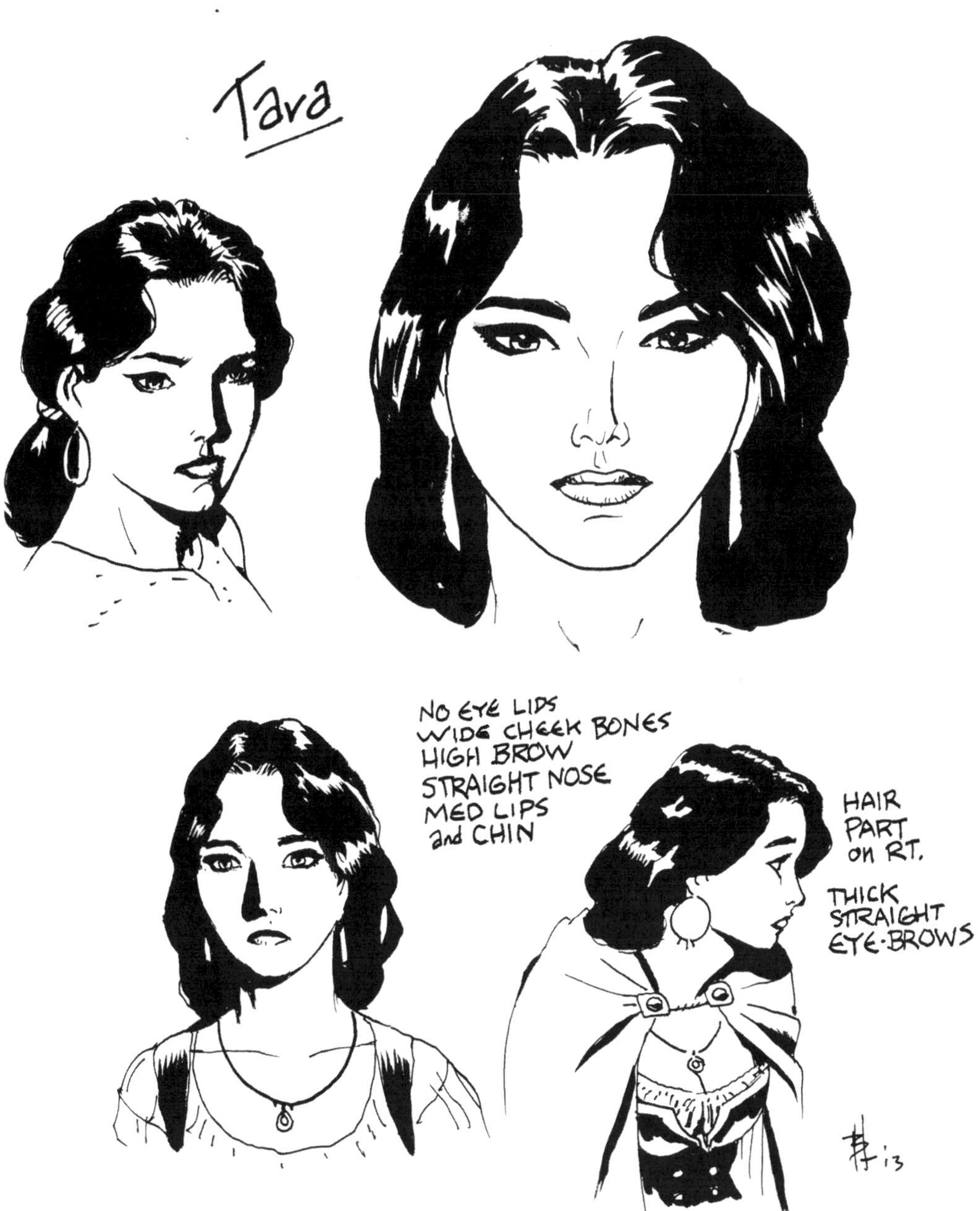
Tara
NO EYE LIDS
WIDE CHEEK BONES
HIGH BROW
STRAIGHT NOSE
MED LIPS
and CHIN
HAIR
PART
on RT.
THICK
STRAIGHT
EYE-BROWS

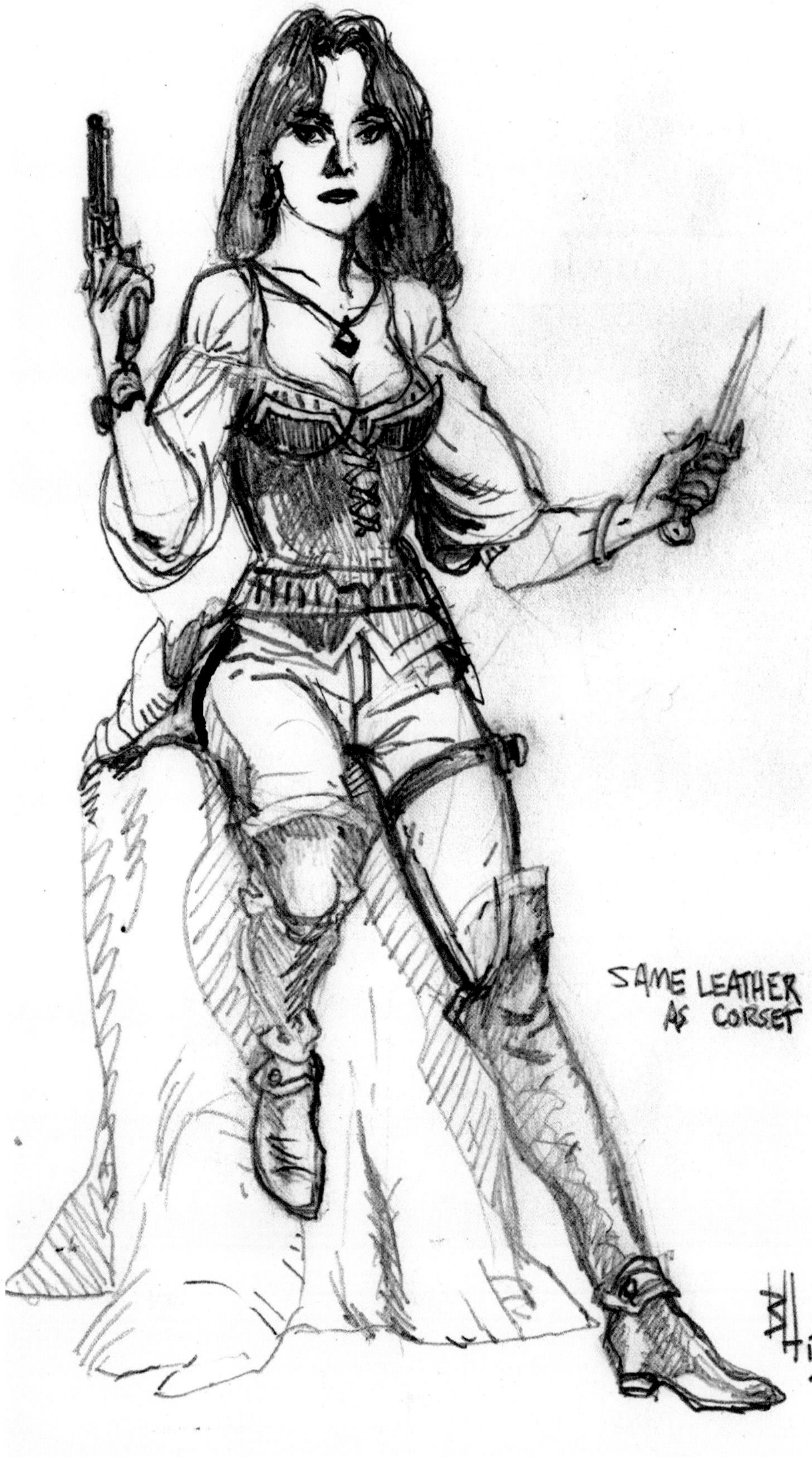
SAME LEATHER
AS CORSET

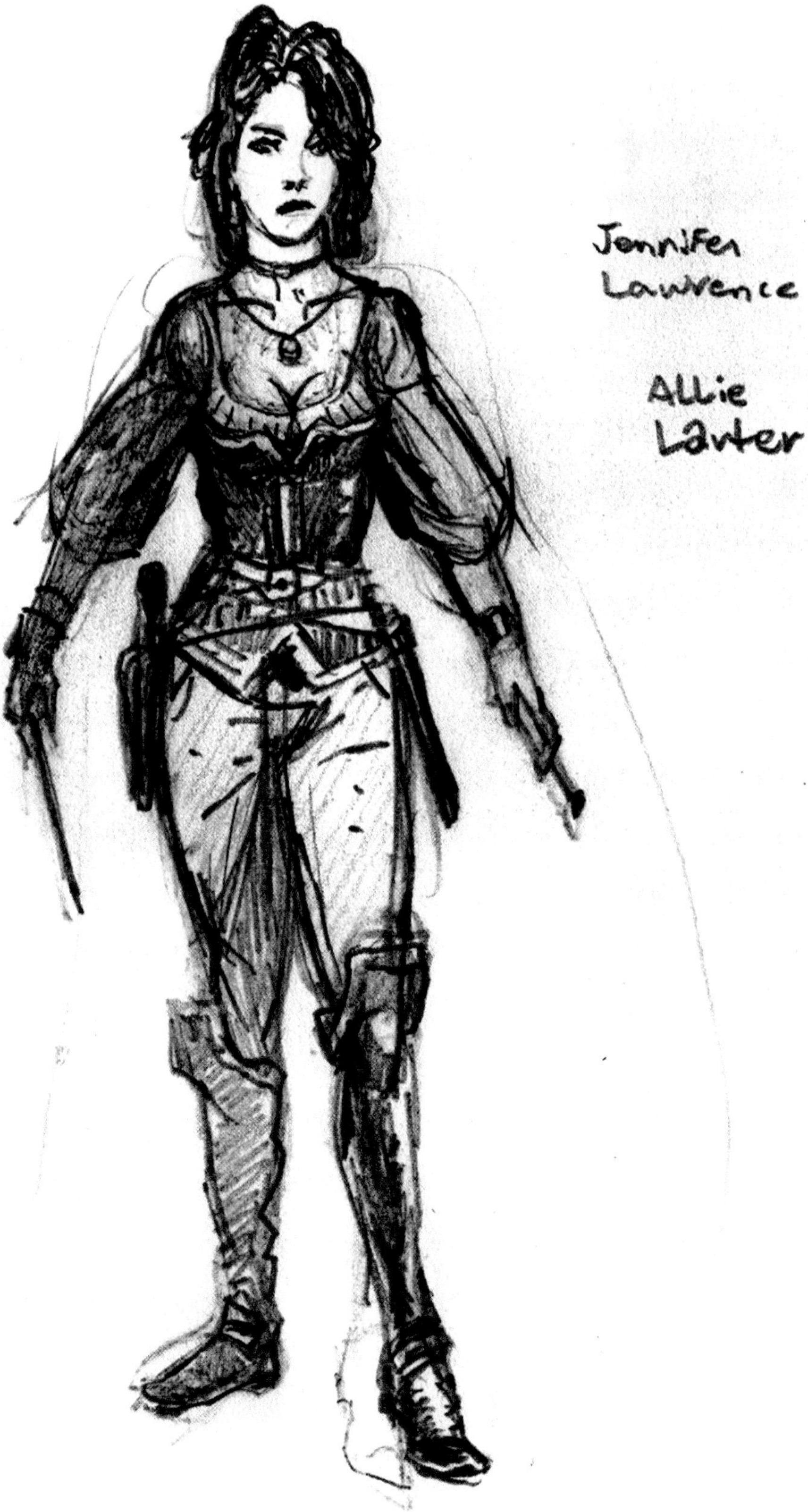
Jennifer
Lawrence
Allie
Larter

She wound up based on Karen Gillan. –B.H.

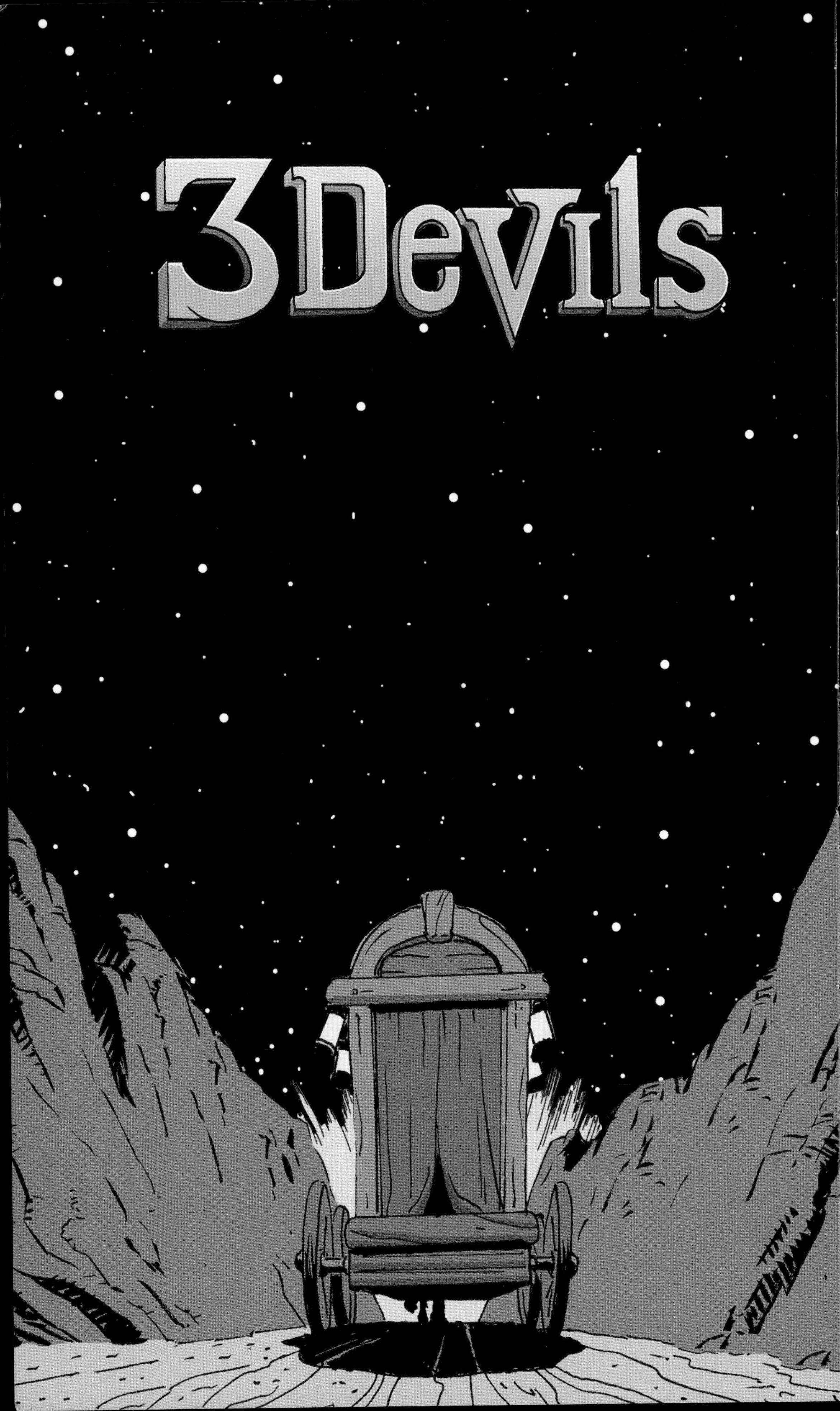
3 Devils